CATCHING UP?

SUNY Series in International Management
Andrzej Kozminski, Patricia Sanders, and
Sarah Sanderson King, editors

Catching Up?

Organizational and Management Change in the Ex-Socialist Block

Andrzej K. Kozminski

State University of New York Press

Published by
State University of New York Press, Albany

For information, address the State University of New York Press,
State University Plaza, Albany, NY 12246

Production by Bernadine Dawes
Marketing by Dana Yanulavich

Library of Congress Cataloging-in-Publication Data
Kozminski, Andrzej K.
    Catching up? : organizational and management change in the ex-
Socialist block / Andrzej K. Kozminski.
        p.   cm. — (SUNY series in international management)
    Includes bibliographical references and index.
    ISBN 0-7914-1597-X (hc : acid free) — ISBN
0-7914-1598-8 (pb : acid free)
    1. Organizational change—Europe, Eastern.   2. Privatization—
Europe, Eastern.   3. Strategic planning—Europe, Eastern.   4. Post-
communism—Europe, Eastern.   I. Title.   II. Series.
HD58.8.K685   1993
658.4'06—dc20   92–40891
                                                                    CIP

1 2 3 4 5 6 7 8 9 10

Contents

Acknowledgments

T he book is based on dozens of Polish, Hungarian, Russian and Czech cases illustrating its main themes. The origins of these cases are different: some of them were totally researched and developed by the author, while some were prepared in collaboration with other researchers. Some profiles are based on consulting projects prepared by MBA students at the International Business School in Warsaw, others on materials published in the Russian, Polish, or Western press. Case material is supplemented with available surveys, statistics, and analysis prepared both in the West, and in Central and Eastern Europe. It must be noted, however, that the author remains highly skeptical with regard to the reliability of Eastern European statistics.

The book has multiple roots in the author's activities:

- Consulting and business experience in the government and private sector in Poland

- Research in the field of economic reforms and business strategies in the communist and post-communist economies

- Experience in management education and training in the United States, Western Europe, and Poland

Many people and institutions made this book possible. My special thanks go to Professor Donald Cushman from the State University of New York, who persuaded me to start working on the book and whose inspiring remarks helped me to develop and structure my ideas.

In 1990, 1991, and 1992, I spent one trimester a year in Los Angeles at the Anderson Graduate School of Management, at UCLA. Research grants from the Center for International Business Education and Research (CIBER) at UCLA enabled me to concentrate on the book. Professor Jose de la Torre, director of CIBER, was among the people who made this work possible.

A lot of inspiration and encouragement came from my MBA students at UCLA and at International Business School in Warsaw, Poland.

Fragments of the book were discussed in the seminars at Warsaw University with my collaborators from the Management and Organization Department of Warsaw University.

I owe a lot to Dr. Alexander Shaposhnikov from the Russian Academy of Sciences in Novosibirsk, and to Dr. Ferenc Ternovszky from the Institute of Labour in Budapest, for their support in researching their respective countries and for helping me to understand them. Dr. Monika Kostera and Dr. Aleksander Nowak, from the School of Management of Warsaw University, helped me to conduct my research in Poland. Valuable materials were made available to me by Professor Andrzej Matczewski from Polish Academy of Sciences.

Professor Stefan Kwiatkowski from Warsaw University, Professor Andrzej Korbonski from UCLA, and Professor Alice H. Amsden from MIT read the manuscript and gave me their opinions and remarks, which helped me to prepare the final version. I want to extend to them my thanks. Naturally, the author takes full responsibility for the content of the book.

Finally, without the help, understanding, love and tolerance of my wife Alicja, the book would not have materialized at all.

Introduction

Events in Central and Eastern Europe, or rather the incredible speed of change, have taken by surprise not only expert Sovietologists and politicians, but also Western business leaders and managers. A lack of understanding of the mechanics of the processes taking place in the former Soviet bloc, and in the former Soviet Union, may lead to costly trial-and-error—or even more costly wait-and-see—strategies.

This book aims to explain this transition process in the making. By focusing on the changes taking place in post-communist enterprises, the transition will be explained by describing the management processes taking place in these enterprises in terms of Western management theory and practice. Are they going to catch up? How fast? What are the main factors determining the pace and speed of change? Which countries, industries, and enterprises are more rapidly becoming compatible with the West, and why? These are some of the questions addressed in this book.

There are no simple answers to such questions in the highly unstable and turbulent environment of the former Soviet empire. There are, however, some more or less certain assumptions that may be considered as foundations of the analysis presented in this book. Let us discuss them briefly:

1. Communism is gone forever—discredited as economically not viable, a cruel and morally evil system forceably imposed on the people.

Even political parties that include members of the old communist parties do not dare to defend openly the Soviet model of the one-party state and centrally planned economy. Even in the deepest crisis, as in Russia during 1991, there is no political base for a return to the old communism. This does not mean, however, the elimination of communists from economic and political life, and even less the elimination of communist mentality.

In democratic elections, political parties representing excommunists (transformed into social democrats, socialists, etc.) consistently get well above 10 percent of the popular vote, and these percentages might easily increase under conditions such as recession and unemployment. It is also well known that a number of successful, purely capitalist, enterprises have been founded by the members of the old communist "nomenklatura"—

quite often with the party's money. Quite often, "black privatization"—the unlawful transfer of state property into private hands—was used to establish these enterprises. Does that mean that "good communists" have become "good capitalists?" How are they going to use their political and economic leverage?

Communist mentality seems to be based on two pillars:

- A "one best way" philosophy, along with a deep-seated belief in the moral right to force others to follow "one best way," even if they don't want to.

- In exchange for their compliance, "ordinary people" feel entitled to the total protection and services provided by the "communist welfare state."

The political elites of post-communist countries have inherited the first of these two principles of the communist mentality. Ordinary people have inherited the second.

2. Communist mentality is difficult and slow to overcome, especially under conditions of recession, unemployment, and permanent disequilibrium.

Due to the archaic structure of the economy (e.g., a high percentage of low-value-added smokestack industries), combined with outdated technology, the transformation into full-fledged democracy and a full-fledged market economy is certain to be long and turbulent. This process will be longer and more turbulent in countries where ethnic tensions have re-emerged after decades of ruthless communist domination.

Political stability, restructuring the enterprises and the economy, and promoting export-led growth are the key, mutually reinforcing factors affecting the transition. Countries where political stability is being achieved, due to the emergence of a few relatively strong, democratically minded "political families," are more likely to restructure and rebuild their economic systems. Post-communist Hungary is an example of such a country. On the other hand, the more economically stable countries—able to restructure their industry, and to control both unemployment and inflation—are much more likely to develop stable and democratic political structures.

3. Post-communist countries are gradually joining the global economy dominated by the "triad"—North America, Western Europe, and the highly developed Far East.

Participation in the global economy can reach different degrees, and take different forms, in the case of different post-communist countries. In some cases, economic participation may be limited to receiving humanitarian and military aid (*African model*). Other post-communist countries will be offering the Triad markets their lower-quality products, cheap labor, and natural resources (*South American model*). Some countries will gradually move from the role of subcontractor to the role of exporter through their efficient use of borrowed technologies and management skills, as well as accelerated savings and investment (*Asian model*).

The post-communist governments have a key role to play in shaping the form and degree of participation of their countries in the global economy. It's up to the government to create conditions that will enable the country to become a home base for successful global competitors in higher-value-added market segments and industries (Porter 1990:20). Such enterprises are more likely to be created when a massive inflow of foreign capital occurs, and when viable domestic partners of foreign capital emerge. Conditions that facilitate or inhibit foreign capital involvement, on the enterprise level, are presented below.

4. Integration of post-communist economies and post-communist enterprises into the global market system can be perceived as a cycle composed of several phases:

- POLITICAL–elimination of communist domination, resolution of ethnic conflicts, consolidation of political parties and democratic institutions

- EARLY MARKETIZATION–liberation of prices, internal convertibility of the currency, lifting legal barriers to private entrepreneurship

- INFLATION CONTROL–restrictive monetary policies, elimination of subsidies, reduction of budget deficit

- MARKET INSTITUTIONS BUILDING–developing and starting a privatization program, identifying government functions in the market economy and restructuring the government, tax reform banking system reform, creation of capital markets, partial marketization of some social services

- ANTI-RECESSION ECONOMIC POLICY–stimulation of economic activity through fiscal and monetary policies, promotion of small business development, putting in place an employment policy, massive modernization and development of the infrastructure, formulation and implementation of an agricultural policy, stimulation of the modern distribution channels development, creation of favorable conditions for the foreign capital inflow)

- GROWTH POLICY–formulation and implementation of the comprehensive industrial policy promoting export-led growth, including: selection of the most prospective industries and enterprises, putting in place a system of incentives and subsidies based on monitored export performance, formulation and implementation of a flexible trade policy protecting domestic industries without compromising access to the most lucrative foreign markets

Successful completion of the whole transition cycle clearly leads toward the Asian model (Amsden 1990, 1991). Even in the case of the most advanced post-communist countries, this process will take a long time.

A few countries, such as Hungary and Poland, started the political and early marketization phases under communism. Hungary even initiated the inflation control and market institution building phases while still under the communist regime. These countries are the leaders of the pack, and have considerable advantage over the others. Some countries—including the former USSR republics, Yugoslavia, and Albania—did not complete the political phase until the end of 1991. Bulgaria and Rumania are experimenting with early marketization without completing the political phase (i.e., "hurriedly repainted" communists are still in power, and ethnic conflicts have not been resolved).

Sequencing and timing of the phases is crucial for successful transition. More advanced phases of the cycle cannot be successfully completed without prior completion of the earlier phases. For example, privatization cannot really be started without banking system reform and start-up of the capital market. Foreign capital is not likely to come into the economies hit by inflation and recession, and where the market institutions' building phase has not been completed. The relative success of Hungary and Czechoslovakia in attracting foreign capital clearly confirms this general rule.

Once a phase is completed, the next one must be initiated without delay. Fixation on one of the phases is due, in the most cases, to its unprofessional and only partially successful completion. For example, Poland was fixated on the anti-inflationary policy phase through 1990 and 1991—and market institution building (e.g., banking reform) has been considerably delayed.

Delays, and the lack of proper sequencing, can easily lead to dangerous "loops" in the transition process. For example, the lack of an energetic and efficient anti-recession policy may compromise political equilibrium and cause a return to the political phase. This danger was clearly visible in both Hungary and Poland—and especially in Poland—at the end of 1991. Many such loops involving political destabilization increase the probability that the African model will develop. Yugoslavia is a very instructive example in this respect.

The last two phases—anti-recession and growth policy—require government with a long-range view. Such a vision can only result from a deep understanding of the realities of today's global competition, permitting the country to be positioned in a global context. Without this vision, only the South American model can be achieved, at best. For the time being, only the Hungarian government seems to have developed and consciously implemented such a vision. It is likely, however, that long-range development programs also will be generated in other post-communist countries when the more advanced phases of transition are successfully completed.

The transition process is seen and analyzed below from the management perspective, focusing attention on the enterprise level. Such a perspective helps us to understand and explain the dynamics of the transition process—how the real fabric of the economy is transformed on the enterprise level. This perspective has practical utility for Western managers entering into business deals in the post-communist countries, or who are considering such a possibility. It enables them to understand an exotic, foreign business environment by comparing it with their own. This understanding is crucial for the proper assessment of business opportunities and threats, as well as formulation and implementation of the right strategy.

In Chapters 1 and 2, different types of post-communist enterprises are presented:

- DINOSAURS–big, state-owned enterprises in heavy industries

- PRETENDERS–more technologically advanced, state-owned enterprises in higher-value-added industries with the potential to export

- MIXED MARRIAGES–joint ventures with Western capital participation

- MOM-AND-POP SHOPS–privately owned small businesses

- GROWING SHARKS–big, private firms already existing in some post-communist countries

Typical profiles of different types of enterprises are used to present the most important problems they are facing in the highly unstable and differentiated (i.e., between countries) environments of transition.

In Chapters 3 and 4 strategies of different types of the enterprises are discussed.

Chapters 5 and 6 are devoted to the change of organizational cultures and transformational leadership.

In Chapter 7, the most likely scenarios are presented for the future development of a business environment in the post-communist countries.

Viable strategies of Western firms operating in Central and Eastern Europe are identified, in Chapter 8, as possible scenarios for the future. A list of "dos and don'ts," relative to the implementation of these strategies, completes the book.

1
State-Owned Enterprises

Types of Enterprises in the
Post-Communist Economies

In the market economies, entrepreneurs and enterprises are traditionally believed to be the most important agents of the economy—creators of wealth, sources of innovation and progress. This view of an enterprise was challenged by Karl Marx. The Marxists believed exclusively in macro-economic rationality attributed to the society as a whole, and represented by a central planning board responsible for securing maximization of that kind of rationality. Marx himself often used a metaphor of the national economy as "one big factory" (Marx 1951:677). Within this framework, only macro-economic rationality counted.

The very notion of macro-economic rationality is also specifically understood: as the maximum possible satisfaction of the needs of society. Such formulations, found in all standard communist textbooks of political economy, require further refinements. The central planning board is given supreme authority to decide the needs of society (interpreted as an itemized and fully detailed list of products and services), and how priorities should be ranked (or which, and whose, needs should be satisfied first).

In a system designed according to a Marxist dogma, classical economic calculation problems (what to produce, how, and for whom?) were not solved on the enterprise level, but decided by a central planning board for the national economy as a whole. In other words, enterprises were not considered economic agents making economic choices—but merely "production units" or "the factories" (as they were often called in the communist countries), where the only problems to solve had a strictly technical and socio-political character. What really counted was the economic system as a whole.

Such a holistic view of an economy has serious practical consequences directly related to the way enterprises are perceived and operated. To illustrate that point, a few characteristic definitions of a "socialist enterprise" may be quoted:

> By enterprise it is meant not financial value important for the capitalist owners, but living organism: a group of working people. (Sarabianov 1924:4)

> By enterprise we mean a group of people united by common material interest, founded on the basis of a system of material production means, constituting a technical and economic entity, created to satisfy a type of needs of society. (Chelinski 1964: 48–49)

The Soviet Encyclopedia, published under Stalin, defined enterprise as "a set of tools and production means, inventories and other material funds used by people to produce or to perform any kind of work. Special nature of an enterprise is determined by type of a social system" (*Bolshaya Sovietskaya Encyklopedia* 1952, vol. 34:408).

Among the most important features of "socialist enterprises," the following seem to deserve special attention:

1. *Maximization of economic surplus, or even the production of goods and services, were not considered the only and the most important functions.* Serving political priorities directly (for example, by providing components for heavy or armament industries, or by supplying revolutionary movements or "brother countries" abroad) were considered much more important, to the extent that cost effectiveness did not count at all.

2. *Socialist enterprises were supposed to provide for the needs of their employees, such as medical care, housing, vacation, recreation, and— first of all—political indoctrination.* These activities were often favored and over-developed at the expense of not only economic efficiency, but also production itself. They remain an important part of the activities of the big state-owned enterprises, even in countries considered to be the most advanced on the road to a market economy. Their elimination carries a risk of compromising the social equilibrium of these enterprises, especially during the economically difficult period of transition. In 1991, for example, East German workers strongly opposed elimination of social welfare activities of their enterprises.

3. *Enterprise was supposed to execute the plan targets decided at the level of the central planning board.* Such plan targets had to serve the needs and the interests of the national economy, not "particularistic" interests of the enterprise itself. Consequently the management of the enterprise could not know the full extent of, and could not evaluate, planning decisions taken above it. Its role was to obey, to execute, and to "mobilize" the workers and personnel of the enterprise to meet, and if possible to exceed, the plan targets. As N. Grossman put it, as early as in 1924, "enterprises did not know the markets and the markets did not know them" (Grossman 1924). This statement remains valid. In-

terviews conducted by the author with managers in Poland, Hungary, and Czechoslovakia in 1990 and 1991 clearly indicate that marketing knowledge is one of the weakest points of their skills, and that a "sellers market" mentality is still alive. In emerging market economy conditions, such a mind-set considerably inhibits performance of the enterprises.

4. *Initiatives of the enterprise management and the workers should be directed toward input rationalization.* This meant producing more with the same amount of input, or minimizing the input necessary to produce a given amount of output. Such an understanding of rationalization of the functioning of the enterprise is rightly considered to be one cause of the poor quality of products produced by socialist and post-socialist enterprises.

5. *Enterprises were also considered to be "accounting units," where production costs and input structures were calculated.* It is significant, however, that the enterprises themselves were not supposed to be the users of the accounting systems—because economic calculation and resource allocation decisions were done above them, on the central planning board level. That is why the enterprise accounting systems built in the communist economies were always aimed at the government agencies supervising the enterprises. This strange accounting logic has not yet been overcome, and remains one of the major obstacles to effective cooperation between western and socialist or post-socialist enterprises. Passing to international accounting standards and training of people accordingly, seems to be a major problem and long and difficult process because it involves complete turn-around of the accountants' and managers' mind set: switching from "bookkeeping" to accounting in the modern meaning of the word. This process is far from being completed even in the most advanced countries such as Hungary or Poland.

Two aspects of the enterprise concept were ever present in communist theory and practice:

- Technical or "technocratic"–an understanding of an enterprise primarily as a system of material production factors, such as machinery, equipment, buildings and technology (clearly visible in the definition taken from the Stalinist encyclopedia)

- Social–an understanding of an enterprise primarily as a group of people jointly contributing to the realization of the plan targets (reflected in other, more recent definitions)

At different stages of development of the communist economies, different degrees of importance were attributed to these two aspects of the notion of the enterprise. During the Stalinist period the technical aspect was given absolute priority, while communist reformers active since the late 1950s stressed the social side of a socialist enterprise. Development of industrial sociology in the USSR and other communist countries in the '60s and '70s is due to this shift in understanding of the nature of the enterprise. It is obvious, however, that under the communist system, the enterprise was never understood to be an independent economic agent acting in a market environment.

Analysis of post-communist enterprises, from the perspective of a highly developed market environment, seems quite difficult. It requires precise discrimination between the different types of enterprises coexisting, at the present time, in the post-communist economies:

- Big state-owned enterprises (mainly in heavy and machine industries) that still maintain an upward orientation toward government, and act as much as possible according to the old "rules of the game"—the "dinosaurs"

- More market-oriented state-owned enterprises, with a relatively high proportion of exports, that try to act in a business-like manner—the "pretenders"

- Joint ventures with foreign capital participation—the "mixed marriages"

- Small privately owned companies—the "mom-and-pop shops"

- Large privately owned companies—the "growing sharks"

Dinosaurs emerged as a consequence of Stalinist industrialization dogma, which focused on heavy industries and those related to the military complex. Stalinist dogma stipulated the enormous size of production facilities, as well as their social and political functions (e.g., cultural, recreational and social welfare activities). Such industrialization programs were often carried out a long time after Stalin's death—in the 1960s, '70s, and even in the '80s.

Pretenders have been formed mainly under the influence of decentralization and the parametric reforms undertaken by communist reformers in the '60s and the '70s.

Most of the existing mixed marriages were born out of the "eleventh-hour" communist reforms directly preceding the fall and total disintegration of communism, and the first period of early marketization of the post-communist economies.

Mom-and-pop shops were always present in some of the socialist countries (e.g., Poland, Hungary, and East Germany)—but even there, these shops were subjected to a number of drastic restrictions by the communist rulers, and remained marginal until the end of communism. In order to survive in a hostile, bureaucratic, and corrupt environment, small private entrepreneurs had to develop a considerable part of their activities in the "shadow economy." The experience of the post-communist countries shows very clearly that the mere existence of a legal private sector under communism, in some of them, played a considerable positive role in laying the ground-work for a market economy.

Growing sharks are clearly carrying the message of completely new times. It is also obvious that the economic system, which must simultaneously accommodate such different economic entities, has to be incoherent and unstable. Dinosaurs are still responsible for the lions share of employment and industrial GNP in the post communist countries. They are the main source of the economic problems, along with the undeniable difficulties experienced by most pretenders when they try to adjust to global market conditions.

Recent examples and cases will be presented in order to demonstrate how enterprises of different categories actually respond to unique conditions created by the transition from centrally planned to market economies.

Dinosaurs

Most of the "dinosaurs" resulted from the "socialist industrialization" drive initiated in the USSR by Stalin under the first five-year plan, in 1928, and followed obediently by other socialist countries (with exception of Hungary) practically until the end of communism. Such ambitious industrialization programs created large populations of enterprises for whom the label "dinosaurs" is justified for two reasons:

- They were over-sized and extremely vertically integrated, nearly to the point of self-sufficiency.

- They were inefficient and employed polluting, often dangerous technologies.

From the perspective of the structures of the post-communist economies, the Stalinist industrialization drive left behind a large proportion of low-value-added smokestack industries unable to turn out world-class products at reasonable cost.

Post-communist dinosaurs are exemplified by two cases: a Polish coal mine, ''Rainbow,'' and a Soviet truck engine factory.

Rainbow. Coal mine Rainbow[1] is situated in the mining region of Silesia, near the major industrial town of Katowice. Built in the 1960s, it still sits on relatively abundant coal reserves. Rainbow employs around 7,000 people, including more than 5,000 miners who work in difficult conditions nearly 3,000 meters under the surface. By comparison, British coal mines of comparable capacity employ about one-tenth the manpower under the surface—and yet have close to five times higher daily production. The British advantage is due mainly to modern efficient equipment, more efficient work organization, and a much lower percentage of administrative personnel dictated, until recently, by the requirements of the communist economic bureaucracy.

In order to understand present situation of Rainbow, one has to bear in mind the specific circumstances of the coal mining industry in communist Poland after World War II. Until 1990, coal mining had escaped all reform attempts, and had kept a management system close to the ''classical Stalinist'' model. This was due to two factors.

First of all, close to 80 percent of the country's energy needs are met by coal and lignite—along with a large chunk of the country's hard currency earnings. This resource is especially vital, since Polish industry is two-to-five times more energy intensive than Western European industry (Karpinski 1986). The management system sheltered the industry from international competition, through a highly developed system of direct and indirect subsidies, and gave considerable pay and benefit privileges to the miners. Such a system was especially beneficial to the communist *nomenklatura* in the industry—but the miners also benefited from it.

Second, coal miners were consistently perceived as a political power base by all governments, including those led by Solidarity. The party leader of the 1970s, Edward Gierek, rose to power from the Silesia mining region. He clearly gave high priority to primitively understood (Stalinist-style) further industrial development of the region—which resulted in catastrophic degradation of the environment, depletion of natural and human resources, and devastation of the infrastructure. In spite of being perceived as a ''workers' aristocracy'' in communist Poland, miners took an active part in the Solidarity movement of 1980–81, and actively opposed the imposition of the martial law. (Seven miners were killed when police stormed one of the mines in December 1981).

After the imposition of martial law, however, communist authorities had to turn to the miners again for more coal and new privileges, and pay increases naturally followed. Nevertheless, the mining region of Silesia remained one of the strongholds of Solidarity—and in 1988 and 1989, miners again played a crucial role in the final overthrow of the communist regime. This gives them considerable political leverage with the new postcommunist governments. It must be noted that miners in the Ukraine and Siberia, in Russia, played a very similar political role in 1990 and 1991.

The "shock treatment" therapy implemented by Vice Prime Minister Balcerowicz, in 1990, necessitated an end to the exceptional situation of coal mining. Subsidies were gradually eliminated and the costs of supply dramatically increased, which dangerously narrowed the margin of competitive advantage enjoyed by Rainbow's coal on the international market. At the same time, deep recession limited domestic demand in a way that was completely new to the polish coal mining industry.

The shock of the new economic situation was combined with very profound organizational changes within the industry. The highly centralized monopolistic structures controlling the whole industry were dissolved—and replaced by a population of individual coal mines acting as separate state-owned enterprises. The reforms had two objectives.

First, they were supposed to lead to a massive exchange of managers and the dismantling of the "old boy networks" of the formerly communist *nomenklatura*.

Second, the reforms were meant to facilitate a restructuring of the industry by closing inefficient, exploited mines—and enabling the remaining mines to compete in domestic and international markets. While this would require considerable capital investment in modern equipment, the new equipment should make possible a more efficient work organization and a higher degree of processing of the output. The industry would produce the "cleaner," more energy-efficient and standardized product required both by foreign and domestic users, and would secure higher prices and advantageous contracts (i.e., large, steady orders).

Local chapters of the Solidarity trade union, as well as Solidarity-controlled workers self-management organs (the "workers councils"), were very active in promoting these changes. At the same time, however, union officials were under strong pressure from rank-and-file members to protect jobs and the real value of wages.

In the context of Eastern Europe, protection of jobs has a specific meaning and significance because of very low, or practically nonexistent, labor mobility—the result of both the housing shortage and the long tradition of lifetime employment of the miners in the same mine. The need to protect the workers' interests, as felt by trade union leaders in the coal mining industry, is made even more urgent by the rivalry between Solidarity and the communist trade unions, OPZZ.

Communist trade unions were created by the party in 1982 after the declaration of the martial law and the banning of Solidarity. They were, and still are, perceived by many as "traitors." But in order to keep and attract membership, they have become aggressively militant. At the same time, Solidarity has neglected typically trade union activities and has become, to a much greater extent, a political organization. Moreover, since all the non-communist governments emerged from Solidarity, it began to be perceived as an official government trade union. As such, Solidarity bore part of the responsibility for the hardships—unemployment and the reduced purchasing power of the working class—resulting from the "shock treatment" measures applied by these governments. As result, the communist trade unions have kept, and often increased, their membership and influence at the enterprise level.

Industrial problems, as presented above, are very closely related to regional policy issues. Silesia is traditionally a heavy industry region similar to the Rhur valley in Germany, Alsace-Lorraine in France, or the Appalachian region in the U.S. It has built its relative economic prosperity on coal mining, steel making, and bulk chemicals. It's environmental situation is, at present, close to a catastrophe. It's economic and industrial base is shrinking dramatically as a result of the transition to a market system (especially through the "shock treatment" of eliminating subsidized pricing) and the opening of the economy to international competition. The whole region—until recently, the most economically advanced—is threatened by massive unemployment.

The political significance of these regional issues can be understood when one takes into consideration crucial the political role of the region in national politics. Furthermore, the region's massive concentration of blue-collar workers is torn between Solidarity and the communist, or post-communist, political formations—such as OPZZ or the social democratic party, which emerged from the communist party in 1990.

All the problems mentioned above were clearly visible at the Rainbow coal mine. Paradoxically, they were even more pressing because of the relatively recent construction date of the mine. Capital investment was not yet paid off, which considerably increased "dividend"—a fixed assests-value tax imposed by the government on state-owned enterprises. The Polish-made equipment used by Rainbow was not technologically advanced enough to provide the labor-efficient organization and technology of extraction that would enable coal mines operating in geological conditions similar to Rainbow's, to remain competitive on world markets in the '90s.

The comparison with British coal mining is especially relevant. Using traditional equipment and work organization, Rainbow had to conduct extraction on 18 levels in order to reach its full capacity of 18,000 tons of coal per day. This required very high employment levels and a very complex production management system, which further increased the cost of extraction. To make a bad situation worse, the technology and equipment used at Rainbow did not guarantee the quality of output required by more discriminating buyers, and which would have justified higher asking prices.

Due to its relatively high production costs and outdated (but still not paid off) equipment, Rainbow was experiencing serious problems that were reflected in a highly variable production volume well below its full capacity. Rainbow also paid lower wages than older neighboring mines. This situation became intolerable for both the trade unions and the workers' self management council. Under the enterprise law of 1981, workers' councils at state-owned enterprises have a say in selecting and dismissing CEOs. At Rainbow, all of these workers' organizations jointly initiated the return, and nomination as CEO, of Miroslaw Maron.

Mr. Maron had been a chief engineer, or technical director, at Rainbow in 1982. He was known in professional circles of the industry for his technical knowledge and competence, and also held a Ph.D. in engineering. Maron was well acquainted with the most advanced mining technology used in Western Europe and the U.S. When martial law was imposed in 1982, Maron was still a communist party member—and remained in the ranks until the party dissolved itself in 1990. Nevertheless, he had been dismissed for political reasons: he had openly expressed support for Solidarity. In spite of these political issues, even the communist authorities could not afford to waste Maron's technical knowledge and expertise. Shortly after his dismissal from Rainbow, Maron was appointed chief engineer at one of the worst (i.e., the most run down) mines of the region. His assignment was to "save" the mine, and to ensure a steady production flow. When he succeeded in this nearly hopeless situation, another similar appointment followed—and the "rescue mission" was again successful. Maron became quite famous in Silesia, and it was this reputation that brought him back to Rainbow.

Immediately after his nomination, Maron came up with an attractive restructuring plan. He proposed to buy immediately one—and later, three or four—of the latest-generation foreign-made coal mining combines, which would make possible the automated extraction of high-quality coal. At first glance, the whole project looked financially unrealistic because of the high cost of the equipment: the estimated cost of one machine was about $25 million. Maron's business plan took that into consideration: it called for the purchase of only one machine initially to be paid off through exports of the additional coal produced. A British manufacturer of coal mining combines, Anderson-Longwall, was interested in supplying one of its latest-generation machines, and also secured the participation of Royal Dutch Shell in the sale of coal from Rainbow on the international markets—which provided for advance financing of the purchase.

Anderson-Longwall wanted to start a joint venture with two Polish manufacturers of coal mining equipment, Famur and Glinik, to produce the next machines jointly. The new enterprise would supply the machines on continuous basis to other Polish, Eastern and Central European markets, and would also offer them to the former USSR republics and China (which traditionally bought its coal mining equipment from Poland). Such a complex agreement, involving two major multinational corporations, was negotiated by Maron as early as November 1989. Complete autonomy of the Rainbow coal mine as an independent enterprise was clearly a precondition for success of the whole venture. Such autonomy had not yet been granted at the time Maron's business plan was originally presented. Coal mines were still under the umbrella of the State Coal Agency and Ministry of Industry. All imports of mining equipment and machinery were handled by the state-owned foreign trade company, Kopex. All exports of Polish coal traditionally went through another state-owned monopoly, the foreign trade company Weglokoks.

All of these powerful agencies were vitally interested in maintaining their influence over the whole coal mining industry and each one of the mines. Maron's plan clearly went against their interests. The state agencies were able to counterattack and to harm Rainbow and it's managing director in many different ways—even without openly using their administrative powers. Instead, they relied on the quasi-monopolist position they still maintained. Such repressive actions might include blocking or slowing sales of coal from Rainbow, or making it more difficult and expensive for Rainbow to purchase other equipment.

Maron was too experienced to take such a risk, so he worked out a compromise: both Weglokoks and Kopex became partners in the proposed deal. Weglokoks was given its share as intermediary, for selling Rainbow's coal to Shell. Kopex received a similar share of the transaction to import equipment from Anderson-Longwall to Rainbow, and eventually to other Polish coal mines. Commissions promised to the foreign trade companies made the whole project more expensive for Rainbow—but Maron considered it to be a fair price for a compromise enabling him to get the OK from the State Coal Agency and Ministry of Industry. The letter of intent was finally signed by all parties in July 1990. The contract with

Anderson-Longwall was scheduled to be signed in August 1990, and installation of the first machine was expected in early 1991.

The whole restructuring program had to be approved, however, by the workers' council of Rainbow—and in the summer of 1990, such approval was very unlikely. A personality clash and rivalry between Maron and Mr. Karcz, who was president of the workers' council, greatly contributed to this situation. Karcz was an engineer who had worked at Rainbow for many years, recently as a foreman. It should be noted that most workers' councils are headed by middle managers or engineers—who often use that kind of activity as an opportunity for quick advancement, and to climb to managerial positions that are often still occupied by the old communist *nomenklatura*. This was clearly the case with Karcz, who wanted to take Maron's place.

In order to achieve his goal, Karcz initiated a thorough examination of the restructuring program by the workers' council. He did not criticize its technical validity, but raised doubts about its financial feasibility—and pointed out that restructuring would lead to considerable layoffs.

At the beginning of 1990, a session of the workers' delegates (a large body composed of several hundred democratically elected delegates, who elect the workers' council) supported Maron' program, and by the same token forced 12 members of the workers' council to resign. This meant that a new election of the workers' council had to be called. The election produced unexpected results: Karcz skillfully played on the fear of layoffs, and raised suspicions of financial manipulations involving Maron and the consulting firm preparing the financial feasibility study. Thus, Karcz reinforced his position and gained an absolute majority within the workers' council. This enabled him to block approval of Maron's restructuring plan until November 1990, under the pretext of a thorough examination by the workers' council.

Meanwhile the idea of a new open competition for the director's position, launched by the workers' council, slowly gained acceptance among the workers' representatives and trade union leaders. In November 1990, it had become clear that Karcz was going to run for director—and that with the support of the workers' council, he had every chance of winning. With his restructuring plan blocked and his position challenged, Maron handed in his resignation, effective immediately, and left for an overdue vacation.

Mr. Karcz's triumph was short-lived, however. Immediately after Maron's resignation, the bank froze Rainbow's account and stopped financing its operations. Dropping sales and the lack of a viable restructuring plan, backed by signed contracts, substantiated the bank's decision.

Workers' wages could not be paid on time. The whole community was terrified by the immediate threat that the mine would be closed. A local priest said a mass in anticipation of Maron's return. Karcz and his supporters were put in the coal carts by an angry mob of miners and driven out the Rainbow grounds. The next day, Karcz sent his resignation, which was accepted. A delegation of miners visited Maron's house and asked him to return to his duties.

After a day of hesitation, Maron accepted. A newly elected (again!) workers' council approved his restructuring plan, which enabled him to sign the contract with Anderson-Longwall and Shell—which, in turn, resulted in the resumption of financing for Rainbow's operations. The Minister of Industry created a special commission to inquire into workers' council activities under Karcz's presidency. As of March 1991, the restructuring plan was off the ground again. But the foreign partners started to have second thoughts, and exactly a year was wasted—making Rainbow's situation even more critical than before.

SovTruck. The next description of a typical communist dinosaur faced with contemporary challenges comes from the former USSR. "SovTruck"[2] is a dinosaur typical of the Soviet automotive industry. In 1989, it employed 120,000 people in 15 plants and produced more than 200,000 trucks annually—a quarter of the total Soviet production volume. SovTruck is an almost completely self-sufficient and fully integrated truck manufacturer, that performs all of the key production operations, from raw casting to finishing. It also produces wide range of appliances, such as refrigerators, kitchens, and microwave ovens. SovTruck has its own hospital, technical schools, network of factory stores and canteens, research and development institute, vacation centers, and apartment complexes.

In contrast with similar enterprises in highly developed market economies, big Soviet enterprises contract out as little as possible and try to do everything themselves. This leads to unused production capacity in many areas, prevents the factory from getting top-quality components from highly specialized suppliers, and considerably increases the production costs per unit. It also the diverts the attention of the managers from key issues. This tendency results from the chronic lack of reliability of domestic suppliers, the nonconvertibility of the currency, and the bureaucratic rigidity of the planning process. In such an environment, a high degree of self-sufficiency (meaning, in fact, autonomy and independence) is considered to be one of the key factors of the enterprise's prestige and success—especially since production costs were neglected to the extent that (as the author's interviews with Soviet managers indicate) production costs per product and per unit were not even calculated.

Labor shortage has always been one of the most difficult problems facing socialist enterprises, especially in big industrial centers. Up to the end of 1990, only those countries more advanced in the transition process, such as East Germany, Poland, Hungary, and Czechoslovakia, had started to experience unemployment problems to different degrees.

In Russia, umemployment was unknown until the end of 1991. The labor shortage was due to very strong tendencies toward over-employment. It is author's estimate that an enterprise similar to SovTruck, operating in a highly developed market economy, would employ less than one-third of SovTruck's work force. Over-employment resulted, in turn, from low labor productivity (due to outdated and poorly maintained equipment, irregular inflow of input, and poor organization of work), from the high proportion of administrative jobs (due to the high degree of bureaucratization of the overall economic system), from the wide range of unrelated and auxiliary activities (where labor cannot be used efficiently), and from high absenteeism, turnover, and lack of work discipline.

Enterprises in the big industrial centers competed to attract and maintain the better workers. Since wages and rates were closely controlled administratively, activities providing for the workers' welfare were the only means of appeal. Enterprise housing was the most attractive, along with—under conditions of severe shortages of consumer goods—factory shops and services. Recreational and medical services also played a role. Enterprises enjoying high prestige and high visibility developed such activities very intensively, which in turn helped them to foster even more prestige and visibility. It is clear that social welfare activities not only increase costs, but also create new needs to employ new people. The vicious circle of over-employment can be observed when: a work force deficit creates a need for development and the extension of social services, which in turns creates new sources of labor shortage. The SovTruck example, where on any given day up to 10 percent of the work force might be absent, clearly illustrates this argument.

Vlachoutsikos and Lawrence (1990) describe a process of appointing managing directors in one of the factories situated in the main Moscow complex of SovTruck. In 1989, factory X produced 900 gasoline engines a day and employed about 2,300 workers (450 of whom were part-timers, because of the labor shortage mentioned previously). Factory X received its production targets from the central management of the Moscow complex, and coordinated the main assembly line with the production of components.

The job of the factory manager was to ensure that these targets were met. It was not an easy task—not only due to the shortage of labor, but also because of the run-down equipment. There existed a long-range plan to convert the factory to production of diesel engines—but it did not materialize for years, and the old equipment was not properly maintained and replaced. In such a situation, an effective manager of the factory had to possess both technical and human skills.

The factory manager since 1981, Mr. Ptichkin, performed well for a couple of years. But around 1985, he could no longer handle the technical problems related to deteriorating equipment, in addition to personnel problems such as absenteeism and the shortage of labor. Ptichkin had to be replaced because factory could not fulfil its production plans.

He was replaced, in 1986, by Mr. Priakhin—who even received some assistance from headquarters, in the form of new equipment and an increased wage fund, which enabled him to pay better wages and hire new workers. These resources did not help him enough, however, and Priakhin resigned in 1988 following a conflict with the workers over compensation for overtime he was trying to force them to put in.

In 1987, the new enterprise law was enacted by the Soviet parliament, giving the workers' council the power to elect managers—who had to be confirmed, however, by SovTruck headquarters. The vacancy left by Priakhin was filled by workers' council candidate, Mr. Tumanov, who was popular among employees because of his activities as union representative. Headquarters had his own candidate, Mr. Gorian, and raised objections related to Tumanov's insufficient technical knowledge (he was not an engineer, but a mere mechanic). Under pressure from the workers' council, however, headquarters decided not to force its own candidate. Tumanov was approved—but after a relatively short time, it became evident that he really was not qualified for the job. Tumanov understood this himself, and handed in his resignation. This time the headquarters candidate, Gorian, was elected—and with headquarter's support (e.g., new, more reliable equipment that enabled him to keep to schedules and improve quality) he performed relatively well.

Both cases presented above enable us to draw some general conclusions covering the whole population of dinosaurs in post-communist economies.

All the issues related to the "dinosaurs" are highly political because of two reasons:

1. "Dinosaurs" were created by communist regimes as strong political entities with large and important party and trade union organizations. Political factors always played an important role in their functioning (for example managers were always political appointees called "nomenklatura"). The same patterns tend to be repeated in the new situation with new political forces (such as new political parties which emerged from "Solidarity" in Poland) and new institutions (such as workers' self-

management councils technically entitled to participate in management including the process of selection of managers).

The new situation of disintegration and collapse of the communist system creates strong uncertainty and strong emotions. These new tensions can be attributed to the strong resentment of the old nomenklatura and the new opportunities and the new perspectives of promotion discovered by new people. Complete lack of institutionalized industrial democracy tradition makes these tensions highly destabilizing and provides for even more uncertainty.

Appointments of managers tend to become emotional issues concentrating all hopes, ambitions, animosities and hates. It can easily lead to the waist of the most scarce resource: existing managerial talents and experience often possessed by the people related to the "old regimes". It also creates very insecure situation for the managers. "Over-democratization" of the big state owned enterprises in the post-communist countries is clearly evident. It takes form of a "populist industrial democracy" (discussed below in the Chapter V). Different countries experience it to different degrees.

Poland with its 12 years long tradition of militant "Solidarity" backed workers councils seems to be an extreme case. Problems of workers council interference with the management process is clearly perceived as a threat by the government. Polish minister of industry declared in an interview in March 1991 that intended transformation of the legal form of the state owned enterprises into joint stock companies wholly owned by the state treasury has two objectives: to prepare grounds for privatization and to eliminate workers council (not allowed in joint stock companies). Even if this operation will be fully successful two or even more trade unions competing on the enterprise level might complicate enough management process.

Ex-USSR republics facing explosive political issues have inherited an old tradition of political activism on the enterprise level. In a political tradition of the Russian empire democracy is often understood and practised as a synonym of anarchy and order as a synonym of tyranny. In such a context "over-democratization" problems seem to be especially serious.

In Czechoslovakia workers councils were introduced by the communists in the lats attempt to save the system through partial populist-minded reforms. Because of that communist inspiration they never became a real factor and were relatively easily removed in 1990. Trade unions, however. and other workers political organizations seem to be quite active in the big state-owned enterprises endangered by "shock treatment" and restructuring processes, especially in Slovakia.

Hungary, as the only country practicing "gradual transition" and capitalizing on earlier communist reforms, had for a relatively long time been clearly inclined toward a technocratic model of management—and has always discouraged political activism on the enterprise level. Such an attitude on the part of government and management saved most Hungarian enterprises from the worst problems of "over-democratization," despite the fact that workers' councils are also required by law in Hungary.

Massive, emotional and often disorderly participation of workers in the management process seems to be a characteristic feature of post-communist dinosaurs during the transition period—before better organized institutional forms of worker participation and industrial democracy eventually emerge. Institutions of industrial democracy will certainly differ from one country to another according to tradition, cultural differences, and different experiences. During a period of systemic transition, people tend to experiment with newly acquired democracy on the enterprise level, too. Dinosaurs are the most likely places for such experiments because of their large concentrations of blue-collar workers, a tradition of political activism (both communist and anti-communist), and the dinosaurs' clearly endangered position in the process of industrial restructuring.

A second reason for the highly political character of the dinosaurs in post-communist economies has to do with their role in the economy, and their competitive position on domestic and international markets. The analogy with "smokestack" industries in the West is visible. In some countries and in some industries, restructuring triggered violent conflicts, such as famous British coal miners strike of 1986. The differences are rather evident as well.

Post-communist economies are characterized by under development of modern high-value-added industries, and even more so of agriculture and the tertiary sector (i.e., services, retailing, banking, insurance). It means that the relative importance of dinosaurs is greater, and that the rest of the economy is not able to generate the resources necessary for restructuring and for cushioning the social shock. Such a situation rules out the rapid elimination of dinosaurs. The east German experience of 1990 and 1991, and especially the wave of strikes and social unrest in the spring of 1992, show that even the strongest European economy cannot afford—economically, politically, and socially—the sudden elimination of dinosaurs.

In the highly developed western countries, heavy industries and the regions where they are located (as well as the militant trade unions) were gradually losing ground. Political scenes of these countries were always dominated by middle-class politics. In post-communist countries, middle classes are nonexistent. Moreover, in some of these countries (e.g., Poland, Russia) blue-collar workers employed in the dinosaurs, and their free trade unions, played an absolutely decisive role in weakening and removing communist regimes.

In all the countries of the region, however, no matter how important or unimportant the role of blue-collar workers in the overthrow of communism, the relative political role of dinosaur workers is much greater than it ever was in the West. Since transition inevitably hurts them, both communist and extreme right-wing elements are likely to seek their support, and to exploit their bitterness. Bitterness results from the sudden change of the situation—as yesterday's pools of "socialist economic development" are transformed into the most depressed regions, and the "workers' aristocracy" or "avant garde of communism" into the unemployed.

Low income levels, in absolute figures, and the difficult conditions of life (e.g., ecological catastrophe) of the workers employed by the dinosaurs, make this situation even worse—taking into consideration the extremely low, practically nonexistant labor mobility. Political results are already visible. In the Slovak town of Martin, where 16,000 workers are employed by a tank factory. The Communist city council and mayor were democratically elected in 1990, and still enjoy massive popular support[3]. In Polish Silesia in the fall of 1990, miners and steel workers voted overwhelmingly for a rightist demagogue presidential contender, Mr. Tyminski, who came to Poland from Canada and Peru. After a campaign of less than two months, Tyminski was able to challenge the legendary charismatic leader, Lech Walesa. In East Germany, both the fascitis and the communists are on the rise.

It is relatively easy to discover that virtually all the post-communist dinosaurs are many times over-staffed, technologically backward, polluting the environment to a degree intolerable by objective biological standards, and hopelessly loosing their traditional markets (the Soviet bloc military complex or, until recently, the "easy" COMECON markets). Their only asset is highly qualified and cheap labor including bright and well-trained engineers. By and large, dinosaurs are unable to compete on international markets. Only a relatively low percentage of them can be rescued by "Rainbow"-type therapy—including massive capital investment in new technology and equipment, adjustment of output to the standards acceptable to international markets, and massive layoffs. Only very few of the dinosaurs can attract foreign investors. Over-democratization, generally hostile attitudes of the workers toward foreign ownership, and the highly political character of the issues related to transformation of such enterprises, are certainly among the reasons substantiating this statement.

For example, in November 1991, Warsaw Steel Works (closed since the previous August) was sold to an Italian group, Lucchini. Although the factory was sold to a European steel industry leader for a very good price, including a minimum $250 million investment by a foreign partner, the deal was temporarily blocked by the workers' council because of the lack of employment guarantees. Experts believed that the sale was the only chance to save the steel works, and finally the deal went through[4].

Do these statements mean that the dinosaurs will be quickly eliminated? Certainly not. None of the post-communist countries could afford it, either economically or politically. Some kind of long-range industrial policy will have to be worked out that calls for the gradual elimination of dinosaurs, creation of new jobs in depressed regions, and massive modernization of a few factories carefully selected as the most promising.

Realistically assessing situation, funds for such a restructuring program can come from two sources: the state budget, or foreign help allocated for such purposes by organizations such as the World Bank or the EEC. In both cases, government will have to play a significant role in the formulation, implementation, and securing of financing for such a policy. This would require, in turn, a deep transformation of government bureaucracy from the old model to the new one.

The old model, inherited from the communist bureaucracy, was based on daily interference of the government agencies and party apparatus with the functioning of the enterprises, combined with patronizing them: "protecting" from threatening environment, securing resources to enable the "dinosaurs to survive. Such an approach means nothing more than further promotion of the waste of resources.

The new model, practised in Western Europe and in newly developed countries of Far East, means industrial policy. It requires radical change in the government structures, skills and mind-sets of the government officials. Such reforms were undertaken only in Hungary in the 1970s, and in the '80s by the "last hour" communist reformers. Central planning in physical units was eliminated, and all sectorial ministries were consolidated into one policy making agency. Such reform brings results. Hungary was able to practice a reasonable "gradual transition" strategy, and to find relatively easily a "common language" with corresponding agencies in Western Europe, both on national and supra-national (EEC) levels.

In the countries practicing "shock therapy," all government intervention in the economy seems to be associated with the old model—and is considered contradictory to "textbook principles" of the market economy. These attitudes, however, will inevitably change under strong political pressure from the dinosaurs. Under such pressure, the Polish government in 1992 had to soften its position considerably toward falling dinosaurs (at least the most politically explosive, such as the Ursus Tractor Works in the Warsaw suburbs). Vice Prime Minister Balcerowicz, responsible for the "shock treatment" policies, had to go. Czechoslovak President Vaclav Havel could not live up to his early promises to completely withdraw his country from international arms deals. The same applies to Russian President Boris Yeltsin. In 1992, the Russian government did not dare to start massive closings of dinosaurs, in spite of pressure from the International Monetary Fund. Unfortunately, Russia did not have a comprehensive restructuring plan, either—the new dogma of an abstract "free market economy" prevents it.

Pretenders

Pretenders are state-owned enterprises that were able to develop, under communist system, a product mix responsive to the requirements of contemporary market economies. These companies built a name for themselves and established commercial contacts in the West. Such enterprises are considered prime candidates for privatization, foreign capital investment (both direct and portfolio), and further expansion in the emerging market environment. Since the number of pretenders is relatively limited in the post-communist countries, they are able to attract management talent. Usually they also build on local reserves of highly trained workers. At the same time, however, transition confronts the pretenders with previously unknown challenges—which they often have problems confronting. Typical problems facing the pretenders will presented here with the help of two examples: Gold Mark S.A. in Poland, and the Star department store in Hungary.

Gold Mark was created[5] in 1945 in the Polish textile industry town of Lodz, sometimes called the "Polish Manchester." The outfit was established to produce clothing for the army. Starting in 1949, Gold Mark expanded its production and sales to include men's winter and spring overcoats sold on the internal Polish market. In 1956, when capital investment in new buildings and equipment made further expansion possible, Gold Mark began to specialize in all-season men's garments.

By the end of the 1950s, exports to the Soviet Union had started. Further export orders came from West Germany, France, England and the U.S. In the '70s, new production facilities were acquired in the Lodz region (smaller enterprises administratively incorporated into Gold Mark by the Ministry of Light Industry) and the new factory building in Lodz was completed. Gold Mark's considerably increased production capabilities made possible deeper penetration of foreign, mainly Western, markets. In

1991, Gold Mark had major clients not only in the Western countries previously mentioned, but also in Great Britain, Denmark, Finland, Italy, Canada, Sweden, Holland, Australia, and Belgium. In short, the company covered all of the most difficult and discriminating markets. During the last couple of years, Gold Mark's volume of exports to hard currency markets consistently exceeded $10 million per year. Exports accounted for 31 percent of the company's sales in 1989, and jumped to 69 percent in 1990.

This dramatic change was, in part, due to the introduction of the new exchange rate, which strongly devalued the local currency. Devaluation was part of the "stabilization plan," introduced on January 1, 1990, known as the Balcerowicz Plan (for the viceprime minister responsible for economic affairs in the first non-communist Polish government). The Balcerowicz Plan provided, among other things, for "internal convertibility of the currency." Internal convertibility means that local currency can be freely exchanged for any foreign currency inside the country—but it still cannot be used as a means of payment outside the country, and is not quoted on the international currency markets.

Gold Mark built a reputation as a high quality manufacturer by targeting the upper segments of the market. It won a considerable number of prizes at international clothing fairs and exhibitions.

In spite of the attention it focused on lucrative foreign markets, Gold Mark has the most prestigious trademark in garments on the Polish market. It still controls more than 25 percent of the men's winter overcoat market, and 38 percent of the men's spring overcoat market. Gold Mark has a smaller share (5–10%) of the markets for men's short jackets and women's overcoats.

Poland, with its population of 38 million can be considered a major market for garments—even if, under "shock treatment," demand has fallen because of the drop in purchasing power of close to 30 percent. Garment prices have risen slightly less than prices in the economy as a whole, but have still exceeded the growth rate of per capita income. In 1985, the average monthly salary could buy five men's spring overcoats made by Gold Mark—but only 3.3 coats in 1991. In 1989 Consumers spent 17 percent of their income on clothing in 1989—but only 9.5 percent in 1990. At the same time, however, the emerging middle class in Poland and other Eastern European countries is offering new opportunities for high quality men's garment manufacturers, such as Gold Mark.

Gold Mark's foreign customers are mainly big retail chains, such as C&A, or wholesalers specializing in garments, such as Bourges in France. Fifty-one percent of the company's exports, by volume, and 29 percent by value are made under "cut, make and trim" (CMT) contracts. The sales manager of Gold Mark, Mr. Kowalski, believes that such contracts are beneficial for the firm because they provide access to new designs, manufacturing techniques, and markets. Domestic distribution channels are in temporary disarray because of disintegration of big state-owned retailers undergoing privatization, under which individual stores are being sold to private owners. Due to the relatively low importance Gold Mark attached to the domestic market—where, until 1990, it could easily sell its second tier lower-quality production—the company did not create its own retail outlets, as did some of its domestic competitors.

The garment industry in Poland is highly fragmented. Garments are produced by over 30,000 enterprises, of which 700 are the larger state-owned enterprises. Only four or five of these companies can be considered Gold Mark's competitors according, to Mr. Kowalski. Fifty percent of the domestic demand for overcoats is covered by imports. In 1991 low tariff barriers, combined with the effects of currency convertibility, resulted in a considerable rise in imports of consumer goods (including garments).

In 1990, even before the privatization law was passed by the parliament in July, Gold Mark has been identified as a prime target for privatization. Preparations started with the help of a local private consulting firm (owned and staffed by assistant professors of management, finance, and marketing at Lodz University), and British consultants brought in by the Ministry of Ownership Changes. The foreign consultants were generously financed by the "Know How Fund," established by British Prime Minister Thatcher to help transition process, which facilitated the transfer of knowledge to Poland. The move to privatization move was initiated by Gold Mark's Solidarity-backed management, which was appointed in the fall of 1989. In particular, the young vice president for finance, Ms.Skrobot (who had graduated from Lodz University in 1982, and was an activist in the underground Solidarity under martial law) was instrumental in preparing the privatization plan and getting support from the ministry. She won the support of the workers' council using three arguments:

1. Privatization would liberate the company from the wage increase limitations imposed administratively on all state-owned enterprises. The wage restrictions take the form of highly progressive (up to 500 percent) taxation of wage increases above the modest limit, decided by the Ministry of Finance, of only 60 percent of the price increase. This anti-inflationary economic measure, included in the Balcerowicz Plan, raised a lot of controversy because it blocked increases in production. For obvious reasons, the limitations were unpopular among workers, and were fought by both trade unions (Solidarity, and the communist-controlled OPZZ). The measure was, however, applied only to the state-owned enterprises in order to stimulate and accelerate the priva-

tization process. Workers hoped to have their wages substantially increased as result of privatization.

2. Funds received from the public offering of shares were supposed to be channeled, at least in part, back into the enterprise in order to upgrade its equipment and to buy better, more reliable western-made machines.

3. According to the privatization law workers were offered 20% of the first emission of shares at the preferential price (50% of the market price) and could apply for credit to acquire them.

Preparation of a viable public offering of Gold Mark shares required careful examination of the company's strong and weak points in the turbulent environment it was facing, and the elimination of the most evident drawbacks.

All products manufactured by Gold Mark were carefully analyzed from the perspective of profit-generating potential. As a result of this study, several marginal product lines (mainly underwear) were eliminated.

In early 1990, Gold Mark rationalized its production facilities by closing one plant situated in the suburbs of Lodz and merging two plants in Lodz. A large equipment modernization program had been under way since 1987 (financed by Gold Mark's hard currency earnings), and the results were already visible: productivity per hour increased by more than 25 percent and, consequently, unit costs went down by an average of 10 percent. But the British management consultants, who specialized in garment industry production management, maintained that Gold Mark was still over-staffed by at least 20 percent. Savings were certainly possible in administration and support: in the fall of 1990, Gold Mark employed 313 administrative and 565 support personnel (e.g., maintenance, social services), and 1,601 employees directly involved in production. Such an employment structure was typical of communist enterprises. Management did not intend to conduct massive lay offs—because it wanted to sustain the workers' support for the privatization program.

It has to be noted that Gold Mark did not experience any major problems in labor relations. During the 1980s there were no major strikes, (except for Solidarity-inspired political demonstrations during and after martial law. The company was able to develop efficient procedures for consulting and negotiating with trade unions and the workers' council.

The skills, knowledge, and experience of Gold Mark workers—supervisors, designers and engineers—as well as their commitment to product quality, were considered to be the firm's major assets. There were quite a few second and third-generation Gold Mark workers. The company had founded its own vocational school to ensure that the required degree and range of skills would continue to be available in the future.

As a result of a careful evaluation of the company (by external consultants preparing the prospectus for the public offering of shares), the following risk factors were identified:

- The major components of the company's costs for the first nine month of 1990 were: raw materials (45 percent), labor (22 percent), and interest on bank credit (10 percent). Profitability of the company (which approached 20 percent of sales, by volume) could be reduced, to the extent that a significant rise in any of these costs could not be recuperated by higher prices for products sold.

- On the domestic market, the company was faced with shrinking demand due to economic depression and the increasing threat of foreign competition. Imports were becoming increasingly attractive, since the exchange rate was stablized at (9,500 zlotys to the dollar between January 1, 1990, and May 15, 1991, when a slight adjustment of 17 percent took place) (Gabrish et al. 1992: 81)— despite high inflation of more than 260% in 1990. In addition, import duties were liberalized. By the same token, export sales were becoming less attractive for Gold Mark, and more vulnerable to trade barriers.

- A high share of the company's domestic and export sales is handled by intermediaries. Gold Mark has very limited direct access to retailers and consumers, making it dependent on the performance of intermediaries. This dependence also reduces its margin, while preventing the company from knowing well its final users, retailers, and intermediaries.

As a result of the company's careful evaluation, a new strategy was formulated and presented to prospective investors. Key elements of this new strategy included:

- Gold Mark committed itself to continuous quality improvement. The same high quality product was to be supplied to both domestic and foreign markets. This improvement was to be achieved by more careful selection of better quality fabrics, and further development of Gold Mark's own designs. The gradual elimination of CMT contracts was announced.

- Gold Mark decided to decrease its reliance on intermediaries by promoting competition among them, and by developing its own network of exclusive retail outlets in the biggest Polish cities. An effort would be made to gain direct access to large foreign retail chains, especially in the U.S. Gold Mark's management realized the need to protect actively and pay more attention to its home market base.

- The company decided to constantly review of the profitability of its different product lines order to eliminate the least profitable items, and to concentrate on the most profitable (''cash cows'') and the most promising (''stars'').

The prospectus prepared on the basis of the firm's analysis and evaluation was sufficiently convincing for investors, and all Gold Mark shares were sold in November and December 1990—most of them to small, private investors. Employees purchased their 20 percent of the shares on preferential terms. Since Gold Mark was part of the ''pilot privatization'' initiated in Poland before May 1991 opening of the stock exchange in Warsaw, and the enactment of the securities exchange law by parliament in March 1991, the shares were offered to the general public by selected banks.

Once privatization was accomplished, however, Gold Mark suddenly found itself in a more difficult, instead of an easier, position. Several factors contributed to that situation:

- The last two months of 1990 and January 1991 brought sharp increases (close to 40 percent) in the prices of fabrics and raw materials used by Gold Mark.

- Increased inflation caused a further tightening of money supply policies, and interest rates went up (to more than 80 percent in the beginning of 1991)—and a considerable increase followed in the general cost of credit and capital.

- Administratively, the exchange rate was firmly maintained at the January 1990 level in 1991—over-valuing the local currency, while considerably reducing the margin on export sales and encouraging foreign competition.

- Recession continued to reduce the internal demand for Gold Star's products. The Eastern European markets collapsed completely, and did not offer any viable alternatives.

- Income from the sale of Gold Mark shares went to the state treasury, and did not finance further modernization of the company.

As a result of this financial squeeze, the workers' wages could not be increased and did not even keep pace with inflation. The workers felt betrayed and went on strike—forcing Ms. Skrobot to resign. To reach a temporary compromise with its own work force, company had to turn to the banks for a "rescue package loan."

Gold Mark's story seems to be a typical example of a pretender enterprise operating in the macro-economic environment created by the "shock treatment" program. It is true that such enterprises, in spite of their relatively good starting point and strong market position, are still not competitive by western standards. They employ too many people—especially administrative and auxiliary personnel—their production management is not highly efficient, and they visibly lack marketing skills. (Until recently, marketing was a completely useless function in sellers' market situation, where selling was the easiest thing in the world.) A question imposes itself, however: will the continuous and increasing pressure resulting from increasingly restrictive monetary policies force such enterprises to accelerate their restructuring process, or will it paralyse and destroy them? Destruction of such "exemplary" enterprises might have a powerful negative impact on the whole transition process, because such enterprises are the "flagships" of a privatization drive intended to stimulate small investors' confidence and attract foreign capital.

In order to provide an example of a "pretender" under a gradual transition scenario, we will use an example of a large Hungarian department store, Star[6], situated in the center of a big city.

Star is by far the biggest retail outlet in the city. It is situated close to the railway station and subway, which makes it easily accessible for shoppers from the city and for visitors coming from other towns. In approximately 7,000 square meters of floor space, it offers a broad assortment of garments, apparel, textiles, shoes, appliances, electronics, and furniture, and also operates a food supermarket in the basement. The department store belonged to the "union of consumer cooperatives" (a communist pseudo-cooperative organization that was, in fact, controlled by the state bureaucracy). During the 1980s, when the "last hour" communist reforms were in progress, it gained considerable autonomy in such areas as purchasing, pricing, sales organization, and promotion.

In 1988, the firm was transformed into a joint stock company. This experimental move was undertaken by a still-communist government committed to the transition to a market economy—but hoping the communist party would be able to retain at least part of its political power. The substantial transformation of Star into a joint stock company was motivated by three factors:

1. The need for complete autonomy and technical flexibility that was impossible for state-owned or cooperative firms

2. The need for new capital to upgrade and modernize the store

3. The need to secure closer and smoother cooperation with key suppliers who intended to be shareholders.

Star's strong commercial cooperatives, major wholesalers and suppliers became shareholders. Foreign investors (mainly German and Austrian commercial firms) acquired 38 percent of the shares when the offering was placed on the Budapest stock exchange, which opened in 1988. Only one percent of shares was owned by individual Hungarian shareholders. Capital raised through the public offering of Star shares amounted to close to one billion Forints. The funds were used to completely remodel the store and increase its working capital.

As a result, Star looks almost exactly like similar department stores in the West. The presentation of merchandise, selection, and brand names are very similar. Prices, however, are at least 30 to 40 percent higher than for the same items in Germany (and for electronics, considerably more). In spite of the price differential, shoppers pour into Star because Hungarians do not have as free access to hard currency as do Poles, and cannot as easily buy abroad or import.

An analysis of Star's operations enables us to discover the reasons for its higher prices:

- Star employs up to 50 percent more personnel than similar department stores in the West (700 sales people, plus nearly 500 administrative and auxiliary personnel).

- Star's inventory management remains relatively inflexible: price reductions and sales do not take place often enough, are not deep enough, and come too late. Orders are too seldom placed and not updated often enough, and the computerized inventory management system has not yet been installed.

- Compared to leading Western retailers, Star certainly did not master the art of "sourcing": finding the most attractive and the cheapest sources of supply all over the world.

- Star's promotional techniques and customer relations handling still retained some of the flavor of socialist clumsiness and arrogance. In particular, customer complaints are processed through a "red tape" system, and with considerable delays.

• Star lacks storage facilities in its main building, which considerably complicates logistics and merchandise handling.

In spite of these weaknesses, Star can certainly be ranked as one of the most impressive "western looking" retail outlets in the post-communist countries. It's profit margin came close to 20 percent in 1989, but it was shrinking during 1990 due to the stagnating purchasing power of Hungarians, and increased competition. Specialized retailers, both domestic and smaller foreign firms offered high quality imported goods that were available, until recently, only at Star in relatively broad selection.

In 1990, the Hungarian government announced the gradual transition to convertibility of currency. Such a change, combined with tightening anti-inflationary monetary policies, could put Star in a much more difficult situation where competition, and cost of capital, will increase. The transition to convertibility of the currency is gradual, however, which gives economic agents time to adjust. The plan for 1992 calls for the creation of an interbank currency market, and limits the possibilities of paying for goods and services in Hungary with foreign currency. In 1993, the rules governing Hungarians doing business abroad are expected to be liberalized, and internal converibility broadened. Only in 1994 foreign exchange market will be opened to individuals. In Poland it hapened immediately in 1990.

Until 1991, Star was purchasing hard currency, at auctions, for 15 to 20 percent below the free (black) market exchange rate. The store had relatively good access to credit from the state-owned banks.

Comparing Gold Mark with Star, one can identify relatively easily the different effects of the "shock treatment" and "gradual transition" approaches on the enterprise level. Gold Mark was suddenly exposed to a very difficult business environment (i.e., recession, restrictive monetary policies, and full-fledged foreign competition on the domestic market). Star, on the other hand, went through the same process gradually. At the beginning of the process of opening of the economy, it remained sheltered as the protective shield was gradually removed.

Such a policy is intended to give time to potentially high-performance enterprises, such as the pretenders to improve and strengthen gradually, and to protect them from destruction by sudden exposure to unrestricted market forces.

In the case of "shock treatment," the analogy is often recalled of teaching children how to swim by suddenly throwing them into the water. Under the "shock treatment policies," however, it is not children—but elderly pupils, who never swam before—who are being thrown into the water.

It must be remembered that pretenders—in spite of the fact that they are the best and the most promising post-communist enterprises—carry much less political clout than the dinosaurs. This is mainly because their workers are less numerous, less concentrated, less organized, and less politicized. Pretenders do not have the same ability to defend themselves using political pressure. By the same token, their workers are more vulnerable and more likely to be sacrificed.

Nurturing and cultivation of promising pretenders becomes, once again, an industrial policy issue requiring highly sophisticated government agencies that can formulate and implement individualized and flexible policies addressed to specific enterprises. At a time of turbulent transition, only Hungary seems to have, to some degree, that kind of modern administrative capability. In other countries, less experienced in reforming a communist system, such capable public administration could not be developed prior to the final destruction of communism. Moreover, consecutive waves of political turmoil, purges, and witch hunts destabilized and paralyzed public administration (which, by definition, requires some degree of stability). It will certainly take a long time for these countries to develop new patterns of administrative action that are well adjusted to a modern, open-market economy.

2

The New Breed of Private Enterprise

Mixed Marriages

Joint ventures were undoubtedly one of the favorite "fads" of the "last-hour communist reformers." They were supposed to solve some of the most difficult problems of the ailing communist economies:

- Joint ventures were believed to be an opportunity to attract technology and know-how and capital for modernization of production facilities and acquisitions of foreign equipment.

- Joint ventures also were perceived as opening access to foreign markets and distribution channels.

- Communist reformers intended to use joint ventures as a way to withdraw some of the most dynamic and promising enterprises from the overwhelming power of the state economic bureaucracy—but without changing too rapidly the overall economic system. From such a perspective, joint ventures could be understood as large-scale economic experiments that would lay ground-work for further, more radical reforms leading toward the "socialist market economies."

- Joint ventures also were considered as a rich source of modern management techniques used in highly developed market economies.

- Younger, more dynamic, better-educated and more widely travelled communist officials and managers looked at joint ventures as good opportunities for lucrative careers under the new socio-economic and political circumstances.

Such an approach—which regarded the joint venture as "an enclave," "experiment," or "exception" creating unusually favorable conditions for economic activity—emerged in the last years of the communist regimes, and did not completely change until now.

These hopes and expectations associated with joint ventures by the communist reformers never really materialized on anything like massive scale. Even Yugoslavia, which started experimenting with joint ventures as early as in 1967, or Hungary, which is consistently ranked as the most attractive country in the region for foreign investors (Merrill Lynch, 1990), were never able to attract substantial amounts of capital. In recent years, none of these countries (Russia included) has attracted substantially more than $1 billion in direct investment, while Spain is able attract more than $6 billion a year (OECD, 1989). Only Hungary remains an exception: in 1991, foreign investment reached nearly $1.5 billion, offsetting interest payments on Hungary's foreign debt (Gabrish et al., 1992: 39). Even if, by some miracle, a post-communist country did as well as Spain in attracting foreign capital, even such a considerable inflow of capital would be marginal when compared to the actual investment needed.

Investment needs of post-communist countries have never been carefully calculated, except for East Germany. Economists believed that in order to close the gap between the two parts of Germany, some DM 300 billion would have to be invested within the next five years. During the process of German unification, these figures were proven to be too low. In 1991 alone, the total net transfer from West to East Germany totalled about DM 120 billion. This aid package included programs such as: infrastructure improvements (DM 27 billion), promotion of investments by the corporate sector (DM 6 billion), financial assistance for enterprises (at least DM 24.7 billion), measures promoting housing construction (DM 8.7 billion), employment-related measures (at least DM 12 billion), borrowing authorization for enterprise restructuring, clean-ups, and subsidies for exports to Eastern Europe (at least DM 20 billion) (Deutsche Bank, 1991).

Based on these figures, one can estimate the investment needs of a country like Poland, whose population is much bigger than East Germany's, population wise and whose infrastructure and industrial base are considerably weaker. Respective figures for the former USSR would seem to be astronomical, no matter how uncertain they may be. The only sure thing is that they are extremely high, and that direct foreign investment will certainly not be able to match them to any significant extent. Every country has to develop its own capital formation mechanism, based on its own resources. Then, foreign capital can come in and accelerate the development process which has already been started.

Qualitative objectives of attracting foreign investment set by communist reformers and post-communist governments were achieved to different degrees in various countries, industries, and periods. For example, a survey of the approximately 1,000 joint ventures registered in Hungary showed that more than half the foreign investment involved sales, marketing and trade, while less than 10 percent went to industrial manufacturing enterprises (see table 1).

**Table 1. In Hungary, a survey of 319 out of approximately 1,000
registered joint ventures gave the following distribution by industries:**

Sales, marketing & trading	56.74%	(181 companies)
Industrial manufacturing	9.4%	(30 companies)
Construction industry	5.96%	(19 companies)
Tourism	4.7%	(15 companies)
Software development	2.82%	(9 companies)
Management & business consulting	2.51%	(8 companies)
Transportation	1.88%	(6 companies)
Agricultural production	1.88%	(6 companies)
Raw materials production	1.25%	(4 companies)
Education	0.94%	(3 companies)
Banking & insurance	0.31%	(1 company)
Others (e.g., entertainment, press)	11.6%	(37 companies)

Figures for the USSR and Poland are similar (Degtyarenko 1991; Sadowska and Olszewski 1991). In the former USSR, most of 3,000 registered joint ventures are dormant and (or) have very little capital invested (Hertzfeld 1991).

Overall, the evaluation of existing joint ventures in post-communist countries by their host governments is rather negative. Among the reasons for such negative evaluation, the most commonly quoted are the following:

- Low amounts of capital invested. For example, in Hungary, more than 60 percent of the joint ventures surveyed by Ternovszky (1991) had assets of less than 10 million forints ($150,000). In Poland, more than 60 percent had assets of less than $50,000 (Sadowska and Olszewski 1991).

- Low preference given by foreign investors to manufacturing and high-value-added industries. The strong tendency to invest in trading or disguised barter has sometimes even been described as "predatory."

- Lack of the expected transfer of management know-how.

Despite such generally negative evaluations of joint ventures, Eastern European countries have several times changed and rewritten their foreign investment legislation, each time making it more flexible and providing more incentives for foreign investors. The USSR did this twice (in 1987 and 1989), Poland four times (in 1986, 1989, 1990, and 1991), and Hungary three times (in 1972, 1980, and 1989).

Foreign investors have their own complaints about the business environments in post-communist countries. The most common reasons for such complaints are the following:

- Insufficient business infrastructure (e.g., telecommunications, office space, banking services, insurance)

- Bureaucracy, red tape, constantly changing regulations and government officials

- Accounting procedures and standards that are incompatible with the Western methods

- Nonconvertible currency and restrictions on credit drawn from abroad, money transfers, exports, and imports

- Unclear and difficult-to-establish real estate property rights,

- Underdeveloped and costly distribution channels

Such a "common body of complaints" applies, to a lesser or greater extent, to all the post-communist Eastern and Central European countries (Mergers and Acquisitions 1991). Nevertheless, new joint ventures continually emerge—and some competent western authors remain optimistic about them in the long run, even in the conditions of extreme uncertainty prevailing in the former USSR (Hertzfeld 1991). Natural resources and millions of customers, with generally not enough industries to serve them, remain the main attractions for Western investors.

Cheap, educated labor is also looked upon as an attractive opportunity. On the first page of the Merrill Lynch publication devoted to investment opportunities in Eastern Europe (September 1990), hourly compensation rates are announced such as: East Germany—$4, Czechoslovakia—$2.05, USSR—$1.84, Yugoslavia—$1.71, Hungary—$1.7, Poland—$1.35. It remains an open question how long such differences will persist in a unifying Europe, where the West German wage rate is approaching $20, and the Spanish rate $10.

The figures quoted above confirm once more how misleading are the Eastern European statistics. Hourly wages in the former USSR are indicated as higher than in Poland, Hungary, or Yugoslavia. The artificially low official exchange rate of the Soviet ruble has been used, even though it is many times lower than free market exchange rate. And in Poland, internal convertibility of the currency, which equalized the official and free market exchange rates, was introduced in January 1990. As a result, tens of thousands of Russian Ukrainian, Belorussian workers come to work illegally in Poland for one-third of the Polish wage rate—and still bring home much more than they could have made in their home countries. However, Western managers and business leaders have a deeply entrenched tendency to respect figures, and to accept them at face value. Therefore, some of them come to Eastern Europe in search of cheap and disciplined labor.

In response to foreign investors' complaints, a more or less common scheme of foreign direct investment legislation has been worked out—modeled on the Hungarian legislation of 1989—and is gradually being adopted by other countries in the region. The most important elements of this legislation are:

- Foreign ownership permitted up to 100 percent

- Gradually relaxes local management requirements

- Repatriation of profits in hard currency permitted up to 100 percent (in Hungary, Poland, Russia)

- Tax incentive packages, including tax holidays, loss carry-forward privileges, and increased depreciation rates

- Increasing protection of foreign investment (Domanski 1991)

Two joint venture enterprises are presented below: the Soviet-Mauritius SOVMAV, and the German-Hungarian HUN PUMP.

The Soviet-Mauritius joint venture[1] was started by the cooperative Vremya and registered in Moscow in 1988. Cooperatives were a dominant form of private ownership in the former USSR after the law on private economic activity was passed in 1987, and until the end of 1991. Vremya had 20 members, and after 2 years of activity had profits of 300,000 rubles per year. It has to be remembered, however, that in such enterprises what really counts is not profits, but the additional earnings of members who usually keep their jobs in the state-owned enterprises, government agencies, universities, or research institutes.

At the beginning, Vremya was involved in theater productions, exhibitions, art auctions, and concerts. But after more than a year of activity, it started to look for other profitable opportunities and for foreign partners. Creation of a joint venture is especially desirable for Soviet entrepreneurs because it gives them not only higher incomes, but also extended freedom of travel abroad.

In 1989, Vremya's management ran across a representative of Depsa Marin Ltd., a Mauritius-based company looking for business opportunities in Moscow, and serious negotiations began.

Depsa Marin Ltd. was founded in 1968, and its scope of activities covers trading, transportation, and consulting services. It has been doing business in the USSR for many years as a trading intermediary, and has accumulated experience on this market. By looking for promising opportunities in the knitwear market and in management consulting, Depsa Marin had attracted two partners: a well-known European management consulting firm, and a textile company with several plants in Mauritius. Textile company sells $6 million a year worth of knitwear in Western Europe and has developed its own network of sales representatives in France, England, and Germany.

After preliminary market study and negotiations between the parties, the Soviet and Western firms decided to create a joint venture company, domiciled in the former USSR, that would first produce T-shirts and sell them on the Soviet and Western European markets. Later, other activities were to be undertaken, such as management consulting, trading and retailing, and production of optical devices and other product lines.

The business concept behind the first proposed venture was quite simple, and quite common in the USSR: to take advantage of the cheap Soviet labor and chronically under-supplied Soviet consumer market, to cover operating expenses through the sale of some percentage of the output at a high price on the ever-hungry local market, and to make money in hard currency through exports to Western Europe.

The Western partners agreed to supply equipment for T-shirt production: a unit valued at $130,000–150,000, plus a steady supply of material valued at $20,000–25,000 per month. Vremya was to be responsible for labor, securing of factory buildings, warehouses and office space, production management, and sales in the USSR. Monthly production capacity of the equipment supplied was estimated at 200,000 T-shirts. The wholesale price for such a product on the Western European market was $1.5–2 apiece, and in Russia a minimum of 10 rubles.

After presenting all the required documents—the charter, cooperation agreement, and feasibility study—and having them approved by the Ministry of Finance, the joint venture was registered with the Moscow City Council. The formalities took relatively little time—from November 1989 to January 1990—probably because of the small size and importance of the venture, and the good local contacts developed by Vremya. Ownership of the company was split 50/50 between the Western investors and Vremya, giving each of the parties four seats on the board of directors. The president of Vremya was nominated as CEO. The Western contribution was valued at $83,000 in cash, capitalized technology and office equipment, plus $130,000 in production equipment. The Soviet contribution was valued at 50,000 rubles in cash to start operations, plus 300,000 in working capital.

It was decided that during the first seven months, only 25 percent of the output would be sold on the Soviet market, enabling the enterprise to cover all operating expenses—including workers' wages that were nearly double the average wage in Moscow, and handsome salaries for managers—plus before-tax profits of 350,000 rubles monthly (a sales volume of 500,000 rubles, less 150,000 in operating expenses). At the same time, the Western partners would be able to recover their investment in totality, plus $600,000 cash in before-tax profits.

The whole operation, then, is characterized by a high rate of return, which makes it unimportant to search for local supplies of materials that—in the highly unstable environment—might turn out to be unreliable and below required quality standards.

Vertical integration seems to be a must for the "more serious" joint ventures operating in the former USSR. McDonald's, which took an incredible amount of time and effort to develop local supplies of potatoes and meat patties for its Moscow operation (by securing sources of supply and building a state-of-the art plant and distribution facility near Moscow) offers the most spectacular example of such a strategy (Hetrzfeld 1991). This strategy, however, is becoming increasingly difficult as the Soviet system disintegrates. As a result, the number of such "serious," already operational joint ventures is very limited, and growing slowly (Gardner 1989; Degtyarenko 1991).

Separate accounting in rubles and hard currency also seems to be a characteristic feature of this type of joint venture. Non-convertible currency is one of the basic assumptions underlying such business concepts. When the situation suddenly changes and a country decides at least to introduce "internal convertibility," as Poland did in 1990, enterprises built on this concept find themselves in serious difficulty. It is too early to assess the impact of the steps toward convertibility taken by the Russian government in 1992, and to compare it with Polish experiences.

HUN PUMP[2] was initiated as early as 1980, when the German inventory of a very sophisticated circulating pump for central heating-and-water systems in individual homes visited Hungary, and in particular, an electric motor manufacturer in Budapest: Electra. Electra was a large factory with over 100 years of experience in electro-mechanical industry, was relatively well-equipped, and had a highly skilled labor force. The idea of setting up a joint venture to manufacture the pump in Budapest for Western Europe markets was born during this visit.

It was an innovative idea because no manufacturing joint venture existed in Hungary prior to 1980, in spite of the fact that following the "very timid" joint venture legislation of 1972, some half dozen such ventures were established in the industrial services and banking sectors. Such an innovative idea had to overcome serious difficulties related to the monopoly of foreign trade jealously guarded by state owned foreign trade companies serving exclusively certain branches of industry (heritage of the stalinist system) and stiff regulations on imports and exports. Since JV is still in existence its development can illustrate evolution of that kind of enterprise in "late communist" and post-communist environments.

German partner was motivated mainly by the access to low cost production facility and highly skilled low cost labor, monopoly for supplying JV with the highest value-added components and product development, possibilities of new markets' penetration. Hungarian partner was motivated by possibility to start new, modern, high value added production line, technology transfer and access to hard currency market.

In order to accommodate still powerful and influential with the economic bureaucracy foreign trade companies, two of them were offered symbolic shares (3 percent and 1 percent in newly created JV as well as informal guarantees of getting lion's share of its import and export business. Emig took 50 percent of shares and remaining 47 percent German partner. Emig's contribution was composed of manufacturing rights (acquired from German inventor), cash and the lease of production facilities. German partner provided equipment enabling serial production of standard basic model of a pump as contribution in kind and some cash.

Company was registered in 1981 and full scale production started in mid-1982. Beginnings were very difficult, however, because of still restrictive at that time JV legislation: German partners' contribution in kind was not duty free. Not only considerable duty was imposed but the company had to go through lengthy process of import licensing. Tax holidays were also not granted as it is now. It took company three years to make profits enabling to compensate for the costs sunk into establishing the company, importing and installing equipment.

Once production started marketing strategy had to be adjusted. Originally targeted market was Western European but by the time production started market situation has changed. Demand for the product offered by Hunpump shrinked considerably because of slowing down of construction business in Western Europe. To make bad situation worse, company was offering only a single model of circular pump (due to the equipment supplied by German partner) and only producers offering full range of product to traders, wholesalers, and builders could survive on the market. Facing difficulties on the foreign markets, the company had to turn to the domestic market, discovering that it was large, untapped, and profitable. In early and mid-1980s Hungary was experiencing a boom in individual home construction and supply of modern heating equipment was very limited because of hard currency shortage. Hunpump was offering on this rapidly expanding market a very advanced and reliable product perfectly fit for middle-size homes at very attractive price (less than a half of the price of the cheapest import pump). Warranty and relatively reliable service were also considered as serious advantages offered to Hunpump buyers. Because of undeniable competitive advantage on domestic market more than 400,000 pumps were sold between 1982 and 1990.

Full command of domestic marketbase enabled further export expansion. Foreign trade company holding 3 percent of "Hunpump" equity organized sales to Scandinavia, Italy, Greece, and Austria. Good quality and competitive price made product attractive on these difficult markets. German partner included Hungarian pump into the wider range of his products and successfully offered it on the German market picking up again in the mid and late 1980s. After passing all the tests required by the US government product was also admitted to the American market and 25,000 pumps were sold between 1985 and 1990.

Between 1983 and 1989 company had healthy annual sales volumes growth rates of 30 percent and the employment raised from 20 to 120. "Hunpump" has two managing directors: one nominated by Hungarian and another by German partners. Organizational structure is very simple and consists of sales manager, technical manager and plant manager. Company employs 6 engineers and 13 qualified technicians. The wages are about 50 percent above average for the equivalent type of job. Margin is well above 25 percent. In order to overcome differences in accounting standards and procedures company has to produce two annual reports and profit and loss statements: one Hungarian and one German. Both have to be accepted by external auditors, which relatively easy since big international accounting firms such as Price Waterhouse or Ernst & Young have opened their offices in Budapest. Double accounting is still necessary since Hungary is only gradually moving toward European accounting standards and intends to fully implement them within the next couple of years.

In 1988 Hunpump was registered in the Foreign Trade register, which enabled it to import and export directly. This license is used only for exports of spare parts and components delivered to foreign customers under sub-contracting agreements as well as for imports of equipment, spare parts and components. Exports of the main product: pumps are still done on commission basis through the foreign trade company—one of the Hunpump partners. This due to constant pressure from foreign trade company arguing that it has distribution and service network too expensive for Hunpump to develop and to maintain. It is becoming evident, however, that distribution channel is costly and inefficient.

Hunpump was selling the same product during the whole decade of the 1980s. Without development product has become obsolete: it remains the only pump on the market without speed regulation. Due to the unique design of the pump necessary development work can be only done in German partners' labs, which are busy developing their own products and Hunpump did not even have a chance to place an order for development of badly needed speed regulation system.

To compensate for shrinking sales of its main product company is supplying components (driving units) for American and Japanese manufacturers of more advanced pumps. According to the company's sales manager Mr. Kaldor that kind of strategy can be hardly perceived as viable in the long run because of slim margins and fierce competition among subcontractors of major manufacturers. Mr. Kaldor is absolutely positive that radical strategic decisions are needed because domestic sales stopped growing and started to decline in 1989–1990. Such a negative trend is due to the transition-related recession and drastically decreasing numbers of new individual housing constructions. Expected convertibility of the currency will expose Hunpump to tough foreign competition offering much more advanced product.

Strategic decisions require, however, full commitment of German partner who seems to neglect and to forget his relatively unimportant Hungarian Joint Venture as long as it does not loose money. Because of that attitude of German partner Mr. Kaldor remains skeptical about possibility of radical strategic decisions. Asked for reasons he names communication problems between Hungarian and Germans and German partners' attention being completely devoted to new business opportunities resulting from unification of Germany.

Both JV's presented above seem to represent reasonably well population of active and relatively successful ventures with foreign capital participation existing in post-communist countries. Their most important characteristic features can be summarized as follows:

- Relatively small size, both employment and foreign direct investment wise,

- Founded by smaller and rather less sophisticated foreign companies,

- Local partners are predominantly state owned companies and organizations,

- A business concept, often based on non-convertible local currency, that can be called "disguised barter" or "leveraged barter"

- Lack of a long-term strategy

- The foreign partners' lack of knowledge of the local market, often combined with the lack of marketing skills of the local partner (part of the heritage of long decades of a "sellers' market" and "repressed inflation").

The bigger joint ventures founded by larger and more sophisticated foreign companies, which can be perceived as exceptional (such as McDonald's and the Moscow City Council, Tungsram and GE in Hungary, Skoda and Volkswagen in Czechoslovakia, or Zamech and ABB in Poland) have different sets of characteristics:

- Long-term commitment and long-term strategy of the foreign partner

- Considerable investment in new production capabilities and new technology

- Careful study of the opportunities offered by local and international markets,

- Domination by the foreign partner, who makes the strategic decisions

It has to be remembered, however, that widely publicized negotiations seldom lead to creation of a joint venture. For example, Gardner (1989) cites 18 huge American ventures under negotiation with Soviets, among them American Express (who wanted to install automatic teller machines in Moscow), Occidental Petroleum (who wanted to build a $6 billion petrochemical complex near the Caspian Sea, jointly with the Italian ENI and Japanese Marubeni), and Combustion Engineering and McDermott International (who were willing to build two large petrochemical complexes in Western Siberia). None of these ideas ever materialized.

High risk potential due to instability of business environment, complete lack of compatibility between Western business enterprises and local bureaucracies and state organizations, as well as complicated and lengthy procedures, are mainly responsible for the failure of such negotiations. Many Western negotiators raise the issue of a lack of clear financial commitment on the part of locals who unrealistically expect that the Western partner will provide total financing for the project.

Unsuccessful joint venture negotiations are not unknown among Western companies, to cite Ford and Fiat. A large percentage of registered "dormant" enterprises seems to be a characteristic feature of East-West joint ventures. It is worth studying. Interviews conducted by the author indicate that unrealistic expectations from both sides, lack of adequate financing, and the rapidly changing business environment are responsible for this specifically Eastern European syndrome.

Comparing East-West joint ventures with the "strategic alliances" formed by Western multinational and global enterprises (Perlmutter and Heenan 1986; Hamel, Doz and Prahalad 1989), the opportunistic character of the second category seems to be the most striking difference. In the case of East-West joint ventures, all involved parties seem to lack a long-term strategy and commitment. When the strategy is present, it is unilaterally developed by a Western multinational that has formulated some strategic objectives in this part of the world, while the local party is passively adjusting and following. Examples of ventures formed in Eastern and Central Europe by such multinationals as ABB, GE, McDonald's (and which are quite exceptional, among thousands of others) clearly confirm that statement.

This lack of strategic depth among East-West joint venture results from the fact that nearly all of the Eastern European partners are state-owned enterprises, or state or local bureaucracies. Such organizations were not accustomed to developing any strategy independently. If a strategy exists at all, it came from the upper levels. Post-communist governments do not have a more elaborate strategy related to the enterprise or industry level. At best, they were able to develop macro-economic stabilization plans and monetary policies. They "want to attract foreign capital," but do not have the slightest idea where, how, and even why to channel it. Hungary (to the least extent), and Poland and Czechoslovakia illustrate this situation—which comes as a result of ideological reasons (a market economy, but without any government intervention), a lack of adequate skills within the bureaucracy, the destabilization of a civil service that has not had time to renew itself, and the general pressure of political, social, and economic issues demanding constant attention. At the worst, the countries are "drifting," unable to take any coherent course of action. This situation is closely linked to the "violent conflict scenario" illustrated by Yugoslavia and some former Soviet republics in Asia.

The managers and officials involved in joint venture deals often change in these turbulent times and places, which makes it virtually impossible to develop the common strategy and "chemistry" between people that is widely believed to be a precondition of successful alliances (Jordan 1990). Managers and officials representing the Eastern European state sector in these deals are very different economic actors from the managers of Western companies and multinationals. They are accustomed to hiding their real intentions behind the "pro forma" plans and strategies presented to higher-level bureaucracies (Kozminski and Tropea 1982). Such an approach, even if understood by the Western partners, makes it very difficult to articulate clearly the objectives, expectations and strategies of both parties. This situation is very likely to occur if the joint venture is really a disguised barter transaction that has to be "properly packaged" in order to be presented to higher levels of the local economic bureaucracy for final approval. It requires the use of such "magic words" as: "transfer of advanced technology and modern management techniques," "enrichment of internal market," "promotion of exports," etc., etc. Approving bureaucrats do not necessarily believe, but they seal the deals if the wording is right and it helps foster their own careers. Quite often, bribes also are expected. Such overwhelmingly cynical attitudes were deeply internalized under communism and cannot be changed overnight.

In the bureaucratic environment of the state-owned industries, conflicts of interests between organizations and their managers are quite common. That explains why Eastern European managers are often willing to enter business deals that clearly put their organizations at a disadvantage: it is simply that such deals benefit them personally. But corruption alone is much too simple an explanation (Kozminski and Tropea, 1982; Kozminski and Zawislak, 1982; Kozminski and Obloj, 1983). For example, any joint venture would considerably benefit a Russian manager because it would give him access to foreign travel, foreign goods (e.g., a company car) and much a higher income than he had before. After 1991, most of this motivation remains. Because of it post-communist managers and bureaucrats—eager to strike the deal—are often willing to give away much more than they should, or have to.

This situation has begun to change recently in Hungary and Poland, and to a lesser extent in Czechoslovakia with development of a local private sector, convertibility of currency and freedom of travel. But in other countries (i.e., the Balkans and many ex-Soviet republics), it remains the same. Such conditions cannot be considered by serious partners as solid grounds for long-range cooperation—because joint ventures built on that kind of latent mutual understanding are extremely vulnerable to attacks from political opponents of the government that countersigned and legalized them. And governments are likely to change quite often in Eastern Europe in the coming years. The Polish presidential campaign and the Hungarian local elections in 1990 provided plenty of examples of the political exploitation of joint venture deals: prices paid by foreign partners for their share of the equity were often challenged as suspiciously low.

The Polish example shows that internal convertibility of the currency, relaxes currency regulations (making transfers abroad easy) and diminishing trade barriers dramatically change the business environment of joint ventures, especially those built on disguised barter. Domestic markets are no longer sheltered and joint ventures now have to face competition—quite often from their foreign partner. HUN PUMP is a very instructive example in this respect. Competition on foreign markets usually requires considerable new investment, and new equipment and technology, as well as access to highly efficient distribution channels and the development of marketing skills that are especially rare in Eastern and Central Europe.

Internal convertibility of the currency and opening the economy will probably reduce the number of newly formed joint ventures. Other forms of foreign capital penetration will develop, of which the following are especially worth mentioning:

- Wholly-owned subsidiaries will enable big foreign companies to retain full control over their considerable investment, saving them from many communications and "culture clash" problems (Coca Cola and Proctor and Gamble choose that strategy in Poland in 1991.)

- Portfolio investments will enable foreign investors to acquire shares of privatized companies on the open stock market, despite the fact that existing and emerging legislation imposes some form of government control over the share of equity owned by foreign investors. For example, in Poland the foreign-owned share is limited to 10 percent of equity of privatized companies offered to the public (but this percentage can be increased to 100 percent by Ministry of Ownership Changes),

- Establishing of limited liability or joint stock companies domiciled in Eastern Europe by foreign investors.

All these forms seem to be attractive alternatives of Joint Ventures for western investors entering Central and Eastern Europe. One can also predict that "new edition" of Joint Ventures much more similar to the "strategic alliances" existing in the West, will slowly emerge.

Mom and Pop Shops

Small private enterprises were allowed to exist in some communist countries such as Hungary, Poland, German Democratic Republic first as "remainings,'' of capitalism doomed to extermination with development of ''superior'' forms of the state ownership. When these ''superior'' forms failed to deliver badly needed consumers' goods and services small private enterprises were allowed to remain as carefully and suspiciously supervised enclaves ''auxiliary'' to dominating and economically ''superior'' state sector. Private enterprises were strictly forbidden to grow beyond limits accepted by communist ideologists, which meant in practice small family owned enterprises with limited number of employees.

For example in Poland limit of the employees private enterprises were allowed to hire was established at the level of 50 by 1947 Nationalization Act but very few private entrepreneurs dared to approach this limit in justified fear of being ruthlessly eliminated by punitive taxes specially designed and used by communist administration regardless the law in order to prevent ''capitalist exploitation of labor''. Private enterprises were often used by communists as a ''scapegoat'' to canalize popular dissatisfaction with shortages and rising prices. Private entrepreneurs were often portrayed by propaganda as criminal black marketeers and speculators. Repressions, ''punitive taxation'' and massive closing of private enterprises always followed such accusations. Stalinist anti-NEP campaign at the end of the 1920s terminating the period of ''socialist market economy in the USSR'' offers an extreme example of such an action. In 1928 all private trade was declared a crime and hundreds of thousands of small entrepreneurs (500,000 of the owners of small retail outlets and unknown number of craftsmen) were deported to camps, where most of them died (Surot 1989: 73). Much ''softer'' but similar actions were taken in Eastern European countries at the end of 1940s and beginning of the 1950s. In Poland in 1947–1948 there was even a propaganda nickname invented for it: ''battle for trade'' (Jezierski and Petz 1982: 41–46).

During the last years of the communist regimes countries who embraced increasingly radical economic reforms (Hungary and Poland) even encouraged private entrepreneurship. ''Last hour'' communist reformers launched the idea of ''mixed socialist economy'' (Kozminski 1990a). Even then, however, private entrepreneurs were treated with utmost suspicion, subjected to discriminating legislation and administrative practices (for example excluding private enterprises from supply sources of the ''socialized sector'' or from contracting and subcontracting for the state) and often to excessive taxation penalizing growth. Higher incomes of private entrepreneurs were often politically exploited by ''hardliners'' fighting ''reformers'' within the party and feeding hostile attitudes of the general public toward private enterprises often associated with fraud, black market and speculation. As result even temporary more favorable attitudes of authorities were followed by new waves of discrimination, persecutions and openly formulated policies to eliminate private sector. Even in such a hostile environment private sector demonstrated amazing ability to survive and grow.

For example in Poland in 1980 16.6 percent of the GNP was produced in the private sector out of which 11.1 percent in private agriculture (dominating in Poland since 1956 and occupying close to 90 percent of agricultural land). In 1989 private sector was already responsible for 19.2 percent of the GNP half of which by private agriculture. Between 1980 and 1989 when production volume in state owned non-agricultural sector decreased by 0.2 percent per year in private sector it increased by 2.7 percent per year. In non-agricultural private sector growth rate was much higher: 6.6 percent per year. After 1986 when more radical reform steps were taken by the communist reformers the rate of growth of private non-agricultural sector considerably accelerated and in 1989 it reached 30.4 percent. The pace of capital formation was also by far the highest in private non-agricultural sector and it averaged 11 percent per year, while in agriculture it was only 2.4 percent and in state sector 3.0 percent. By the end of the 1980s, when communism ended, private sector in Poland employed over 30 percent of the work force employed in the economy, 70 percent of it in private agriculture. Between 1980 and 1990, under continuing depression conditions non-agricultural private sector was the only one where employment was consistently increasing: 11.1 percent per year. (Breitkopf and Gorski and Jaszczynski 1991: 18–28).

All the figures quoted above might seem over optimistic. So it has to be reminded that share of small private business remains still considerably smaller than in the EEC countries and other developed market economies. Comparison of West and East Germany shows it very clearly: by the end of the 1980s over 60 percent of the people employed in West German non-agricultural sector worked for the enterprises employing less than 1,000 persons, the same figure for East Germany was only 24 percent (Statistishes Jahrbuch für die Bundesrepublik Deutschland 1989: 179 and 613, Golachowski 1991: 10).

If privatization consisted of increasing the share of small private business at the same pace as in the past it would take over 50 years for Poland to reach over 50 percent of non-agricultural GNP from private sector.

Private sector is also much worse equipped than state owned, in spite of the fact that some quite modern private enterprises are emerging. (Some of these are presented below.) In Poland, it is estimated that the value of fixed capital per employee is seven times higher in the state sector than in the private, non-agricultural sector. Hourly productivity is only 37 percent lower in the private, non-agricultural sector and that difference is diminishing. The average employment in small private firms in Poland is only slightly higher than two people (Breitkopf and Gorski and Jaszczynski 1991).

Private businesses under communism were concentrated in such industries as: crafts (repair shops, traditional by-hand production of such items as shoes and furniture), services (barbers, tailors), construction (small builders, renovation of apartments), transportation (moving, taxis), small industry (manufacturing of plastic items, spare parts, machine parts), hospitality (bars, restaurants, small hotels) and retailing. Recently, private entrepreneurs began moving into areas such as banking. (In 1990, a couple of private banks were registered in Poland and Czechoslovakia, and this number increased consistently in 1991 and 1992.) Entrepreneurs also are entering trade (export, import), wholesaling, high-tech industries (computer software, measurement equipment, medical instruments), larger-scale production (textiles, garments, cosmetics), large-scale distribution (supermarkets, chains of retail outlets). In countries with highly restrictive monetary policies and prohibitively high interest rates and capital costs, private enterprises tend to concentrate in lines of business providing high capital turnover, such as import trade and commerce. (Gabrish et al. 1992: 47)

More capital intensive industries remain still inaccessible for private entrepreneurs because of the lack of capital and high cost of capital. For example in Poland total volume of savings of the population deposited in the banks and in cash both in hard and local currency were estimated at only $16.6 billion which is less than 25 percent of the total net value of the assets of state-owned enterprises (Breitkopf and Gorski and Jaszczynski 1991, 29–30). Recent public opinion survey conducted in Poland indicated that workers were willing to put 1.4 of their monthly salary in capital investments, middle management—1.7, and top management—2.5. It amounts to $2.2 billion—only 3.5 percent of the value of the assets of the state sector (Jarosz 1990). High interest rates due to tight monetary policy aimed to stop inflation, underdeveloped banking system (dominated by still behaving in the old way more like government agencies) make access to capital very difficult for private entrepreneurs and considerably slow down both development of new private enterprises and privatization of the existing state owned.

Relationship between private enterprises existing in communist and post-communist countries and "shadow economy" merits special attention. In some countries (USSR, Rumania, Bulgaria, Albania) legal existence of private enterprises (even of the smallest size) was not possible. In these countries illegal activities remained the only possibility for private entrepreneurship. Especially ex-USSR is well known for such activities taking very different forms such as:

• Un-reported and un-taxed services delivered by the workers of state-owned enterprises (partially on company time, and with company equipment and materials) in such areas as cars, household appliances repairs, and renovation of apartments)

• Un-reported sales of agricultural products by farmers on small individual plots (gardens surrounding houses), but often produced on kolkhoz time and with kolkhoz equipment, fertilizers, and seeds (Katsenliboigen 1977). In 1985 such quasi-legal activities, according to official Soviet sources amounted to 27 percent of total Soviet meat production, 23 percent of milk and 28 percent of eggs (Gregory and Stuart 1990: 296). This percentage is much higher for fruits and vegetables: in 1979, 60 percent of potatoes and 42 percent of fruit was produced in this way (Seurot 1989: 214).

• Pure speculation (i.e., buying scarce products at subsidized prices in state-owned stores, and selling them on the free market at considerable profit)

• Sales of goods stolen from the state-owned enterprises. It is estimated that thefts consistently account for a significant percentage of total production costs. In 1975, for example, in Kazakhstan 20 percent of the gasoline used by private automobiles was stolen from state-sector enterprises (Seurot 1989: 280). In an official speech at the plenum of the Central Committee of the Party, Brezhnev admitted that the Soviet economy was loosing 25 billion rubles a year because of thefts, and another 25 billion because of speculation (Seurot 1989: 281).

• Massive conspiracies organized by managers in order to divert a part of the output of state owned enterprises to black market or even to exports at their own personal account,

• Illegal transactions in gold, previous stones, narcotics, prostitution,

• Buying hard currency and goods from foreigners,

• ''Commercial foreign tourism''—buying and selling abroad for profit by ''tourists'' from post—communist countries, especially Poles gained themselves a reputation for doing it at massive scale in neighbouring countries: Germany, Austria, Sweden (to understandable discontent of local authorities) but also in the Far East (private import of electronics),

- Illegal work abroad and illegal (without duty or taxation) transfer of earnings to the home country in the form of currency and merchandise (here Poles and Yugoslavs are the champions),

- Medical underground (pharmaceutical and in some countries like Rumania illegal abortions and even sales of children for adoption by foreigners).

Ex-USSR has a reputation for the most drastic forms of criminal economic underground. It seems to be due to the process of decomposition of the Soviet empire, growing chaos and decreasing repressiveness of the system combined with still remaining bureaucratic rigidity, growing inefficiency of the official economy unable to satisfy the most basic needs of the population even at subsistence level. Rumania and Bulgaria seem to face similar set of contingencies. Soviet specificity seems to consist of "imperial dimension" of the problem, long Russian tradition of corruption (see literary presentation of it by Gogol in XIX century), and economic underground able to survive even in the extreme conditions of terror and repression imposed by Stalin. The shortages were aggravated under "perestroika" as state-controlled production and distribution fell apart. With the rapid decrease in repressiveness of the system, the role of the *underground* economy increased considerably. This trend seems to be continuing since the fall of communism in 1991.

In his testimony to a joint economic committee of the U. S. Congress, Professor Wladimir G. Treml of Duke University formulated an opinion that goods and services exchanged in the underground economy might amount to as much as 25 percent of the GNP and involve more than 16 percent of total labor resources (Binder 1991). In spite of the fact that this estimate was not substantiated with exact figures, which are not available, it seems very plausible. Also, outright economic criminality (mainly thefts) has recently seen a constant and sharp rise. In an interview given at the beginning of 1991, the state prosecutor and police chief from Gorbachev's home town of Stavropol admitted that, in 1990, economic criminality in the region increased by nearly 50 percent (Ekonimika i Zhizn 1991: 13).

Countries where market-inspired economic reforms were undertaken, and where the private sector existed under communism (e.g., Poland and Hungary) decided in the last years of communism to "legalize the black market," or at least some part of it. In Poland, which has been a double-currency country since the 1970s, and where illegal currency transactions amounted to hundreds of millions of dollars a year, the last communist government in 1989 issued 2,281 licenses for privately owned currency exchange establishments trading in currency at free market prices. In Hungary, "moonlighting" and second jobs were made legal in 1986. The Soviets tried to follow by introducing special legislation on "individual economic" activity in 1986, but this measure was too restrictive to legalize the powerful economic underground of the USSR.

In the countries where private enterprises were allowed to evade taxes (due to loose record keeping and cash-only transactions), illegal labor and the use of materials illegally acquired from the state sector became a "way of life" for private enterprises. The end of communism does not seem to have put an end to these practices—just the opposite, as the turbulent transition seems to provide fertile ground for economic and business criminality. On April 19, 1991, an article appeared in the *Wall Street Journal* under the significant title "Poland has plenty of one thing: crooks—Thefts, communist scams thrive as economy shifts" (Barry 1991: A14). The author focuses exclusively on ex-communist officials as unscrupulous crooks who take advantage of the opportunities presented by transition. But it is hard to believe that the others are as innocent as angels.

The following factors enhanced this "second economy" in all communist countries:

- Repressed inflation syndrome, of which the two main components are shortages and the administrative mechanism of setting prices

- Non-convertible currency

- Lack of competition, and monopolies in production and distribution

- Rationing and bureaucratic procedures for allocating resources

- Domination of state property, combined with widespread belief that "state property is nobody's property," and that "stealing from the state is much less of a sin than stealing from an individual"

- Restrictive legislation that discriminates against legal private entrepreneurship

All these factors have not disappeared completely with the elimination of communism, and for a long time the second economy will certainly remain closely linked to private entrepreneurship. Only complete "normalization" of the business environment will accelerate the process of eliminating the more drastic forms of this "economic underground." It is well known, however, that even some fully developed market economies are characterized by the important role of an underground economy. U.S. agriculture in the southern states, which uses illegal Mexican labor on a massive scale; sweat shops in New York City; the Italian garment and leather industries, massive production in the Far East of fake brand name products; Italy's notorious tax fraud—these are just a few examples.

Assessing the role of the underground economy's link to the process of forming a market economy is not an easy task, and can lead to ambiguous conclusions. From one perspective, this role must be considered highly positive, since it enhances the development of private entrepreneurship. A number of reasons support that point of view.

In some countries (such as the USSR for example), the underground economy was the only place where entrepreneurial spirit and market instinct have survived. In others (such as Poland or Hungary), it enabled legitimate private businesses to adjust to an extremely difficult environment, to survive, and even to grow.

The underground economy made possible the initial accumulation of capital that was instrumental in the creation and development of larger private enterprises after the fall of communism. In fact, most of the big private enterprises that emerged in post-communist countries seem to share that background, usually in combination with some tradition of legitimate business. Here again, some similarities to early capitalism can be found: first-generation tycoons, such as the "robber barons" in the U.S. were never close to being angels. Even quite recently, German economic reconstruction after the World War II is attributed, to some extent, to the black marketeers of 1945–1948.

Finally, the underground economy helped relatively large groups of people to have better standard of living than was offered by the "official" economy.

As a result of these factors, communist regimes could not really afford, and were not able, to eliminate the underground economy. Governments not only tolerated the second economy, but even encouraged it. For example, even in the 1970s, the hard currency bank savings of private citizens in Poland were practically tax exempt—and no questions were asked about the source of these revenues. This policy could not be immediately discontinued after the fall of communism.

These considerations lead us to the negative aspects of relationship between the underground economy and small private enterprises.

A management culture and behavioral patterns inherited from the underground economy can hardly be considered "sound business practices." Tax evasion is one such behavior, and another is cash transactions that sometimes amount to millions of dollars. Most private entrepreneurs (especially the bigger ones) prefer to remain silent about the real value of their assets. Businesses and properties are often legally owned by "front figures." Customs declarations are often falsified in order to avoid payment of duties. Poland in 1989, for example (when ceilings were imposed on domestic production by ill-conceived anti-alcohol legislation), 1,990 private importers of alcohol ripped off the state budget by hundreds of millions of dollars worth of unpaid duties and taxes. It is believed that some huge fortunes quickly arose that way.[3]

The close links between communist officials and the underground economy represent another aspect of the phenomenon. Especially in the southern and middle-eastern republics of the former USSR, such close relationships were developed and cultivated to such an extent that some authors have described it as "mafiazation of the economy." Obviously, such an excessively corrupt criminal environment cannot be perceived as conducive to the emergence of normal, healthy private enterprises—and rightly becomes one of the major targets of the anti-communist opposition.

Due to the criminal aspect of the underground economy, private entrepreneurship still lacks legitimacy in the opinion of a majority of the people. Many people still associate private enterprise with fraud. It must be remembered that post-communist societies still cherish egalitarian values, and that the conspicuous consumption of the new emerging middle and upper class—especially visible in Poland and Hungary, where the streets of Warsaw and Budapest are packed with brand new BMWs and Mercedes—is shocking and revolting to many. The issue is especially delicate, and even potentially explosive, since the transition to a market economy inevitably requires that serious sacrifices be imposed on a majority of the people—including unemployment, and a serious decrease in the purchasing power of the average family. Such rapidly increasing differences in income and standard of living at a time of deep recession may be easily exploited politically by "neo-communists" or the extreme right, and thus inhibit the transition process. It's worth remembering that in the late 1920s, these issues helped Stalin to replace the NEP market economy—which was based to a great extent on private property—with a totally centralized, totally planned and unbelievably repressive "forced industrialization" system.

The uncertain business environment and requirements for the accelerated accumulation of capital (i.e., the scarcity of capital, high interest rates, and underdeveloped commercial banking and capital markets) divert private entrepreneurs from manufacturing (especially the more capital intensive), and push them toward activities promising a high and quick return, such as trading and import-export. If not corrected by government policies, such trends could be exploited politically to demonstrate the "parasitic character" of private enterprise.

In the most advanced post-communist countries (e.g., Hungary, Poland and Czech republic), the recent development of a private sector is very impressive. In 1989–90, 516,000 new private enterprises were registered in Poland, 300,000 in Czechoslovakia and 250,000 in Hungary.[4]

Three cases illustrate this development of private entrepreneurship: the computer firm Graphisoft in Hungary, a high-class restaurant in the old town of Warsaw, and a small private Jewish restaurant in Moscow.

The founder of Graphisoft[5], Mr. Bojar, was a gifted computer programmer and software developer. He was employed in one of the state research institutes, but left when funding to support his work on modelling software was cut. As did many Hungarians and Poles at that time, Bojar worked abroad (in West Germany) as programmer, gaining experience and hard currency. In 1981, together with a colleague, he started a private software firm.

In 1982, the Hungarian Power Ministry solicited bids on engineering assistance in the installation of a complicated system of pipes in a Soviet-designed nuclear power plant. The designs were inconsistent—the pipes did not fit together—and the Hungarian ministry had to prove this to the Soviets in order to seek compensation. Bojar and his partner decided to bid. Under "normal" circumstances they never would have gotten the contract, because many large, powerful and prestigious organizations (such as Hungarian Academy of Sciences) participated. But this time, the job "really" had to be done quickly—and "Graphisoft" was able to generate 300 drawings, using their new software, before the bidding period ended. They worked nights using a computer rented from the Geophysics Institute, and finished before anybody else had started. The ministry was able to use their drawings to prove the inconsistency of the plans supplied by the Soviets—and won its case. Graphisoft was paid the equivalent of $30,000 for the job: 30 times more than the initial capital they had declared to set up their company. These funds kept them going for next two years. Moreover, they kept the software—which had been developed to generate the drawings—because, at that time, the ministry did not have a computer.

During the next two years, Bojar and his associates took their software to trade shows and computer fairs in West Germany, trying to find a hardware vendor with whom they could cooperate as a software developer. In the beginning they had little success, but they finally began to cooperate with Apple. This cooperation gained momentum when a Macintosh came out specifically equipped for engineering applications.

In 1990, Graphisoft employed more than 50 people, of whom thirty were highly qualified software developers. The firm was selling highly sophisticated CAD and CAD-related products, such as ArchiCAD for architects; TopCAD for mechanical engineers; and PlotMaker, a lay-out program for CAD drawings. Nearly 4,000 units were sold in 1990. In order to penetrate US market, Graphisoft had established a five-person sales office in San Francisco. Its mission was to set up a professional resale network, and to support its customers directly.

Bojar recognizes that his major weakness is the lack of a customer base in his home country, and in Central and Eastern Europe. This is due to the fact that Apple computers are practically unknown in the region, where the market is dominated by IBM and IBM-compatible "clones" manufactured in the Far East. Therefore, Bojar decided to start distributing "Macs" in Hungary, and helped to set up a dealers' network. By concentrating on desktop publishing and engineering applications, he hopes to sell at least 1,000 units in the first year of operation of "Graphisoft Trading." At the same time, Graphisoft plans further development of engineering software packages and sales to Western customers.

The Tartuffe restaurant[6] was established in 1985 in the most picturesque section of Warsaw's Old Town, close to the Old Town Market Square—the most popular place among tourists visiting the Polish capital. The restaurant is located in a beautifully restored, historical stone cave belonging to the cultural workers trade union, which unsuccessfully tried to establish a social club there. In 1985, the premises were leased to a pair of private entrepreneurs, Jan and Eva Pawlowski, who decided to maintain a "club" name for their high-class restaurant. This gimmick, which enabled the couple to refuse service to "unwanted" customers such as noisy drunks or people who were not properly dressed, helped enormously to establish an image of exclusivity and high class that was especially appealing to the most affluent segment of Warsaw restaurant goers: foreign diplomats and business people, and the rapidly growing group of local private entrepreneurs and successful artists. To keep up that image Tartuffe never advertises—relying solely on world-of-mouth—but is always filled, both at lunchtime and in the evening.

Jan and Eva Pawlowski both graduated in the early '70s from the Food Processing Department of the Agricultural Academy, in Warsaw, and took jobs in low-quality state-owned restaurants. They sincerely hated the low quality of the food and service they provided, as well as the overwhelming bureaucracy that made any improvement impossible. They dreamed about running a high-class restaurant, and used their few opportunities for foreign travel to visit and observe such places. Jan is a creative and talented chef who likes to experiment and cook fancy dishes for friends. In 1985, when the Pawlowski's learned about the cultural workers trade union's desire to lease their club in the Old Town—an ideal location for the restaurant of their dreams—they took a chance, quit their jobs with state-owned restaurants, mobilized all their saving plus all they could borrow from family and friends, and strike out on their own.

Jan took care of purchasing supplies and the kitchen, while Eva handled customer service. Both Pawlowskis concentrated on developing the unique features that would connote exclusivity. After a series of experiments with different recipes, Jan identified a number of exclusive "landmark dishes" to project the Tartuffe "image," such as: carp with almond sauce, Russian pancakes ("blini") served with caviar, smoked salmon and sour cream, a traditional Polish beef dish served with heavy sauce in an emptied dark bread loaf, and salads served with specially prepared dressings.

In 1985 the restaurant business in Warsaw was, at the same time, much more difficult and much easier, compared to Western Europe or Warsaw itself in 1990 or 1991. On the one hand, supplying a high-class restaurant was a very difficult job. For example, meat was still rationed and restaurant prices were regulated and monitored (especially in the case of private establishments). This made it difficult to justify much higher prices on the free market, where restaurants were not allowed to buy. So, Jan had to "make friends" among the city government bureaucrats who allocated meat to restaurants and state-owned meat distributors. Alcohol, and especially wines, posed similar problems, since it was not possible officially to change zlotys into hard currency, and purchase the beverages in hard-currency stores. Jan had to rely even more on "friends" from the state distribution system. He managed, somehow, and Tartuffe was consistently relatively well supplied and could feature on its menu all the "house specialities," plus many other items. In order to avoid the risk, however, most of the specialties were not meat dishes.

On the other hand, however, Tartuffe was in a privileged situation being the only high-class private restaurant in the most visited historical part of town. Competition was very limited in the city as a whole: a couple of state-owned and state-run hotel restaurants, along with one or two private restaurants that were not as conveniently located and lacked the high class image. The telephone never stopped ringing at Tartuffe. It became a "must" for all the foreign celebrities visiting Warsaw. The owners were getting a pretty good return on their 60–70 hours of hard work a week. The Pawlowskis drive good cars and moved to a new house in a nice section of town. They also were able to hire a chef, whom Jan trained, and a female manager. These arrangements gave them more free time to spend with their two sons.

The biggest problems were related to the quality of service. Waiters and waitresses were paid well and could count on good tips—but still it was difficult to find qualified people who spoke foreign languages and could to ensure a western standard of service. As a result, Tartuffe was (and still is) over staffed—one waiter serving a maximum of three tables—and turnover of personnel was high. After some time however, Eva was able to select two excellent hostesses (one of whom had worked for the Polish airlines as stewardess) who were generally liked by the public, along with a handful of young waiters and waitresses. Eva has discovered that only young waiters and waitresses could be upgraded to her standards—the older ones had too many "bad habits" they couldn't loose.

Since 1989 the situation has changed for Tartuffe and its owners: all the restrictions and shortages disappeared, and supplying the restaurant has become less of a problem. Nevertheless, Jan still gets up at four in the morning and goes to the market to select the best quality of produce, meat and fish. Everything is available now, and Tartuffe proudly features a pretty good selection of fine French wines. But at the same time, a lot of competition has emerged: at least half a dozen of fine restaurants have opened in Warsaw, some of them foreign owned (the Greek "Parnas," for example) and located closely to the most popular places in Warsaw. The upper segment of the restaurant market in Warsaw is certainly growing because of the new emerging middle class and constant flow of foreign visitors. Nevertheless, decreased internal demand in general (due to austerity measures implemented within the framework of the "stabilization plan") has eliminated the "normal" Polish customers, who cannot afford to go to restaurants anymore.

Jan and Eva have to meet new challenges, but they seem ready for them. They had planned to open a branch on the Old Market Square by buying or leasing a very beautiful, but run-down state-owned restaurant where they could have a night club or a cabaret. Unfortunately, the local government of the Old Town section of the city—which desperately needs revenues to build up its budget—demanded unrealistically high lease payments, so Jan and Eva decided to wait.

Moscow's private restaurant, Joseph's[7], seems to have quite different problems. When the 1987 law on individual economic activity was passed by the Soviet Parliament, Joseph Perezowskij decided to open the first and only Jewish restaurant in Moscow. He openly admits that it was not only a simple business venture for him, but also a matter of political and religious conviction.

Joseph Perezowskij's background is quite interesting. In 1991 he was 43, a Soviet Jew who never joined the Communist Party. He had studied medicine, law and literature, and took many different jobs: teaching, personal services (barber), work for a Moscow concert agency. From 1972 to 1975, he spent three years in prison. (Perezowskij believes that he has

been one of many victims of the persecution of Soviet Jewry under Brezhnev.) He has a reputation of being a knowledgeable art collector. His connection to the underground economy is very likely.

On May 11, 1987, Perezowskij registered his "cooperative" (or private enterprise, in Soviet legal terminology) under the name of "Zamosk-
voretchye," and leased the premises of a run-down restaurant that had
been closed for many years. The restaurant was conveniently located near
one of Moscow's major railway stations. His license called for a self-
service popular restaurant serving a typical Russian dish: dumplings.

After a considerable amount of money (40,000 rubles from Joseph's
personal funds) were already invested in the renovation of the premises,
the local authorities learned about Perezowskij's "Jewish project." The re-
action was quick: the premises were seized and sealed, and Perezowskij
was given three weeks to find a new location. The managers of the enterprise from which the premises were leased (some of them Jews themselves) were, according to Joseph, afraid to be labeled as "Zionists"—
which was deadly in the USSR. As a result, Joseph was not able to find
anything for quite some time.

In March of 1988 he finally found a place, which belonged to a private
(cooperative) firm. Renovation took some time and in the summer of that
year—(when Ronald Reagan visited Moscow)—Joseph's restaurant was
officially inaugurated. It was quite an event in Moscow, and representatives of foreign embassies and enterprises, artistic circles, and religious
organizations participated.

At that time, however, there were very few people in Moscow who
knew anything about Jewish kosher cuisine. In the beginning, one of the
dishes on the menu was "Borshtch with . . . pork." Nevertheless, Joseph
was determined to live up to his reputation of "genuine Jewish food." He
started to look for old Jewish women who could remember old recipes. He
paid them well, a minimum of 25 rubles a day, while they often lived on
pensions of 60 rubles per month. The results were better than anyone's
expectations. Over ten of Joseph's recipes are already included in foreign
cookbooks, such as *Kosher Kitchen Cabaret,* edited by Anit in New York.
He is especially proud of his jewish-style stuffed fish. At present, he features at least 33 Jewish dishes on his menu, some of them unique.

The most jealously guarded of Joseph's secrets are his sources of supply. This is understandable, since buying food has become one of the most
difficult things in Moscow. He only revealed that he bought veal at a high
price from a kolkhoz near Moscow.

Employee compensation has become one of Joseph's major problems.
He started by paying waiters 500 rubles per month, plus a bonus. This is far
better than the average monthly salary in Moscow, which was less than 200

rubles. However, he kept the tips for himself. The system did not work. Waiters tried to hide the tips, and service was not much better than in the state-owned restaurants. This says a lot to say—since Russian waiters have earned the reputation of being the worst in the world. When he started giving them 10 percent of the value of the checks, nothing really changed. Finally, he worked out a compensation scheme which he finds satisfactory. Waiters receive a modest monthly salary of only 150 to 200 rubles, but are allowed to keep their tips. Guests' complaints, however, result in fines imposed on waiters and/or kitchen personnel (chef included), depending upon the nature of complaint. Now Joseph's has a reputation for the best service in town.

Service includes discretion: from time to time, the restaurant is closed for the public and private meetings take place at Joseph's. This may explain why Joseph is not interested in advertising to the general public. In well-informed circles, he has a reputation for being an intermediary in many serious business deals. He remains silent about this, however. His business card says not only restaurant, but also "International Club of Business Contacts." The club is not officially registered and its activities are limited to gatherings of carefully (and purposely) selected local and foreign business people. From time to time, Joseph's restaurant or one separate room is used by foreign representatives (especially Israelis) for talks and negotiations.

Joseph put an advertisement in Moscow's *Jewish Gazette* announcing that he can help in sales and purchases of houses, apartments, and dachas. In 1991, he became a partner in first private real estate agency registered in Moscow.

Joseph has been visited a couple of times by local mafia representatives who tried to impose their "tax" on him. He flatly refused, and still maintained his prices surprisingly low for the (unusual in Moscow) quality of food and service he is providing. A couple of times his car was set on fire and his windows were smashed, and his employees have been harassed and beaten. He says he kept on refusing to pay and finally, after nearly a year of harassment, was left alone. He commented on it in the following way: "Italians and Jews never paid the mafia. They are the mafia themselves."

Joseph remains discrete and pessimistic about the financial results of his enterprise. This is quite understandable for someone talking to a Soviet journalist in early 1991. He admits to an average 37,000 rubles monthly turnover value. In 1990, he had an additional $5,000 from credit cards, which he does not consider a considerable income. Joseph points out that his lease went up from 6,000 rubles in 1990, to 29,000 rubles in 1991. Most other cost elements such as electricity, gas, and laundry also increased considerably. His profits are taxed up to 50 percent, and he jokes that he was quite well-to-do before he started his business.

Expansion of the legitimate business is not easy, however. Joseph has negotiated a joint venture with the British David Schreiber, a specialist in kosher foods, to open a strictly kosher restaurant and supermarket in Moscow, but he could not obtain a location for it from the city government. He has also acquired five automated lines for bread production and two for bottling beer. None of them can start operation because of the lack of space, which has to be allocated by the city government. Fear of "zionism" seems to be quite alive, though. On February 25, 1991, Perezovski was badly beaten and robbed by the Soviet militia when he entered the U.S. Embassy in Moscow for a scheduled meeting with the commercial attache of the Embassy.

All three cases of small private businesses in Central and Eastern Europe, presented above are as different as the countries in which they operate. By western standards, the Hungarian case seems the most normal, the closest to the way similar enterprises operate in the West. Tartuffe has recently also become quite similar. The Russian case is the most exotic. Nevertheless, all three cases seem to have some common elements:

1. Individual enterprises in Eastern and Central Europe are often started by individuals who were maladjusted to the communist system and strongly valued independence, individual success, and high quality work. These values could not be realized in the "normal" setting of the state-owned communist enterprises.

2. Private enterprises under communism could not survive without close ties to the second economy. These ties are not likely to be discontinued completely or immediately when communism is gone. For example, in Czech republic all 500 workers of one of the largest privately-owned companies declared themselves self-employed in order to avoid huge wage tax and benefit payments. As a result, the owner can pay them much higher salaries and still increase his own profits considerably.[8] Even now, it would be difficult to find even in the most advanced post-communist countries (Hungary), a private enterprise which is not using a couple of such tricks. These tricks enable it to increase the margin and to grow under conditions of tight monetary policies, such as high interest rates and high taxation, resulting from various stabilization plans implemented in the region. But one can also easily come to the conclusion that, after decades of communism, such ways of doing private business have become deeply internalized. They have become a cultural factor.

3. Private enterprises in post-communist countries have difficult access to credit and in most cases, their creation and development has to be financed from private savings. This is rightly considered one of the major factors inhibiting the development of the private sector, and especially acceleration of its capitalization, modernization of its equipment, and technology-enhancing competitiveness. Such difficult access to capital is due both to the monetary policies mentioned above and to the underdevelopment of the commercial banking sector. Surveys conducted by the Research Department of the Polish National Bank indicate that investment in small business carries more risk, and banks have to charge higher interest rates and keep bigger reserve funds, than when financing small business (Domanski R. 1991: 5). The Bank of Bohemia opened in Czechoslovakia on April 1, 1991 with a capital of $10 million and the explicit mission to finance small business from its ten regional branches. Such an institution is still quite unusual in the region.

The further economic development of Eastern and Central Europe seems to depend to a great extent upon its ability to finance small private enterprises. This is also the main difference between small business in post-communist countries and small business in the West, where highly efficient and relatively easily accessible financing is available. The fact that post-communist entrepreneurs are seldom able to prepare a business plan or a feasibility study—as required by western banks—is also due to the fact that financial institutions serving the needs of small businesses are still virtually non-existent, and that a part of expected revenues still comes from sources which cannot be explicitly or formally indicated (the second economy link).

Private businesses, which were allowed to exist under communism in countries such as Hungary, Poland or East Germany, were quite restricted on the input side (employment and supply limitations) and unable to grow beyond certain limit: However, they enjoyed the same status of protected market as the state-owned enterprises. Lack of aggressive and innovative marketing is a direct consequence of such privileges. It makes adjustment to shrinking market conditions more difficult and increases the mortality of small businesses. For example, in Poland in 1990, 516,000 new private businesses were created, but 165,000 closed (Gorski and Jaszczynski 1991: 35).

Surprisingly enough, private entrepreneurs in Eastern and Central Europe (especially in Hungary and Poland) seem to have much more extravagant life styles (cars, houses, vacations, etc.) than their counterparts in the West. It is obviously more visible when compared with the average

self-management. The Communist *nomenklatura* management of the shipyards has been successfully challenged by the workers and replaced. Under the present law governing state-owned enterprises, workers' organizations (trade unions and workers' self-management councils) have an important say in the selection of managers. They also have the power to recall managers.

In the shipyards, where workers are active, mobilized and militant, management is a weak partner. It has to be receptive to workers' demands, and be able to accommodate changing requests from the changing authorities of the trade unions and workers' councils. Such an arrangement makes consistency in strategy difficult to achieve. No wonder foreign investors are discouraged. In 1989, the Polish heir to the Johnson & Johnson fortune, Barbara Piasecka-Johnson, signed a letter of intent stipulating her $100 million investment in the Gdansk shipyard. A year later she had to withdraw because of the unclear power structure in the company and the workers' demands for pay increases and no layoffs. Also, the Komuna Paryska shipyard in Gdansk negotiated with a German investor for a year and a half without results. The German investor left them in near bankruptcy after holding them for a year or so, under a preliminary contract forbidding negotiations with other prospective partners.

Legal transformation of the state-owned company into a joint stock company, wholly owned by the treasury, helps to solve the problem. In joint stock companies, regardless of who owns them, the workers' council is automatically eliminated and management is appointed by the board of directors. The state treasury, however, is reluctant to accept direct financial responsibility for financially troubled companies, and requires a viable business plan providing reasonable guarantees of profitability in the not-too-distant future. In 1991, shipyards had problems providing such guarantees.

In 1990, eight ships out of 11 planned by the Warski shipyard in Szczecin were still contracted by the Soviet Sudoimport. In a couple of months, all of these contracts were cancelled, and the Soviet importer refused to pay for the ready-to-deliver ship built for him, which was worth $13 million. Interest on the loan taken to finance construction of this ship cost $1 million a month. Five more ships for the USSR are sitting on the building slips in different stages of construction. Some of these ships are highly specialized, like the nearly fully outfitted biological laboratory ship.

All the shipyards are in a similar situation because of the loss of the Soviet market. In some instances, however, the situation is aggravated by mistakes committed by Centromor when negotiating other contracts. For example the Wisla shipyard in Gdansk has delivered two small vessels to

Iran and has not been paid. The Warski Shipyard in Szczecin is bound by an ill-conceived contract, which carries an obligation to deliver a series of ships to the United Kingdom and to India at a considerable loss. To make things worse, prices of energy and raw materials have nearly tripled, and interest rates have gone up to more than 70 percent. All the subsidies were completely eliminated. As a result, all the shipyards found themselves in the red, and accumulated enormous debts. For example, in July 1991, the Komuna Paryska shipyard in Gdansk owed the equivalent of $130 million to its suppliers, to the banks, and to the state in unpaid taxes. At the same time, however, both drastic restructuring with massive layoffs and the closing down of operations, as a consequence of technical bankruptcy, were difficult because of the political leverage of the workers' organizations. Delays in solving this situation only aggravated it (Mering 1991).

All the interested parties (workers' organizations, management, ministry of industry, suppliers, contractors foreign clients, and prospective investors) knew that the writing was on the wall, and that something had to be done. Some parties, such as foreign clients negotiating contracts and prospective foreign investors, were visibly trying to take advantage of the situation in order to get even better deals. All the parties inside the shipyards, however, were desperately looking for solutions.

The most common strategy adopted in this sinking industry was to put more pressure on the government, in the hope that the government would resume subsidies. The Shipbuilding Forum, which took place in Szczecin in June 1991, indicated that shipbuilding industries are subsidized all over the world. In 1987, subsidies averaged 28 percent of the ship's value; in 1991, they still amounted to 15 percent on average. The Japanese government was cited as spending $1 billion a year to subsidize its shipbuilding industry (Mering 1991). The Gdansk shipyard, which produced eight ships in 1991, compared with 32 in previous years, and still maintained the core of its work force, was especially active politically in putting pressure on the government. This is probably due to the fact that the Gdansk Shipyard is President's Walesa's home base, where he started Solidarity in 1980 and was employed as an electrician for many years. This strategy was not initially successful. Until the early fall of 1991, the government remained unimpressed, and did not want to sacrifice its stringent monetary stabilization policies for the sake of the ailing and overgrown shipbuilding industry. When pressure mounted, however, the government agreed to transform shipyards into joint stock companies, which was equivalent to a form of financial guarantee.

Only the Warski Shipyard in Szczecin was relatively successful. In July 1991, Warski was transformed into a joint stock company wholly owned by the state treasury. Two banks assembled a $100 million loan package for Warski; $35 million made available immediately in order to pay off the most pressing debts to the suppliers. This rescue package was certainly inspired and backed by the government. What was unique in Warski's strategy? What message did the government want to send to the other shipyards, and to other dinosaurs in danger of extinction?

The main difference between Warski and other Polish shipyards is that Warski has a full portfolio of orders. Instead of waiting for the sloppy and unprofessional, yet expensive, services of Centromor as others did, Warski went out on its own and signed $1 billion worth of contracts. The company was also able to negotiate relatively high advance payments from the clients. In the second half of 1991, advance payments of $50 million were secured. Only 5 percent of these orders came from Russia. Warski intends to specialize in chemical and container carriers for western clients.

A comprehensive business plan was also presented that included streamlining the company by selling out or leasing some production facilities, equipment, and land. Special programs of cutting material and labor costs were put in place, along with the new accounting system and new stringent financial policies. Warski is developing its own marketing department. The company also intends to considerably reduce the burden of social services it traditionally carried as a communist dinosaur. Two thousand apartments belong to the shipyard, but only 25 percent of them are inhabited by the people who actually work for the company. Also, state-regulated rents are so low that they do not cover even 50 percent of the maintenance costs. Management hopes that the new law regulating tenants' rights will enable them to increase the rent, to remove some of the tenants, and to sell some apartments at free market prices or use them as collateral for bank loans. Representatives of two Polish banks were impressed with Warski's plan and decided to finance it. Nobody had yet talked about privatization. Warski intended to remain state-owned until its economic viability in the new environment is on solid ground.

In Mintzberg's terms, Warski's strategy as a plan can be clearly presented as a sequence of objectives: attract western clients and sign contracts that maximize advance payments, prepare a viable business plan and restructuring program, secure financing from the banks, and implement a restructuring program. One aspect of Warski's strategy contains a ploy: "Make good impression on western clients—don't let them know how desperate the company's financial situation is." A kind of pattern also can be inferred from Warski's behaviour: an absolute priority is given to securing a new, viable client base. Warski wants to position himself as a differentiated marketeer: as a highly specialized constructor of chemical and container carriers. A desperate financial situation might also force the company to assume a cost leadership position when negotiating badly needed contracts. Strategy, as long-term perspective, is more difficult to infer when the company is concentrating on simple survival. One might suspect, however, that Warski wants to become a market-driven firm.

The Lublin Foundry of the Ursus Tractor Works[2] was evaluated by World Bank experts in 1991 as one of the finest and most technologically advanced, and most ecologically safe, production facilities of its kind in Europe. The Lublin Foundry, situated 120km southeast of Warsaw, is a part of one of the most notorious communist dinosaurs in Poland: Ursus Tractor works, a giant composed of 13 production facilities all over Poland. In the summer of 1992, the 13-headed-monster still existed, but was going deeper and deeper into debt.

In the early '70s, a high-level political decision was made to transform the pre-war Ursus tractor factory into the biggest tractor manufacturer in the world, with a capacity of 100,000 tractors per year produced under British Massey Ferguson license. At that time, both tractor and automotive production were under the same administrative umbrella: the Association of Tractor and Automotive Industry. The Lublin Foundry was designed to serve the needs of the whole association, with a projected yearly output of 100,000 tractors and 500,000 cars. As a consequence, the Lublin Foundry was designed for an unbelievable output of 120,000 tons yearly.

Ursus was one of the communists' lunatic industrial pyramids. Nobody cared that the maximum estimated domestic demand for Massey Ferguson-size tractors was only 35,000 to 40,000 units a year, or that the export of tractors was difficult considering the intensive competition, or that such incredible overcapacity would kill the enterprise economically. Irresponsible communist decision makers wanted something big and impressive and they got it—along with an astronomical deficit! The Lublin Foundry is a part of this story.

Construction of the Lublin Foundry was started in 1979 and is still not completely finished. In spite of economic difficulties and political turbulence, construction continued throughout the whole decade of the '80s. Although there were stoppages due to hard currency shortages, it nonetheless continued with central financing from the state, confirmed as late as September 1990 by the non-communist government. Such a long construction cycle made the investment even more costly. It still continued, although throughout the '80s, production of Massey Ferguson tractors was never higher than 20,000. The Lublin Foundry was still being built with a capacity of 120,000 tons.

The most advanced equipment was purchased from such manufacturers as the Swiss Brown Boveri and Georg Fisher, the Danish Disamatic or the British Stone Wallwork. Depreciation on the new equipment was only 20 percent. A 16-hectare (more than 32 acres) air-conditioned production facility was built (used only in 50 percent), a water and purified compressed air supply was built, along with modern computerized energy distribution systems for electricity, heat, and gas. The most advanced environmental protection systems (unusual in Poland) were put in place. In the middle of 1991, the production capacity of the foundry was 55,000 tons, even though some sections could handle much higher volumes (up to the full planned capacity of 120,000 tons, in some instances). The cost of the Lublin Foundry was never precisely calculated. The outstanding debt resulting from unpaid investment credits plus accumulated interest that amounted to $30 million in July 1991—and this was only a fraction of the total construction cost.

The break-even point for the foundry was calculated at the level of 38,000 tons. Using full existing capacity of 55,000 tons would generate $10 million worth of profit. During the first five months of 1991, production volume was only 4,600 tons. At that production level, the operating loss amounted to the equivalent of $10 million. Being so clearly threatened, the factory management implemented emergency measures, such as reducing employment from 2,850 to 1,950. Inventories were slashed considerably to two-weeks' output in finished product, and to $2 million worth of materials, components, and spare parts (the absolute minimum required technically). Paychecks were reduced to much below the average in Polish industry to the equivalent of $120 per month. In order to increase production volume, exports to the West worth $150,000 were undertaken in June 1991. These exports are expected to reach $400,000 monthly by the end of 1991.

All these measures, however, could not prevent a major disaster. Because of the sharp decline of the Polish tractor and automotive industry in 1991, major clients considerably reduced their orders to Ursus Tractor Works (by 60 percent) and the Warsaw Automotive Factory (by 20 percent). Orders from the truck factories Star and Jelcz were completely cancelled. Being a part of Ursus Tractor Works made things even worse for the Lublin Foundry. Ursus ordered it to reserve production capabilities according to its over-optimistic production plans—thus preventing the foundry from negotiating with the outside customers—and at the last minute cancelled the orders. Being part of the larger conglomerate with an unclear degree of autonomy, made all kinds of negotiations with outside clients, suppliers, bankers, and investors extremely difficult for the Lublin Foundry. Its management was tied to the sinking giant, which was visibly falling apart, and did not have enough courage and determination to cut the rope before it was too late.

While the client base was shrinking dramatically, the costs of energy and materials were constantly rising. All of this contributed to the foundry's operating deficit. Already, in 1989, it was slightly in the red. In 1990, the deficit amounted to $3.7 million. During first five months of 1991, the operating loss was already well over $3 million. Debts accumulated, including $30 million in unpaid investment credits plus interest, $10 million unpaid suppliers bills, $4 million electrical energy bills, and $3 million fixed capital rent due to the state treasury. The Lublin Foundry lost its liquidity and credit worthiness in April 1991, but continued to operate at a reduced scale on day-by-day loans from Ursus Tractor Works. In June 1991, Lublin electrical Utility cut off the electricity because of unpaid bills. Ursus Tractor Works could not come to the rescue, being deep in the red itself.

At the last moment, the general manager of the foundry, Mr. Swirk, launched dramatic appeals for help to the Ministry of Industry, asking for a subsidy, and to the Ministry of Ownership Changes, asking for authorization to issue stock and sell it to foreign partners. At the same time, unconditional offers were sent to well-known international firms that previously were seriously interested in the foundry: Krupp GmbH, Thyssen GmbH, Steyer AG, Caterpillar, and others. It must be added that the physical closing of the foundry would cause irreparable damage, because it has to be operated on a continuous basis. Within a month or two, such a closing would shut down completely the entire Polish tractor and automotive industry, and export contracts would have to be cancelled with due penalties. In order to prevent the closing, an immediate emergency loan of at least $12 million was needed. The foundry manager proposed to repay it from the income generated by sales of the foundry's shares to foreign investor or investors.

Let's leave the story at that moment, July 1991, and try to describe the strategy of the Lublin Foundry management using Mintzberg's categories. Elements of plan are difficult to detect in the foundry's management's behavior. It was just focusing on survival, passively responding to contingencies without any far-reaching goals in mind. The Foundry's management's behavior was also seriously restricted by the still existing superstructure of Ursus Tractor Works. The ploy element was certainly present in the foundry's behaviour: all the time it wanted to force government to come to help. Looking for a pattern or consistency in the foundry's behaviour, one can describe it as asking for outside help—from the government, from foreign investors. The concept of ''market position'' was still alien to the foundry's management. It was only trying to position itself vis-à-vis Ursus and the government. Its perspective or driving force, in analyzed behavior, was purely defensive—lacking vision and far-reaching goals.

The case of the Lublin Foundry illustrates pretty well the dominating behavioral patterns of post-communist dinosaurs. For decades they were never concerned about the financial aspects of their activities and even in the most restrictive conditions of macro-economic monetary stabilization and transition policies, they still seem to wait for a "post-communist white knight," someone who will give them money: government, foreign investors, or preferably both. Such "given" financial resources should enable them to continue their privileged existence and perhaps gradually improve economic performance. Such attitudes are still pre-dominatant among dinosaurs, and clearly have led to the physical destruction of sometimes valuable and quite modern industrial plants that are badly needed for the economic reconstruction of devastated post-communist economies. The Lublin Foundry case clearly illustrates that aspect.

Macro-economic policies alone (even the most restrictive) are not capable of changing such passive, defensive attitudes, and lack of strategic thrust among the managers on the enterprise and factory level. Government has the responsibility of initiating and closely monitoring the process of restructuring the dinosaurs. It has to reduce them to manageable and technologically self-sustaining enterprises, commercialize them (through transformation into joint stock companies), clearly and precisely determine the authority and responsibility of the management team, select proper managers, economically support viable and financially sound business and restructuring plans, and eventually initiate privatization.

In the case of Lublin Foundry, the Polish government did not live up to its responsibilities and risked wasting a valuable piece of the nation's industrial wealth. The lack of a clear and precise understanding of industrial policy—in the market economy emerging from the communist heritage—seems to be responsible for this, along with a narrow concentration on macro-economic (especially monetary) policy, without taking into consideration the real responses of the enterprises.

Dinosaurs—huge capital-intensive industrial complexes in heavy and machine industries—are the heritage of the Stalinist's forced industrialization policies, which continued up to the end of the '80s. They exemplify the communist passion for gigantic industrial pyramids, and are built with total neglect of economic and market considerations as well as, in most cases, environmental ones. Such an over-investment policy is widely believed to be one of the main sources of cyclical fluctuations and crisis in the communist economies (Seurot 1989: 322; Bauer 1978). The existence of dinosaurs, which in most cases are highly inefficient operations, creates a need for subsidies and distorted pricing, and petrifies an unfavourable economic structure with a high share of low value-added industries. Most of the dinosaurs will have to be eliminated by market forces and international competition. They must be phased out in an orderly way, however, to prevent an uncontrolled wave of bankruptcies. New jobs have to be created, especially in the factory towns where dinosaurs are the only employers.

Micro-economic strategies on the enterprise and factory level are extremely important to minimize and cushion the devastating impact of such radical structural change. Cutting dinosaurs into economically and technologically viable units, and letting management teams try rescue operations through streamlining, restructuring, and market re-positioning might make parts of the dinosaurs competitive, in some instances, or at least delay massive lay-offs and factory closings in others. The Warski case, presented above, indicates that such possibilities do exist. Using such opportunities on a larger scale calls for an elaborate industrial policy, well coordinated with a privatization drive and a big effort in management education. Post-communist governments, fascinated by a rather primitive version of a free market economy based an exclusively on a macro perspective, are only starting to realize it.

The issue is especially pressing in the countries practicing "shock treatment" therapy: Germany and Poland. That's why the cases presented above were taken from Polish industrial practices. (Germany was a special case of "highly assisted transition," financed by the German government up with to $80 billion in 1991 alone). Czechoslovakia and other post-communist Eastern European countries had still not dared to touch their dinosaurs by the end of 1991. Czech republic, which enjoys a relatively high reputation among foreign investors, visibly counts on them to cushion the shock of the pending radical structural change. Hungary, the only country in the region which conducted relatively reasonable pro-market economic policies under communism, started to divest its dinosaurs in the '70s.

The ex-Soviet Union undoubtedly is facing the most difficult problem, considerating the number and size of its dinosaurs, as well as their share in the GNP. The problem had not even been addressed yet, on the practical level, at the end of 1992, and has certainly been aggravated by the size of the military industrial complex. In most cases, conversion of highly specialized armament manufactures is not very likely. In 1992, the Russian military industry was still producing and trying to sell whatever it could. Conversion and restructuring is imaginable to some extent, but only in the case of the most technologically advanced enterprises.

Soukhoi Aircraft Works, which produces the pride of the Soviet Air Force—the supersonic SU-27 jet fighter—provides an example of conversion and restructuring. In cooperation with an American firm, Gulfstream Aerospace Co., and the British Rolls Royce, Soukhoi will produce a small executive mini-jet, capable of developing a speed of MACH, 2.4 designed and manufactured on the basis of the SU-27 fighter. The same Soukhoi has already started to sell the most advanced acrobatic aircraft yet constructed of a new material, carbon fiber.[3] Such deals, however, can hardly sustain a giant employing 80,000 workers and 20,000 of the nation's best engineers.

Communist dinosaurs—like all big state-owned enterprises in basic industries all over the world—were, are, and will remain highly politicized, both in their internal and external relations. Until some of them are at least partially privatized (which seems to be very difficult), strategic reorientations and restructuring of these enterprises will remain highly contingent on national politics. To turn them around—or just to save the most valuable parts of them—will require a combination of politics, macro-economic policies, and reasonable strategies on the enterprise and factory level. The probability of such a fortunate combination is not very high in the post-communist countries.

Pretender Strategies

''Pretenders'' are those post-communist enterprises that have some competitive advantages, and which can become international players in relatively high value-added industries. To what extent this potential competitive advantage will become a reality depends upon the strategy of these enterprises. The pretenders' management teams have to overcome their communist heritage, to make their enterprises global market—oriented, cost efficient, and technologically up to world standards. Only some of them will be successful. In each individual case, the fit between the firm's strategy and its international and domestic business environment will decide the outcome. For the next couple of years, the domestic business environment seems to be more important because of the local or regional (Central and Eastern Europe) nature of most post-communist enterprises. An environment conducive to the emergence of a relatively large number of strong competitors—successful pretenders (among other categories of enterprises)—will also facilitate the successful reconstruction of post-communist economies and their association with highly developed core western markets.

For an explanation of pretenders' strategy, two examples will be used: Mera Pnefal, an industrial automation company in Poland; and Glaser, a Czech luxury glassware company.

Mera Pnefal[4] is a private measurement instruments company that was founded in 1945 and nationalized in 1953. Since 1961, company has been manufacturing and supplying control and measurement instrumentation, bellows, thermostats and systems for industrial process control. It is the only Polish company that specializes in supplying, installing, and servicing complex industrial automation control systems. Mera's scope of activity covers production and service. The most important items in the production sector are: bellows and thermostats, pneumatic instrumentation, electronic instrumentation, control panels, and process control cubicles. In the service sector, Mera provides systems designing (including software development), site installation, start-ups and commissioning, product service, and customer staff training. In 1990, pneumatic instrumentation was responsible for 57.5 percent of Mera's sales, electronic instrumentation for 24.8%, bellows and thermostats for 9.2 percent, control panels and cubicles for 8.0 percent, and services for less than 1 percent.

Mera offers these products and services to the following industries: petrochemical (refineries), chemical (fertilizers, pharmaceutical), metallurgy, food processing (especially sugar mills), paper and pulp, glass and, recently, electrical power generation and environmental protection.

During the last 30 years, Mera has installed over 2,000 complete industrial automation systems all over the world. However, its most important markets are located in Central and Eastern Europe.

In 1990, domestic sales represented 38 percent of the company's revenues and 62 percent of its exports. In 1991, these proportions were almost completely turned around, as exports were reduced to slightly over 30 percent. In 1990, the company had approximately 50 percent of the Polish market. It covers 100 percent of the domestic demand for pneumatic installations, 30 percent for electronic control systems, and makes 50 percent of all complex deliveries of industrial automation systems. Thirty-three percent of the company's domestic sales go to the chemical industry, 25 percent to mining and metallurgy, 20 percent to food processing industry, and 22 percent to other industries.

In 1989, Mera had 15 percent of the East German market, 30 percent of the Czechoslovakia market, 10 percent of the Soviet market, and 15 percent of the Bulgarian market. In the first six months of 1990, 33 percent of Mera's exports went to the former East Germany, 30 percent to Czechoslovakia, 15.7 percent to North Korea, 6.5 percent to Bulgaria, 7.4 percent to West Germany, and only 3 percent to the Soviet Union. Nearly all exports sales were made by the specialized foreign trade company Metronex, which always served it (as a monopolist, until 1988), while only 1 percent of sales were made through the company's own representatives.

Although Mera enjoys a well-deserved and well-established reputation for the reliability of its products and services, as well as the high technical competence of its designers and engineers, the technological level of its products is certainly below the world's standards set by giants that spend millions of dollars on R & D, such as Siemens, Westinghouse, ABB, Rosemount, and Fisher Controls.

Mera is one of Europe's leading manufacturers of the simplest (but still in use) elements of industrial automation systems: bellows and simple pneumatic thermostats. In 1991, Mera produced 3.8 million bellows, while its three competitors (Skodock and Witzemunn in Germany, and Calorstat in France) together turned out around five million. Mera's simplest product is of excellent quality, and the company visibly has cost advantage over its competitors. Clients willing to buy constantly knock on the door. Unfortunately, Mera does not yet have sufficient capacity. Moreover, it delivers irregularly and with considerable delays, due to the malfunctioning Polish railway system and irregular deliveries from domestic suppliers of materials. After the Eastern European markets were lost, bellows generated close to 60 percent of the company's exports. But such a declining and low value-added product cannot guarantee Mera's future.

In 1964, Mera acquired a license from Siemens for the pneumatic control system, Telepneu. This license has been successfully developed over the years, and Mera has become an excellent, experienced manufacturer of pneumatic control systems. This product line became a foundation of Mera's spectacular success in the 1970s. Unfortunately, pneumatic control technology has been declining since the late '70s, and is being gradually replaced by electronic systems. Mera is still producing and installing them, but also offers its services in the development, modernization, upgrading, overhaul, and maintenance of such systems.

In order to keep up with technological progress, a license for electronic control systems was acquired from Honeywell in 1978. This license was not developed as successfully as the previous one. In spite of many trials and considerable effort, Mera's R&D center failed to acquire the proper quality of piezzo-resistive gauges crucial to electronic control systems. This is the main reason for the huge and increasing technological gap between Mera and its foreign competitors. An attempt to develop computerized digital control systems in cooperation with the Industrial Automation Research Institute, of Warsaw—although quite successful on the laboratory experiment scale—did not fill the gap. In the middle of the 1980s, another attempt was made to keep up-to-date with the most advanced technology. Since Honeywell was installing its computerized digital systems in Poland, and in other Central and Eastern European countries, Mera offered its services as a subcontractor installing, programming, starting, and maintaining the systems. The offer was accepted because of the cost advantage, and some of Mera's engineers were sent for training to Honeywell—which enabled them to considerably upgrade their skills in the most advanced electronics. Cooperation with Honeywell was successful and as a result, three very complex systems were sold in Poland and one in Czechoslovakia. One electronic system of Mera's own design was sold to North Korea, which became one of the major clients. In spite of all these efforts, Mera is lagging behind in electronic systems and components. These are the rising technologies of the future and the only ones capable of securing its future survival and growth in the international marketplace.

This weakness, and many others, were demonstrated with full strength when market forces came into play in Poland, and when the protective umbrella of non-convertible currency was removed and the "easy" COMECON markets collapsed. The USSR market practically disappeared in 1990. Most of the East German clients became bankrupt, or are in the process of being taken over and drastically restructured by West German companies. Most of the long-term contracts were cancelled, and some payments could not be collected. Once all transactions between ex-COMECON countries were calculated and effectively paid in hard currencies, Mera lost its advantage—especially for new clients, who usually prefer more advanced electronic systems, even if they are much more expensive. This statement applies not only to the Czech and Bulgarian markets, but also to the Polish market. After the introduction of internal convertibility of the zloty, on January 1, 1990, Mera had to face direct competition from the world's leading manufacturers of control systems. This competition is especially difficult for Mera, which is in deep recession and has considerably reduced its volume of capital investment. Few enterprises that build or modernize their facilities feel that they can afford anything but the most up-to-date equipment in order to stay competitive, even if that equipment is expensive. For this reason, Honeywell, Taylor, Foxboro, Rosemount, and other world leaders are successfully penetrating Polish market and cutting into Mera's home market base.

Mera's financial results in 1990 were still favorable, mainly because of the continuation of old contracts. However, practically no orders for complex systems beyond 1991 were received. This means that if nothing changes dramatically, Mera can only survive as minor supplier of low value-added components, such as bellows and maintenance services for existing systems. In other words, the leadership position Mera once held is fading away forever. Mera's profitability (profit/costs) was in decline: down from 58 percent in 1989 to 32 percent in 1990, and to well below 20 percent in 1991, based on sales worth $35 million. The company employed more than 1,600 people, including professionals—both engineers and skilled workers—who were highly skilled in the design, installation, and start-up of industrial process control systems. Human resources are

considered to be the company's most important asset at the present time—
and its hope for the future. However, sales and value-added ratios per employee remain very low by Western European standards.

The internal weaknesses of the company do not facilitate an adequate response to the external threats outlined above. Production facilities are equipped with 8- to 11-year-old machines that have depreciated
nearly 70 percent. The financial situation of the enterprise, although
still relatively far from insolvency, does not permit massive capital investment in badly needed new equipment. In 1991, credit was too expensive—the interest rate was well over 80 percent at the beginning of the
year, and well over 50 percent at the end of the year—for any investment
with longer payoff time. Mera's outdated and slow accounting and financial reporting systems did not permit the assessment of cost structure
and profitability of different product lines. Marketing functions were
practically not performed until recently. The enterprise was cut off from
its clients and did not have a minimum knowledge of the market, prices,
or the competition. Because the stabilization plan imposed restrictions
on the salaries of employees of state-owned enterprises, Mera had
problems keeping its best engineers and designers, who had been trained
by Honeywell.

The company's new manager Henryk Skawinski who was elected in
1989, realized that a new strategy was badly needed. Being an engineer,
Skawinski understood that in order to turn Mera around, he needed some
managerial training. He enrolled in an American-style MBA program in
Warsaw offered by the International Business School, an independent institution that was an offspring of Warsaw University. At the school,
courses were taught partially in English and partially in Polish by both
Polish and foreign professors (mainly from the U.K. and Denmark).
Skawinski admitted that whatever he learned in the marketing, accounting, strategic management, and human resources management courses, he
tried to implement immediately.

By the time Skawinski received his MBA, in the summer of 1991, a
new strategy for Mera was already in place. The plan's main strategic objective was to regain and maintain Mera's previous leadership position in
industrial automation systems on the Central European markets.

In order to implement its far-reaching strategy, the company had to
survive the recessionary times of 1991 and 1992. Mera had to watch its
cash flow very carefully. The export of bellows was identified as a potential ''cash cow'' for the next couple of years. In order to increase its earnings substantially and to take advantage of the economies of scale,
production volume had to be doubled. This would require changing the

factory lay-out, and some minor investment. In order to assure regular deliveries to the biggest buyer in Germany (Anschutz), Skawinski's plan called for leasing a truck and using it as a shuttle to carry imported components from Germany to Poland.

In order to keep track of the costs and cash flow, the entire accounting and financial reporting system had to be computerized and adjusted to contemporary European standards. Special task forces were created to cut inventories, to rationalize procurement, and to cope with the problem of accounts receivable and notorious payment delays from clients. In 1990, payments often were over two months late, although the legally required payment time was 14 days. Some lay-offs of unskilled labor and administrative personnel, along with early retirement and a no hiring policy, were also implemented. As a result, by the end of 1991 employment was reduced to slightly more than 1,100 workers. The company wanted to maintain and to increase its cost advantage, but at the same time it wanted to keep its corps of highly skilled personnel.

Skawinski carefully studied the market for pneumatic control systems and decided to stay close to Mera's traditional markets and traditional customers, despite political and economic changes which made this more difficult. He assumed that customers in Central and Eastern Europe, who already had pneumatic systems installed by Mera and were satisfied with them, would rather maintain, develop, and upgrade them, rather than replace them with new and costly electronic systems offered by leading Western manufacturers.

In order to keep in touch with such customers, the technological design department of the company—employing the best engineers and designers, who also were familiar to Mera's customers—was reorganized into a sales and marketing department. The new department's mission was to study the market, to contact customers directly, and to increase sales. It was decided that the company had to ''liberate'' itself from Metronex (the foreign trade company), and to start penetrating its major foreign markets directly and studying the new needs of its former customers. In order to keep in touch with the key German market, a sales representative office was established in Leipzig, in the former East Germany, and a cooperation agreement was signed with the Polish-German trading company Metronex Deutschland in Dusseldorf, in the western region of Germany. A sales representative office was also established in Czech republic. In cooperation with Soviet and, later, Russian and Ukrainian trade representatives, a series of seminars and visits with Russian and Ukrainian clients was organized in 1991. Special attention was to be paid to the domestic market. The newly created sales and marketing department was assigned a mission of developing new contacts with former customers and studying their needs carefully. The department was also assigned to acquire new customers. As early as 1990, the penetration of the new market segments in Poland had brought some results. Two contracts were signed with giant electrical power plants undergoing modernization, and with a handful of large chemical plants that were not previously Mera's clients.

The acquisition of new clients was possible because Mera made a big effort to modernize and upgrade its electronic systems. In August of 1991, Mera signed an agreement with American Rosemount Inc. a world leader in the field of transmitters for assembly of the "1151" family of analog and "SMART" transmitters. Mera became the only Eastern and Central European manufacturer having access to that level of technology. Since transmitters are key elements in the industrial processes control systems, its offer to design, produce, and install complex systems automatically became much more attractive. The agreement with Rosemount made possible contracts with new Polish clients. Skawinski hopes a joint venture with Rosemount will be the next step of cooperation.

Cooperation with Rosemount is considered to be just the beginning of the long process of upgrading and developing Mera's expertise in the most advanced electronic systems. Mera is constantly looking for technology transfer opportunities, and negotiations are being held with other technological leaders. The company is participating actively in international meetings and fairs. International firms and organizations (e.g., World Bank, UNIDO) specializing in "match-making" between Polish and foreign firms, also have been approached.

In the meantime more apparent measures, aimed at upgrading simpler technological processes and improving quality, are being taken. More advanced technological processes have been introduced, such as machining, automated deep stamping, automated punching, electro-discharge machining, heat treatment in gases, galvanizing baths free of cyanide, and the fine tuning of micro processor systems. The company has also been forced to invest in environmental protection, in order to comply with more rigid regulations and to avoid steeply increased penalties for water and air pollution.

The company badly needed massive replacement of its outdated equipment. It also needed to purchase modern ones, particularly computerized machining centers. Since credit was prohibitively expensive in Poland, a modernization program was submitted, with an appropriate feasibility study, for financing to the World Bank Mission in Warsaw, which administered World Bank Credit lines for the modernizing of Polish industry. However, credit was not granted until the end of 1991. Such credit is mainly available for private and privatizing companies, because it is intended to stimulate and accelerate privatization.

Mera is preparing itself for privatization and restructuring. According to Skawinski's plan, once privatized it should be transformed into a holding group of four separate companies. Technically independent profit and investment centers, these companies would be responsible for distinctive product lines: bellows and thermostats, simple systems and devices, complex systems, parts, components and services. Such a structure calls for greater decentralization, as compared with the present organization. Financial and strategic management, development of new products and new production capabilities (investment), and strategic partnerships will be left only at the holding level. These functions will be fulfilled with a very small staff (40 people, maximum). Four companies will have complete autonomy in such areas as production, marketing, procurement, R&D, and personnel.

In Skawinski's plan, special attention is paid to training, personnel policies, and human resources management, as well as developing a market orientation and teaching basic marketing skills. Skawinski states: "Discovering that contracts and orders have to be solicited, and that clients have to be persuaded, was the biggest shock for our managers and engineers—who used to care only about production, taking excessive demand for granted." The need for training in accounting and finance, as well as the complete reorientation of the accounting and finance departments, was ranked second on the urgency scale. All the managers were encouraged to enrol in the MBA program, or to attend shorter management development courses focusing on specific topics (mainly in accounting and finance) such as normative cost accounting, inflation accounting, or cash flow analysis.

Preparation of a completely new system of human resource management and compensation has been initiated, along with a thorough restructuring and retraining of personnel who had not played an active role in communist enterprises. Preparations included selection tests, job evaluations, compensation and profit sharing systems, along with job training methods and career planning. Because of the lack of individuals with practical experience in Poland, Skawinski wants foreign experts to help in the preparation of such a human resource management system for Mera. The system will be implemented following privatization of the firm. His ambition is to develop a distinctive company "culture."

Using Mintzberg's terminology, Mera's strategy has all the elements of plan. It is a sequence of precisely formulated objectives and a consciously intended course of action. It maintains liquidity through: increasing exports of bellows; exploiting to the maximum existing and potential markets for pneumatic systems; upgrading electronics and capturing new markets for electronic systems; strengthening the company through new investment in modern equipment; introducing financial discipline and gradually reducing over-employment; and preparing a plan for privatisation and restructuring of the company.

Pattern and consistency in Mera's behavior are clearly visible. It wants to regain the market leadership position it once had. The ploy aspect of the strategy is less visible. It is perhaps seen in negotiations with foreign partners when Mera presents itself as stronger potential partner than it really is. Strategy, as position, is also rather clear. Mera wants to position itself as a supplier of declining (but still in demand, regionally) technologies, and to move gradually towards the higher end of the market by constantly developing its products through technology transfers from market leaders. Strategy, as perspective, is also clear. Mera has discovered market competition as a new key to survival and development. This is quite a discovery for an ex-communist enterprise, whose fate depended until recently on the central allocation of resources by the party-dominated government bureaucracy.

Glaser Company, in Marianske Lazne[5], is one of the very few Czech companies that is fully competitive on the global market. A manufacturer of luxury hand-made glassware, Glaser possesses one of the most prestigious brand names in the world. Glaser was founded in 1863 by Friedrich Glaser, who owned a decorating workshop and glass shop in Marianske Lazne. Glaser's ambition was to produce "the glass of kings and the king of glass." He achieved this by using the best quality materials available: fine crystal and colored glass, decorated with exceptionally complicated classical cut and engraved patterns. More than 70 percent of its 5,000 different products are classical designs from more than 50 years ago. Glaser has supplied royal courts, aristocracy, and the "rich and famous" all over the world since the late nineteenth century. Even after its nationalization in 1949, Glaser products consistently won the highest awards in international exhibitions and fairs.

Due to the unique design and features of its products (table sets, decorative household glass, and unique artistic objects), such as etched and gold-etched decorations, Glaser can successfully compete with such famous brands as Baccarat, St. Luis or Lalique from France, Costa Boda from Sweden, Hoya from Japan or Steuben from the U.S. It is believed that Glaser's products, which are hand decorated by means of gilding and engraving, are unique and cannot be imitated.

The company was never tempted by the prospects of mechanization or mass production. In communist Czechoslovakia, it enjoyed a rather comfortable and privileged status as a national monument of sorts. It remained a small operation with total sales of slightly more than $9.5 million, and employed only slightly more than 500 people—fewer than 150 of whom were the most skilled glass blowers, cutters, and engravers in the world. These trades are hereditary at Glaser, and many of the highest skilled workers are third generation. The company's own development and design shop was always, and still remains, faithful to the old tradition and to Glaser's unique style.

From 1950 to 1990 all of Glaser's exports were handled exclusively by the monopolistic state foreign trade organization, Glassexport, which had an administrative monopoly for all glass exports from Czechoslovakia (of which Glaser's sales were only a small fraction). This was a typical situation in communist countries. Glaser's products are sold in the world's most prestigious luxury shops such as Galleries Lafayette in Paris, Harrods and Selfridges in the UK, Neiman Marcus and Saks in the U.S., and Meiwa in Japan. Over 60 percent of Glaser's sales go the most advanced countries (Japan, Italy, France, Canada, Germany, U.K., U.S.) Sales to other post-communist countries are practically nonexistent. Since 1989, 80 percent of domestic sales are carried exclusively by five company-owned stores located in the centers of big towns. Because Glaser's products are expensive, even in Czechoslovakia, they are mainly purchased by foreign tourists and diplomats.

About 60 percent of Glaser's production consists of special orders from customers, with the rest made up of so-called parallel products. The company was never fully able to satisfy the demand for its products, mainly because of the limited number of craftsmen. It takes 10 to 15 years to become a good glass blower, and only every second or third blower reaches master status. It takes 15 to 20 years to become a master engraver, and only one-fourth of the senior workers reach mastery level. Glaser has a small school that prepares young people for this long-term career. No wonder there are not too many candidates, especially since salaries, although good, are not exceptional. In 1991, there were not enough candidates to fill all the places in the vocational school at Glaser.

The wave of changes and the new economic policies triggered by the "velvet revolution" had an impact on Glaser's operations.

First inflation created strong pressure to increase wages. Simultaneously, Glaser's labor costs increased by close to 50 percent in 1990, compared with 1989.

The rise in unemployment made it easier for Glaser to attract new unskilled workers and to increase labor productivity in auxiliary jobs. Unfortunately, however, these factors were only of minor importance in the company's operations.

The liberalization of domestic prices enabled the company to raise its prices on the domestic market (i.e., closer to the level of world prices).

The devaluation of the Czech crown, from 14 to 28 crowns per U.S. dollar increased company earnings from exports to western markets, and in 1991 made up for the elimination of previous export subsidies.

The abolition of foreign trade monopolies made it possible for Glaser to bypass ''Glassexport'' and sell directly to foreign customers—but required marketing skills that were underdeveloped at Glaser.

The prices of domestic and imported raw materials and components increased sharply, but these cost increase were absorbed price increases on Glaser's products.

In 1991, the company was transformed from a state-owned company into a joint stock company, wholly owned by the state treasury, and represented by the Ministry of Industry. Further steps toward privatization are being considered.

Glaser was not affected by the domestic recession and the collapse of the Soviet, Central, and Eastern European markets, because it sells mainly to the Triad countries. Even temporary recessions in the West, and crises such as the Persian Gulf War, do not seem to affect Glaser, which is conveniently positioned in the upper market segment.

Due to the changed circumstances, the newly appointed management team, selected from experienced Glaser employees, had to come up with a new strategy. The strategic objective for the coming years that was developed by the new management can be formulated as follows: further and more profitable penetration of the highest and most discriminating segment of the world market. The new management wants to preserve and to reinforce Glaser's brand-name image as ''the glass of kings and king of glass.'' It seems to be afraid of mechanization, mass production, mass distribution and possible exploitation of the famous brand name by prospective foreign partners. To prevent this, management is proposing its own privatization plan: sale of the company stock to the Czech bank that finances its activities and to the very conservative British bank that finances some of its export operations. The company's privatization plans also call for the sale of some stock to one of the exclusive Western retailers carrying Glaser's line of products. Twenty-five percent of the shares were reserved for the employees, especially its craftsmen. This solution is intended to motivate core personnel.

Management has a plan of direct penetration of new highly lucrative markets, including Far Eastern countries such as Japan, Hong Kong, and South Korea, as well as the U.S., where Glaser's sales are expected to grow rapidly after Czechoslovakia has been granted ''most favored nation'' status. Glaser intends to increase the percentage of direct sales and save on commission. The company also intends to experiment with pricing, since it is believed that Glaser's products are systematically underpriced on both the domestic and world markets—the result of management's lack of marketing skills and experience. In order to increase the volume available for exports, management intends to raise the prices on the domestic market to the world price level, and to decrease domestic sales. Management also plans to provide more financial incentives for highly skilled workers, and to intensity the process of training new workers.

In order to reduce production costs, management plans to upgrade the technology of glass production. In 1990, maintaining Glaser's proverbial high quality standards required a reduction of its 40 percent rejection rate for semifinished products. Solving this single problem could significantly reduce production costs.

Glaser's strategy can be relatively easily described using Mintzberg's terminology. Its plan involves: further penetration of the highest segment of the market. Management has a sequenced plan of direct penetration of precisely identified markets. There seems to be no ploy aspect to this strategy. Strategy as pattern can be relatively easily derived from Glaser's behaviour: the company is clearly interested only in the highest end of the world glassware market. Glaser is determined to stick to the highest quality standards, to traditional, distinctive models and patterns, to the most discriminating markets, and to the wealthiest clientele. The company has positioned itself in the upper segment of the Triad market, and is not really interested either in the domestic or the Central and Eastern European markets. As a perspective or driving force, this strategy can probably be labelled as elitist and defensive, as opposed to the temptations of mass production and mass distribution.

Danish consultants—who were brought to Glaser in the middle of 1991 and financed by the World Bank loan—came up with different solutions. They proposed to mechanize gradually some of the production operations, including glass blowing, by using the most advanced computer-control systems. According to the program, only the decoration would be done manually. The increased production volume would be sold under the famous Glaser brand name, generating much higher earnings. In order to finance modernization of the company, the foreign consultants called for a joint venture with one of Western Europe's mass manufacturers of glassware, and for management control by foreign investors. Glaser's management strongly opposed such a radical program, and stucks to the original strategy. It is expected, however, that privatization (and especially foreign investment) may lead to another change of the management team—and strategy of the company.

Such a strategy can be only sustained by perfect knowledge of the marketing and distribution channels, by elaborate promotion and advertising, and by expert pricing. Glaser was, for decades, cut off from its markets which had been developed by the monopolistic Glassexport foreign trade company. Actually, Glaser has not practiced any marketing. Sales volume of the company also seemed rather small.

Further development of macro-economic transition policies could also bring some surprises. If in Czech republic, as in Poland, a stable exchange rate is maintained for a long time as an anchor of the stabilization plan, while cost-induced inflation continues on the domestic market, exports will lose their attractiveness and profitability. In such a situation, production costs and tax burdens will sharply increase. The question remains open to what extent Glaser will be able to compensate for these factors by increasing prices on international markets.

Both examples of the pretenders' strategies clearly demonstrate that the quality of management, and its ability to generate and implement proper strategy, plays a decisive role in securing the future of the pretenders—must be tied to the international markets. Governments do not carry such direct responsibilities for the future of pretenders as they do in the case of dinosaurs. Also, politics are not so important for pretenders as for dinosaurs. Once some economic stability is achieved, proper industrial policies may facilitate further expansion of pretenders (for example, the "Asian Tigers"). In transition times, however, when inflation, recession, unemployment, and sinking dinosaurs are top priorities, the pretenders are on their own. Whether they are going to make it or not depends on their own management.

Pretenders were relatively successful under communism because they were able to produce somewhat better, more advanced products than other enterprises. Since costs were not important and prices were always set by the administration below the equilibrium level, these products would always sell on the ever-hungry, undersupplied domestic and communist bloc markets. Monopolistic state-owned foreign trade companies could also sell them to some core markets, especially since prices were not important, only revenue in hard currency counted. Decades of such experiences made these enterprises exclusively production oriented. Turning them into market oriented organizations is the essence of their transformation, as well as survival and development in the new business environment.

Management education and cooperation with foreign enterprises, facilitating technology and management skills transfers, as well as access to external (foreign) sources of financing seem to be crucial conditions to the transformation of the pretenders. These factors, however, can only act as catalysts of sorts, multiplying the positive effects of management talent and the will to change that already exists within these enterprises—and cannot be replaced.

4

Strategies of Private Enterprises

Mixed Marriages' Strategies

Strategies of the joint ventures are somewhat more complex than strategies of other types of enterprises because they have to be perceived as some kind of synthesis, or as the result of the strategies of at least three types of involved actors: western enterprises participating in joint ventures in Central and Eastern Europe, local partners (enterprises and governments), and the "mixed marriages" themselves.

Two generic types of strategies of western companies entering joint ventures in post-communist countries can be identified:

- *Special*-specially designed for a venture in a post-communist country,

- *normal*-resulting from overall global strategy of the firm.

"Special" strategies are usually followed by small enterprises unknown in the West. These enterprises are often specially formed to cooperate with Central and Eastern Europe, and try to take advantage of the exceptional opportunities resulting from the still persisting lack of compatibility between western and post-communist enterprises in the process of transition. Such opportunities are usually tied to non-convertible currencies, corruption, and low or zero prices of some production factors such as clean air and water, and undersupplied markets—facilitating speculation, compromising on quality, combined with high prices. Such joint ventures are the majority of those established during the last years of communist rule and the early stages of the transition processes. They are often linked to the old communist *nomenklatura* and the economic underworld. Sovmav, which was described in Chapter 1, can be considered an example of such joint ventures. A Polish-German joint venture, established in 1989 exclusively for dumping toxic waste in Poland, is another example. Such enterprises often repeat in communist and post-communist enterprises strategies developed in third world countries. For example, one US firm selling clothing in Moscow for hard currency and generating about 60 percent of its revenues from the USSR (and which also operates in Turkey and

Brazil) has formed a joint venture with the Soviet partner to carry out sales in rubles.[1]

In the early stages of transition, western firms following such special strategies certainly outnumber the others, and trigger uneasy feeling or even resentment against foreign investment. In some cases they also fuel populist, anti-capitalist rhetoric. At the same time, however, governments and legislators feel obliged to protect their countries against migrant foreign predators. This explains why in Poland, for example, the new foreign investment law passed June 14, 1991 stipulated that tax holidays are only given to bigger foreign investors investing the equivalent of over two million ECU (Domanski 1991). Hungary earlier adopted a similar solution.

"Normal" strategies are followed by large multi-national corporations looking for legitimate business opportunities in the post-communist countries. They follow their usual logic of evaluating the strategic options of investing abroad and forming joint ventures with foreign partners. Doz identifies winning strategies of major multinational enterprises as "multifocal": achieved through ad hoc and constantly reformulated strategic compromise between the benefits of integration of operations on a multi-national scale, and the requirements of flexible responsiveness to local national conditions.

"Industry economics characteristics can make multinational integration, national responsiveness or multifocal strategies more or less attractive to multinational companies. Economies of scale, experience and location, the basis for product differentiation, product and process technology, the maintenance of export and distribution channels controlled by the firm, and the firm's access to capital are most critical in making a strategy attractive. This list is not surprising; this is the basis for oligopolistic competitive advantages, and theories of foreign investment tell us that multinational companies have been successful largely to the extent they exploited these advantages from country to country" (Doz 1986: 19). When communism in Central and Eastern Europe started to fall apart, the same possibilities emerged.

Economies of scale, experience, and location are usually pursued by such firms as ABB, which installed itself in Poland, or GE in Hungary, who take over existing facilities, expertise, and people and develop and restructure them in order to increase volume and market penetration. In the restructuring process, they take advantage of previously accumulated worldwide resources, knowledge, and experience (Greenhouse 1990; Maney 1990; Taylor 1991).

The strategy of taking control over export and distribution channels is often followed by western partners in the countries with nonconvertible currencies. The operation of a Danish firm, Macroline Technology International, in the former USSR is a good example of such a strategy (Gornov 1991).

Macroline Technology International unites 55 firms from Denmark and other Scandinavian countries in the field of electronics (microelectronics, personal computers, and radio electronics equipment). It runs a computer assembly operation in Thailand, and represents a number of Danish and North European firms on the Soviet market. It reported $100 million in gross profits in 1990. Its Soviet partner is Soveltest, a voluntary association of over 20 leading manufacturing, design, and R&D organizations (industrial enterprises and research institutes) in the fields of engineering, testing, and radio electronics. It was established in 1989 by the States Standards Committee.

Two partners have established a tandem of two joint ventures: one registered in Russia and one in Denmark. Soveltest Europe (60 percent Danish, 40 percent Soviet ownership) will operate in Denmark, while the Macroline-Soveltest International (60 percent Soviet, 40 percent Danish ownership) will handle the Soviet market.

Both firms intend to specialize in the joint development, production, and marketing of radio electronics. The partners believe that their unusual arrangement will enable them to better control both markets, especially the Russian market, and to overcome the still too stringent Russian currency and foreign trade restrictions, such as export licensing. Under this arrangement, the partners are able to exercise the rights of two legal entities at once under jurisdiction of two different countries. This added flexibility takes many forms of free circulation of goods, components, technology and know-how.

It overcomes restrictions on barter deals imposed in 1990 in the form of export licences requirements, as well as hard currency and ruble funds (Gornov 1991). It is evident that changes introduced after the aborted military coup in Russia (August 1991) call for an adjustment of this strategy (mainly currency convertibility issue) but the basic strategy, the creation of two separate entities, still remains viable.

Surprisingly enough, a joint venture with a partner in Central or Eastern Europe can become a source of capital for the western partner. For example, Overseas Private Investment Corporation is a U.S. government agency providing financing and political risk insurance for American businesses investing in Eastern Europe (more precisely in Poland, Hungary, Czechoslovakia and East Germany). When President Bush announced a comprehensive program of $200 million in aid for Europe's new democracies in 1990, the Eastern European Growth Fund was created (initiated by OPIC and managed by Salomon Brothers) to provide capital for new projects with participation of local private capital. A special $100 million fund was developed by OPIC to provide start-up capital for business projects in environmental protection. In early 1990, OPIC wrote investment insurance for $150 million GE-Tungsram Hungarian deal. Between the beginning of 1990 and August 1990, more than 400 American firms, ranging from small to giant-sized applied for OPIC assistance in securing capital for their Eastern European ventures. Similar solutions have been adopted by the EEC.[2]

Product and process technology may also be acquired by western firms, in some instances through joint ventures with post-communist countries. It does not apply exclusively to the Soviet military high-technology (the Gulfstream-Soukhoi joint venture presented above), but also to other countries and other sectors. It is worth mentioning that the first Czech joint venture was the one in which the Czech contribution was patents in the field of bio-technology, while the foreign partner provided cash, equipment, and marketing expertise (King 1990). One of the technical and scientific sensations of 1991 was the Czech Minister of Defense announcement that until recently, Tesla Radio Works in Pardubice produced a top secret unique radio-location system presumably capable of detecting the "invisible" U.S. Stealth bomber[3]. All countries in the region seem to have interesting, untapped, and often not fully developed technologies to offer.

Doz's list of the strategies of multinational companies should be completed with "negative," preemptive strategies aimed to discourage, inhibit or block a triadic opponent or competitor in the post-communist territory (Lewis 1990 a). When GE concluded its Tungsram deal in Hungary, acquiring the biggest Eastern European manufacturer of lighting/ light bulb sources with well-established exports to the EEC, Phillips, the European market leader in light sources visibly accelerated its negotiations to acquire a light bulb factory in Pila, Poland. The move was interpreted as preventing further expansion by GE in the region. Similarly, German buyers of Polish apple juice concentrate began mixing it with German and other apple juices, and sweetening them for exports to the U.S. This blocked American buyers from having direct access to Polish sources of supply.

Strategies pursued by local partners result from their motivations to form joint enterprises with foreign firms. On the enterprise level, these motivations varied, depending upon the individual characteristics of the firm such as, most importantly, the firm's market and financial position. These motivations also seem to be different in different stages of the transition process. During the last years of communism, joint venture were perceived as "enclaves" and experiments, but at the same time were seen as opportunities of enrichment for the most trusted, most resourceful and best connected members of the communist *nomenklatura*. Joint ventures, which emerged out of this climate, exploited their privileged status and opportunities resulting from the widespread economy of shortage and non-convertible currency.

Such "enclave" motivations persisted during the first stages of transition, but with the progress of reforms leading toward the market economy they were gradually replaced by "normal" business motivations. In particular, the introduction of internally convertible currencies and the elimination of shortages played a decisive role in this process. Normal business motivations, however, are still biased by a lack of knowledge and understanding of foreign partners and an inherent tendency toward a somewhat simplified and naive perception of joint ventures as a universal cure for all the weaknesses of the communist enterprises. Local managers and workers expect joint ventures to be the sources of capital and technology, as well as to provide an opportunity to increase considerably the workers' wages and the managers' salaries.

On the level of the national economy, motivations to attract direct foreign investment are well known, and in the case of post-communist economies, do not differ significantly from motivations of other countries which are trying to stimulate their growth and to modernize their economies through foreign investment. The most important among these motivations are: the importation of productivity increasing factors such as technology, equipment, and managerial know-how, external financing of these crucial imports, access to the new difficult and profitable markets, employment, exports, upgrading of domestic markets and promoting competition, and fostering of closer cooperation with core Triad economies. Such statistics as the fact that 32 percent of Irish exports, and 40 percent of Portugal's, are linked directly to foreign investment, and that over 30 percent of manufacturing employment in Belgium, Ireland and Spain, are often quoted to support the policy of attracting foreign investment (King 1990). At the same time, however, some warnings against foreign capital are being voiced, and not only within the framework of populist rhetoric used by some politicians on the extreme left and the extreme right. Such warnings refer to the nationality of investors (for example, the touchy issue of German investors in western regions of Poland, which belonged to Germany prior to the World War II), and to the loss of "economic sovereignty" in general. Another issue raised is the possible reduction of national income resulting from foreign firms or joint ventures taking advantage of their monopolistic position on heavily protected markets (King 1990). Warnings result in specific government regulations, such as restrictions of the percentage of shares offered to foreign investors in companies privatized through public offerings of shares (10 percent in Poland), land ownership by foreigners, or low tariff barriers. All these precautions might seem over-exaggerated, since post-communist countries still remain relatively unattractive for western investors. Such factors as political instability in some countries, still incompatible economic and legal system, and unknown environments can only partially explain that. Still persisting bureaucracy and red tape, combined with the notorious instability of the political, financial, and legal environment, are often responsible for failures of quite promising negotiations.

The case of the Swedish manufacturers of metal office furniture, Dove International Ltd.[4] in Poland seems to be a perfect illustration, because its case is so typical. Dove is a leading manufacturer of metal office furniture, offering a full range of products, including all kinds and sizes of tables, desks, and file cabinets, computer tables, and chairs. It outfits all kinds of offices and conference rooms, from top management down. Dove has more than ten factories in Sweden, and in 1989 reported over $500 million in sales volume. In 1990, Dove got its first big contract in Central and Eastern Europe: the complete furnishing of 20,000 square meters of office space in Moscow. Because of this, they became seriously interested in business opportunities in the region. This interest also included the acquisition of manufacturing facilities, identifying potential subcontractors, business contacts, and marketing channels.

Dove was approached in June 1990 by the general manager of a medium-sized enterprise of 500 employees known in Poland as PUT (Polish abbreviation for Enterprise of Technical Equipment). PUT manufactures mechanical parts of relatively simple lathes, and is situated in a small town 80 kilometers from Warsaw. Until 1990, PUT was a part of Ponar-Remo, a large multi-factory corporation specializing in lathes and mechanical tools. In 1989, the corporation got rid of its technologically weak and under-capitalized provincial factory and created an independent enterprise. It started to specialize in production of simple machine tools and spare parts for lathes used in Poland. It was quite successful in 1989, and even started to prepare for upgrading of its product line. The introduction of a stabilization plan and internal convertibility of the zloty in 1990, combined with very low or non existent tariff barriers, changed this situation dramatically. Demand dropped, due to the recession and the elimination of many industrial clients. Primitive tools produced by the enterprise could not compete with much more advanced foreign imports. The financial situation of PUT deteriorated rapidly, and the company approached bankruptcy. The bank refused further financing in March 1990. In May 1990, the Ministry of Industry decided to liquidate PUT and its director, Mr. Wasiak, was nominated as liquidation executor—with the mission to close operations, lay off personnel, and sell all the assets.

Wasiak had started in PUT as a manual worker 25 years earlier. He later took evening classes to get his engineering degree, and in 1990 graduated from the School of Management of Warsaw University. He was active in the Solidarity movement and, in 1989, was unanimously elected managing director of PUT. Being a local patriot and popular figure in the community, he decided at least to try to save the factory, as it was the biggest employer in a small town already hit by recession and unemployment.

All attempts to find strong partner (domestic or foreign) in the machine tools and lathes industry were unsuccessful. Wasiak decided to penetrate other industries, and found out that PUT was relatively well fitted for manufacturing metal furniture. It had all basic machinery (including a relatively modern paint shop), vast storage surface, a work force specialized in the metal industry, and very convenient railway connections. Design, some technical help, and access to markets were needed. Dove was identified as a potential partner and when it expressed some interest, Wasiak was able to persuade the Ministry to postpone liquidation for sometime—the Industry Restructuring Fund issued some limited bank guarantees. Wasiak bought time to form a joint venture company.

Potential partners for a joint venture company, Dovton SA, were: Dove International Ltd., contributing 60 percent of the $1 million capital; a highly diversified (electronics, food processing, trading, and transports, among others) Polish private "company B," offering a wide network of business contacts and 25 percent of capital; and a group of private individuals (Wasiak and four others company managers), offering expertise, knowledge of local conditions, and 15 percent of the capital. Wasiak prepared himself, working 18 hours a day for two long summer months. By early September, not only were the feasibility study and business plan ready, but also a joint venture agreement, as well as sales and leasing contracts.

Davton SA would buy all equipment and facilities and lease the land of liquidated PUT and immediately start the production of metal office furniture elements. The Feasibility study and five-years business plan called for an immediate start of manufacturing of furniture elements (chair and desk frames), and gradual expansion into a complete line of file cabinets, desks, and chairs. Expansion was conditioned by capital investment financed partially by credit from a British bank (guaranteed by Dove) and partially by the sales of existing equipment. 1991 employment of Davton was projected at 250 people (including 50 administrators, managers, and engineers, including eight foreigners). The projected employment for 1992–1994, would increase to the level of 850 (with only three Swedish engineers remaining). Projected sales for 1991 were at the equivalent of

$8.5 million, over $14 million in 1992, and already $25 million in 1993. Dove committed itself to buy and market all the product of the joint ventures company. A special personnel training program was designed, as well as a compensation plan calling for 50 percent of wages directly linked to productivity. The best workers would make 2 to 2.5 times the average local salary.

In August 1990, all the papers were submitted for approval to the Ministry of Industry. In spite of constant pressure and frequent visits to the Ministry, an answer did not come until the end of the year. On January 1, 1991, all the assets of state-owned enterprises were revalued (corrected for inflation) and, in order to buy the liquidated PUT assets, the partners had to raise nearly $2.5 million, instead of the $1 million initially projected. Dove withdrew—and the deal was cancelled. PUT was liquidated quickly and all the workers were laid off. In 1991 and 1992, they were all collecting unemployment benefits. Wasiak was hired and rapidly promoted to a top management position by another foreign company operating in Poland. Dove International, which realized the magnitude of business opportunities for them in Central and Eastern Europe, started to look for a partner in Russia and Ukraine.

Strategies of the "mixed marriages" themselves can be divided into two generic categories:

- Strategies resulting directly from the remaining elements of the communist system (such as non-convertible currencies, undersupplied markets, discretionary powers of economic bureaucracy and mutual trade agreements between former COMECON countries).

- Strategies resulting from the emerging participation of the post-communist countries in global market environment and global competition. Such strategies result from broadening the scope of penetration of the multinational corporations, and integration of the post-communist countries into the field of their interests. Relatively few global leaders take into consideration the specific and unstable environment in the post-communist countries.

These two types of strategies are often incompatible. Successful adjustment to the remaining elements of the communist system inhibits successful free market competition. It is worth remembering that the best known joint ventures in the region (such as GE-Tungsram in Hungary, and ABB-Zamech in Poland) were developed predominantly under the influence of market forces and the strategies of sophisticated global companies. They are somewhat insulated from the influence of the remaining elements of the communist system. Many weaker joint ventures operating in Central and Eastern Europe, especially the ones founded prior to 1989, were forced to develop mixtures of both types of strategies. Such a mixture (with still dominating influence of the old system) will be illustrated by the case of Elfur International Ltd. (a Polish-Western European joint venture company founded in Poland at the end of 1987), while still under the communist rule[5].

Elfur was born primarily out of initiative of Mr. Kurski, who in 1986 was a managing director of one of the Polish foreign trade companies dealing primarily with the exports of Polish furniture to the West. Kurski can certainly be considered a typical representative of the most enlightened and westernized communist managers. He graduated in 1963 from the Central School of Planning and Statistics Department of Foreign Trade. An activist in the communist youth organization, and then a party member, Kurski was rapidly promoted in the ranks of foreign trade organizations. In the early 1970s, he attended an executive development program in marketing, conducted in English, at a prestigious European business school. Later, he was a Polish trade representative in Sweden, and became managing director of a foreign trade companies. In the '70s, he headed a task force established in the Ministry of Foreign Trade to promote Polish-American trade. He made several business trips to Japan.

By the mid-1980s, Kurski knew the furniture exports business very well, and realized that in order to stay competitive on the international market, and considerably increase the volume of exports, Polish furniture factories needed modernization and considerable capital investment. Such investment had to be financed in hard currency. In 1985, Polish enterprises could not get any western credit and had to sell most of their hard currency earnings to the Polish National Bank. Hard currency auctions initiated in 1985 could not provide larger amounts of investment capital. As a Foreign Trade Ministry insider, Kurski knew that the Joint Venture Act was in the making—and decided to be one of the first to take advantage of it.

A private consulting group—composed of young assistant professors from the Warsaw University School of Management, who were eager to practice some ''real business''—was hired to help to select a partner, develop a business plan, negotiate an agreement, and set up a joint venture company.

The first task was to choose a western partner. Kurski looked for candidates, and a consulting group screened and evaluated them. After some unsuccessful candidates had been interviewed, Kurski brought in for screening Mr. Pawlak, who represented ''X,'' a European computer manufacturer in Poland. X had been in Poland since the late 1950s, selling mainframe and minicomputers to big clients (e.g., bureaucracies and state-owned companies) who could afford to pay in hard currency. Mr. Pawlak, a citizen of one of the EEC countries, was an artist turned salesman who was born, in the West, to a polish emigrant family. In the late '70s, he became X's representative in Poland. Pawlak took full advantage of his knowledge of the Polish language and culture, as well as an unquestionable business talent demonstrated in the difficult period of martial law. At this time, most western firms withdrew from Poland—but X continued selling.

The consulting group and Kurski came to the conclusion that Pawlak and his company were the perfect choice. The business concept of the future Elfur company was born out of the non-convertibility of the Polish zloty. The joint venture would sell Polish furniture in the West for hard currency. This was not difficult, taking into consideration the already established market, quality and price of the product. The joint venture would then buy X computers and sell them for zlotys in Poland. In 1988, a company exporting furniture from Poland could obtain $1 worth of hard currency for about 400 Polish zlotys' worth of total costs (for production, commercial, overhead, taxation, etc.). The same $1, invested in computers and systems imported to Poland and sold for zlotys to Polish customers, could bring as much as 1,200 zlotys. Huge profits obtained in this way from the "leveraged barter" could be invested into the modernization of factories, creating considerably increased volumes and the development of new models suitable for export—as well as promotions, training of personnel, high salaries, and benefits. Under the economic conditions existing in Poland in 1988, clients would wait in line to buy computers for zlotys, even at very high prices, because state-owned enterprises subjected to "soft budget constraints" could be short of anything except local currency, and had very limited access to hard currency.

The joint venture law was passed in November 1986. In 1987, Kurski and his consultants assembled a group of Polish partners. It included four furniture factories representing practically the complete technological cycle of furniture manufacturing (including lumber production), two foreign trade companies specializing in furniture exports, and one electronics enterprise. The electronics firm was capable of assembling computers from kits, building systems, and testing them. The western partner holds 35 percent of the equity, which according to the company by-laws, gives it veto power in crucial financial decisions, such as: dilution of equity; new business ventures, coalitions, on partnerships; and major expenditures. Sixty-five percent of the equity is held by the Polish partners, all of them state owned. The western partner paid for its stake the equivalent of about $800,000 in cash and $400,000 worth of in-kind contributions (advanced computer software). The foreign partner also provided over $3 million worth of bank loan guarantees, enabling an immediate initiation of a modernization program for the factories. Until the end of 1989, Elfur was the biggest employer of all joint ventures in the crumbling socialist block, employing over 6,300 people in 1988.

Polish factories, as state-owned enterprises, could not contribute all their assets to the newly formed joint venture because of the required complicated and lengthy legal procedures involving technical liquidation of legal entities. Therefore, the consultants broke these enterprises into artificial sections. Each factory entering the joint venture leased to it most of its assets, leaving one business unit outside the venture. For example, armchair production was left out in one case, and maintenance in another. Kurski used his leverage to obtain very low lease payments—under contracts that are binding on furniture companies for 10 years. He was also able to obtain another important privilege. Elfur was required to sell only 10 percent of its hard currency earnings to the state, while other joint ventures had to sell 20 percent.

After registering the company in November 1987, a corporate governance and management system was established. The authorities of Elfur are the General Assembly of Shareholders, a supervisory board and a management board.

The General Assembly of Shareholders meets once a year and reviews and approves major financial decisions, such as the division of dividends, compensation of the company's management and board members, bank loans, and investments. It also puts a seal of approval on annual reports presented by management and approved by the supervisory board.

The supervisory board meets every two or three months. It is composed of 12 people appointed by the shareholders assembly but, in practice, proposed by management. The Polish partners, the two Western partners, the two banks cooperating with Elfur, the two academics in the fields of management and economics, the two political parties (active in 1987, under the communist regime, and in practice controlled by the communist party) each have two representatives. Additionally, there is one member representing employees of the company and one representing the consulting group who helped to establish the company. Members of the management board participate in the supervisory board meetings as resource people, providing information. The supervisory board reviews the company's strategies and plans, expresses its opinions, and gives approval. It often becomes, the scene of confrontations between the western partner's representatives and the Polish management, which often feels constrained by X's policies.

The management board is unquestionably the real center of executive power within the company. It was initially composed of three members:

Kurski, president and CEO of the Company; Pawlak, who represents X's interests in Elfur, but also remains its direct sales representative; and Mr. Dobczynski, vice president of finance and CFO. Mr. Dobczynski, who was a communist party member, holds Ph.D. in economics, and for many years was employed as the director of one of the research institutes in the field of economics. In the early '80s, after the declaration of martial law, spent a couple of years as the Polish government representative in one of the international organizations headquarters in Vienna.

Elfur's management system is characterized by strict centralization of import and export operations, and decentralization of most of production management operations. Production planning, however, is centralized because of the necessity to implement export programs. Factories became "production units," following the detailed plan provided by the management board. Strict coordination of operations was needed because many of the factories that joined Elfur supply others with components and semi-finished goods. While in some furniture lines Elfur factories are cooperating very closely, in others they are independent producers.

Day-to-day operations of the factories forming Elfur are completely decentralized and left to the managers' discretion. This applies to personnel policy, procurement, production scheduling, and marketing policies with respect to products sold in Poland. After a while pricing became centralized because the factories visibly lacked marketing experience and used the "cost plus" pricing formula still prevalent in post-communist countries. With growing inflation and constantly rising demand, the factories constantly underpriced their product—and the management board decided to centralize pricing policies. In order to study consumers reactions, a special store with the new products was opened in Warsaw to perform pricing experiments.

The first three years of Elfur's operations were extremely successful. On the shop-floor level, a coherent and uniform wage system was implemented. This system was a complete novelty for Polish workers. The system is based on three premises:

1. Wages are a confidential, personal matter, which means that workers do not know each others wages.

2. Groups of workers engaged in fully integrated technological operations are provided with a budget. If they perform this operation faster than planned (without compromising quality), they are still rewarded with the same amount of money, which they can divide among themselves.

3. Workers' wages calculated in this way are then transferred to private accounts (an innovation in Poland, where wages and even management salaries are always paid in cash).

This new compensation system created strong motivation to increase productivity, which went up by 15 percent in 1989 and 12 percent in 1990. Trade unions initially opposed this solution, but were unable to enforce their opinion because of the workers' approval of the system. Under this system, wages increased considerably, as compared with the state-owned enterprises. Management moved even further: it did not permit union meetings on company time, which is common practice in Poland. After an initial period of limited mutiny and a few short strikes, the unions gave up—so long as workers made much more money for being more productive. But union leaders and the workers' self-management councils retained bad feelings about management. These feelings resurfaced in 1991.

Exports of furniture were at the level of $12 million in 1988, $17 million in 1989, and $32 million in 1990. Domestic sales were also constantly rising during the first two years of operation. In 1988, they reached the equivalent of $27 million, and in 1989 $53 million, but in 1990 they dropped to $47 million. In 1990, Elfur became the biggest single furniture manufacturer and exporter in Poland, occupying about a 6 percent market share and providing 4.9 percent of exports. Profit margins were 16.5 percent in 1988, 33.5 percent in 1989 and 13.6 percent in 1990. The unusually high margin in 1989 was due to the devaluation of the local currency (Polish zloty), which increased the book value of export earnings. Although this measure was introduced on January 1, 1990, it affected the 1989 profit-and-loss statement. Computer sales were always much lower than expected: $1.7 million in 1988, $2.3 million in 1989, and $1.2 million in 1990.

In order to meet the demand for furniture, Elfur leased new factories but was not able to modernize and restructure them. Between 1988 and 1990, Elfur was only able to invest the equivalent of $7 million in badly needed new equipment. At least $15 to 20 million was needed to stay competitive on the international market and to become a real global player. In furniture manufacturing, economies of scale require highly specialized and costly equipment. The inability to finance a modernization drive was due to the specific features of the Polish banking system and capital market in transition times, which was highly representative of "economies in transition." Before internal convertibility of the currency was introduced in 1990, hard currency loans were difficult to get (especially for a newly created and non-state-owned entity, such as Elfur).

Guarantees from the western partner, X, were expected. However, X issued such guarantees for only $2 million, and refused to extend them in spite of constant pressure from the Polish management. Factors such as political instability in Poland, the "exotic" business environment and the "exotic" line of business for a computer manufacturer (i.e., furniture) and perhaps to some extent a culture clash or even personality clashes with the Polish management, were responsible for the consistent refusal to guarantee further loans. After convertibility of the currency was introduced, the restrictive anti-inflationary monetary policy caused extremely high interest rates in Polish banks. Polish enterprises could apply for credits in foreign banks, which in turn required guarantees from one of the two major (internationally recognized) Polish banks. Polish banks were asking for collateral and Elfur could not provide it, because they were leasing nearly all of their production facilities. This explains why guarantees for only $5 million were obtained from one of the Polish banks.

In 1989, Kurski proposed the diversification of Elfur into such new high-return lines of business as hotels, tourism, and supermarkets. The foreign partners, however, expressed some concern about diverting the company's resources from its main lines of business. Once again, financing was a problem. Finally, the diversification idea did not materialize.

Computer sales never reached the level of expectations. In 1988 and 1989, Elfur had not yet built up an adequate sales force, deliveries of kits from Western Europe were delayed, there were some quality problems, and the Polish electronics firm that joined Elfur needed time to iron out all of its assembly and testing problems. In 1990, the situation changed dramatically. Since all potential buyers gained access to hard currency, competition intensified immensely especially when IBM returned to Poland, and huge numbers of Far Eastern manufacturers entered the market. At the same time, the demand from traditional buyers of X's minis (big state-owned enterprises and government agencies) dropped, because of the sudden introduction of hard budget constraints and restrictive monetary policies. Also, Elfur's offer itself became increasingly unattractive for Polish buyers because of the shrinking market share of minis—due to the general trend of upgrading of PCs and downgrading of mainframes—as well as because of the quality problems and low responsiveness of X's European headquarters to changing Polish market conditions (mainly slow adjustment of prices and delivery conditions).

With the introduction of convertible currency, conflicts of interest emerged within Elfur. Since all the sales of computers were done in local currency, Elfur—as required by the new legislation introduced as a part of the "shock treatment therapy" effective January 1, 1990—(a joint venture with X's participation) competed directly with X's direct sales through its sales representation. To make things worse, Pawlak was at the same time Elfur's vice president, representing X's interests, and X's sales representative in Poland. Obviously, both X and Pawlak were interested in increasing direct sales at the expense of Elfur's—which they successfully did. While Elfur's computer sales were constantly falling, X's direct sales increased considerably. At the end of 1990, Pawlak resigned from Elfur's management board and joined the supervisory board as X's representative. His seat on the management board remained empty. The foreign partner did not appoint anyone.

After 1990, X yearly lost interest in the Polish joint venture and concentrated on protecting its investment, successfully blocking all initiatives of local management and consistently refusing financial guarantees. In 1990, X was taken over by a giant Japanese corporation, which did not make any decisions concerning Elfur until the end of 1991, in spite of several letters and memos sent by Kurski. This fact certainly influenced the foreign partner's strange behavior.

In order to compensate for the lost computer sales, Elfur made several attempts at diversification into such high-tech areas as telecommunications (sales and installation of western telephone equipment) and medical equipment (portable electrocardiographs under licence from relatively little-known Danish manufacturer). They all failed because of increasingly expensive credit, lack of managerial expertise, and strong competition on these markets.

In furniture, Elfur had an unquestionable competitive advantage due to its superior designs (which won medals and awards at international fairs and exhibitions), low labor and material costs, and expertise in production and marketing. After 1991, however, the furniture situation also became much more difficult. Among the contributing factors, the most important were:

1. The exchange rate was maintained at the level of 9,500 zlotys for one American dollar between January 1, 1990 and mid-May 1991. In the mean time inflation in 1990 alone was close to 260 percent and in January 1991 it was 12 percent (in the following months, inflation decreased considerably to 2 percent to 4 percent per month). In 1990, the US dollar and all hard currencies in Poland lost close to 70 percent of their 1989 value. Exports to the West (the flagship of Elfur's business) became less and less attractive and profitable. Taking into consideration that the three-year tax break granted to Elfur expired in October 1990, several export contracts became money-losing operations.

2. The costs of local supplies were rapidly increasing, and the prices of energy, gas, and raw materials were skyrocketing. During the first two

months of 1990 alone, they increased by over 45 percent. The low cost of labor—the equivalent of $200 in monthly wages for a skilled worker, a traditional Polish cost advantage in this business—were increasing, due to strikes and the demands of the Solidarity trade union for a bigger piece of the pie. The huge profits of Elfur in 1989 and 1990, the high wages of management (in some cases, 30 times the average Polish salary), and generous fringe benefits (houses, big BMW cars, expense accounts, etc.) were handy excuses for trade union leaders to exert pressure on management, who had been humiliated then in 1988 and 1989. The subject was politically touchy because the management of the company was perceived as members of the old communist *nomenklatura,* still taking advantge of old privileges and connections. In fact, many of them (not only the CEO and the CFO) were party members and held relatively high positions under the communist regime.

3. Hostile relations with trade unions and workers' self-management made restructuring of the factories and layoffs of redundant workers impossible. Over-employment in Elfur's factories was estimated at about 30 percent.

4. State-owned factories that leased their facilities and equipment to Elfur wanted to privatize, but binding leasing agreements (on terms very financially unfavorable to the factories) made this very difficult. Pressure mounted because the worsening financial situation of Elfur did not permit wages to keep up with inflation. Workers hoped that privatization would save their jobs and make further increases possible. From the legal viewpoint, bankruptcy and liquidation of state-owned enterprises could make cancellation of the leasing contract and privatization in the form of employee ownership possible. Such a risky solution seemed tempting for some, but it would certainly have given a final blow to Elfur.

5. The high prices of furniture and the lower purchasing power of the population lowered the aggregate demand for furniture by over 35 percent in 1990, as compared with 1989. Elfur was especially badly hit because their furniture was too expensive for average families—especially in difficult recession times—and in luxury furniture, Elfur was confronted by expensive imports often preferred by the emerging upper middle class. The domestic furniture market did not look promising at all.

Confronted with such an extremely difficult situation, management was virtually paralyzed and until mid-1991, and no real strategic decisions were taken. Elfur drifted.

Using Mintzberg's perspective and terminology, one discovers that Elfur's strategy, as a plan (a consciously intended course of action and sequence of goals to achieve), existed only until the fall of the communist regime and implementation of the Balcerowicz Plan in January 1990. The same applies to strategy as a pattern: "leveraged barter" certainly includes a behavioral pattern that is relatively consistent and easy to infer. When the originally intended behavioral pattern became visibly obsolete and the new strategy had to be formulated, management started to behave inconsistently, exploring many different possibilities and following none.

Elfur originally positioned itself as a privileged intermediary between Polish furniture factories and foreign markets and sources of financing, as well as between foreign computer manufacturers and its Polish clients. Non-convertible currency and all the market entry restrictions which distorted and complicated both the Polish firms' access to the foreign markets and foreign firms' access to the Polish market) justified this intermediary and his huge profits. Once market entry obstacles were removed, the intermediary position lost all economic justification. Elfur was not able to anticipate and to build up a new market position. The joint venture firm visibly had a predator's perception of the business, modeled after the old communist concept of the monopolistic foreign trade enterprise exploiting its domestic and foreign clients. Such firms were never really subjected to competition-enforced efficiency. Elfur visibly followed that pattern.

Origins of the paralysis of Elfur's management are certainly worth explaining. From its inception, the firm was torn by internal conflicts of interest. Furniture factories were forced to join Elfur and to sign leases. Both management and workers felt uneasy about it. Hostility was appeased, so long as Elfur paid better than other firms. When financial situation deteriorated, management could not count on cooperation from the factories and especially from the workers, who had been constantly antagonized by the arrogant and provocative behavior of people from the Warsaw headquarters, who were perceived as remnants of the old communist system.

The foreign partner treated the joint venture exclusively as an additional convenient channel of distribution that considerably increased the Polish market, under the conditions of market entry barriers and non-convertible currency. The foreign partner wanted to maximize computer sales and hard currency earnings from furniture exports, but clearly did not have any interest and expertise in the furniture business.

The exact opposite applies to the Polish management: they were interested in maximizing investment in furniture factories, but did not know much about computers. Mutual mistrust between the Polish and foreign partners resulted from such different interests and perspectives. When the situation changed dramatically, mistrust intensified and the foreign partner developed his own defensive strategy to minimize exposure and protect his original investment. This strategy had nothing to do with the joint ventures success, and actually, was a major paralyzing factor.

Management paralysis is even more striking, since as late as the middle of 1991, Elfur's situation was not hopeless at all. The company could survive by adjusting its product lines to changing domestic and foreign market requirements, restructuring its factories, and building up competitive strength in furniture.

All the classic textbook reasons for joint venture failure are present in this case: the lack of clearly formulated objectives, mutually agreed upon by partners and translated into a common strategy; mistrust and communications problems; initially hidden conflicts of interest; competition in the same market between the joint venture and one of the partners; and different, non-compatible backgrounds and areas of expertise. There is also a specific reason resulting from the conditions of post-communist economies in transition, Elfur was built on the old communist business concept and initiated by the old *nomenklatura,* who were losing touch with a rapidly changing reality.

In the most advanced post-communist countries, Hungary and Poland, cases similar to Elfur's gradually fade away, but in others they will certainly persist for some time. Some of them may even survive if they show more capability to adjust.

Successful strategies of East-West joint ventures will probably have to be developed under the dominating influence of the western partner, who should help post-communist enterprises to formulate their missions, objectives, and strategies clearly. This is due not only to the lack of strategic thinking abilities, patterns, and traditions, but also to the turbulent and unstable business environment in post-communist countries. Local managers tend to be influenced predominantly by the present situation and the opportunities and threats resulting from it. They seem to have problems visualising what a fully developed market economy will look like and what are the consequences of globalization of the markets. Such a dominating role of the foreign partner requires considerable investment in terms of time, effort and material resources. It can only materialize if the western partner is consciously willing to make such an investment after carefully evaluating its magnitude, payoffs, and risks involved. Real commonality of interests also has to be evident. All these conditions are not easy to meet, especially since serious cultural differences have to be overcome. That's why the role of foreign direct investment, and especially joint ventures in the transition of post-communist economies, often seems to be exaggerated.

Strategies of Mom-and-Pop Shops

Small privately-owned companies seldom develop formalized long-range strategic plans. That does not mean, however, that strategies as patterns, positions, and perspectives cannot be inferred from their behavior. These strategies can vary considerably, depending upon country and industry-specific market conditions, macro-economic, financial, political, and legal environments, and even the personalities of entrepreneurs. In spite of all these differences, at lest one common characteristic feature of small business strategies in post-communist countries seems evident: they all follow differentiation strategies offering highly diversified ranges of products and services.

Strategies of post-communist small enterprises will be illustrated below by three cases:

- The Russian phonographic firm, Erio

- R-Z, Polish manufacturer of mechanical elements of electronic systems and anti-break lock systems

- A & D—a Polish construction enterprise

The private phonographic firm, Erio, was registered in Moscow on January 5, 1991 (Gornov 1991). The initial capital investment (in rubles, hard currency, and in-kind), as well as the identity of the owner or owners, were not disclosed. The managing director, Wassily Lavrov, identified the firm's line of business as production, manufacturing, and marketing of records, compact discs, cassettes, video cassettes, and video clips. Until now, there had been only one company specializing in this line of business in the entire former USSR the state-owned monopolistic giant, Melodya. Erio wants to capture 10 to 15 percent of this giant market. Since 1991, however, some other new players have been emerging in the newly independent states.

Starting its activity, Erio employed 30 people in three divisions: production and manufacturing, editing, and marketing. The firm owned advanced imported equipment for manufacturing records, compact discs, cassettes, and video clips. It rented studios and office space in Moscow and in the Baltic States. It plans to open its own stores in Moscow, St. Petersburg, and the Baltic States of Lithuania, Latvia, and Estonia.

Lavrov expects a high return on his investment. According to his business plan the initial capital investment will be paid off in one year, assuming that records sell for an average price of 8 to 12 rubles, compacts discs for 40 to 80 rubles, and cassettes for 10 to 14 rubles, and that prices will be adjusted for inflation. The first two records produced and manufactured by Erio were already available in Moscow shops in January 1991.

Erio's strategy can be summarized as follows:

1. The new firm intends to produce higher quality records than its rival, Melodya, which adds scrapped old records to the material from which new ones are manufactured. This practice compromises quality. Erio is using high-quality imported products, obtained through complicated barter transactions which Lavrov did not want to disclose (one more secret !). The same high-quality requirement, obtained through the use of imported materials and components, applies to other Erio's products such as compact discs and cassettes.

2. Erio does not intend to specialize in any particular kind of music (such as classical music, jazz, or rock and roll). It wants to fill the gaps left by Melodya and to get music and performers who are known to the public (at least informed public), but who are not yet available on records, discs or cassettes quickly to the market. In other words, Erio wants to take advantage of other weaknesses of its giant competitor (besides poor quality of records): its slow decision-making process, its conservative tastes, and its long production cycle.

3. Erio wants to produce a small series (20 to 40 thousand copies) of items for collectors and connoisseurs of contemporary Russian music and famous performers. It intends to attract them, both by the exclusive image of the firm and its higher fees.

4. To build up the exclusive image of the firm, Lavrov intends to control distribution channels by opening the firm's own stores in prestigious places in the biggest towns of Russia, as well as some other C.I.S. countries and by carefully selecting trading partners.

5. Erio started with production and distribution of records and intends to proceed to cassettes. Compact discs are intended to be the next stage of Erio's development. Video clips, considered the most profitable part of the business, will wait until the state TV monopoly is dismantled.

Erio certainly has a strategy fitting all the aspects addressed by Mintzberg in his series of definitions. This includes strategy as a long range plan setting a consciously intended course of action and that is composed of a sequence of objectives. The Russian phonographic firm clearly exposes a pattern of behaviour consisting of high quality orientation combined with careful selection of target publics and appropriate distribution channels. Ploy element is certainly present in Erio's strategy, it had already started its activities as a private firm under communism and it cannot disclose all its secrets, such as sources of initial capital and barter arrangements enabling imports of high-quality materials.

This element of the strategy, which is certainly country and time specific, seems to have been taken from the western management book. Lavrov's firm clearly has positioned itself at the high end of the market, and intends to build the image of high quality and discriminating taste that appeals to the Russian-speaking audiences in the countries that emerged after the collapse of former USSR. Its perspective is dominated by two factors: the weaknesses of the giant competitor it intends to exploit and the prospects of dismantling the Soviet media monopolies, and reinforcement of market forces.

R-Z[6] has an unusually long history for a private enterprise operating in a post-communist country. It was founded in 1961 as a small craftsman shop specializing in the production of spare parts for motorcycles. The rapidly growing sales of Polish-made and foreign (Czech, Soviet, Hungarian, and German) motorcycles in the early 1960s triggered a demand for spare parts. This demand was never satisfied by communist producers, who always had a strong preference for finished goods and neglected parts, because of the "plan fulfilment indicators" system and administratively set official prices. Parts were sold to an already existing network of small private retailers selling motorcycle and auto parts.

The scale of the operation was quite large for a private enterprise in a communist country. The operation has partially hidden in the underground economy. Further expansion was impossible without attracting attention of the authorities, who often imposed additional discretionary taxes on private entrepreneurs who grew too big. The purpose of these taxes was to ruin them and to drive them out of business. Profits could not be reinvested and were mostly spent for consumption. Because of this, in the communist countries where small private enterprises were officially tolerated to some degree (Hungary, Poland, East Germany), tiny private entrepreneurs enjoyed surprisingly high standards of living (the proverbial Mercedes, big houses, etc.). Communist propaganda often exploited this issue, to increase public opinion against private entrepreneurs.

In the early '70s when more freedom was given to private entrepreneurs in Poland, R-Z expanded. It launched a new product: wind shields for motorcycles, which became an instant success. New lines of spare parts and accessories for Polish-made and foreign motorcycles were constantly added to the product lines already carried by the firm. Between 1972 and 1975, the sales volume increased 15 times. Between 1975 and 1980, the sales growth rate was 20 percent a year. In 1980, strong inflationary pressures and huge amounts of "hot money" in the hands of consumers—confronted with mostly empty shelves of the state-owned stores—contributed to another record sales increase for R-Z: over 100 percent between 1980 and 1982.

In 1982, the business environment for small private firms in Poland started to change again. Economic reform introduced in 1982 under the special conditions of martial law, as well as open confrontation with Solidarity and the majority of the population, created a surprisingly favorable and more stable environment for legitimate private businesses. Some black market "sharks," or people who made money abroad and transferred it to Poland at an extremely favorable black market exchange rate, decided to invest in legitimate private businesses. Such new entrants became very dangerous competitors of the already established "fat cats"—traditional private firms well adjusted to the communist business environment. One such new entrant, Bella, challenged R-Z's monopolistic position on the motorcycle accessories and spare parts market.

In 1982 when R-Z still owned 100 percent of the market, Bella came up with a partnership offer. Bella was willing to contribute new foreign style products, technologies, and equipment as well as substantial amount of capital in exchange for a 50 percent share in R-Z, with its well established brand name, distribution channels and existing production capabilities. R-Z's owner rejected the offer, but soon realized that he was not able to face the competition from Bella. The new entrant offered better, more stylish and cheaper products in the most profitable motorcycle accessories line.

By using aggressive marketing and directly approaching private and state-owned retailers, Bella captured 80 percent of the market in two years. The passive attitude of R-Z's owner resulted in sales volume that were 10 times smaller in 1984 than in 1982.

In order to save the firm, it was transformed into a limited partnership with two new partners contributing some new capital and willing to participate in the firm's activities. It was decided that R-Z should continue to specialize in motorcycle spare parts and accessories in order to capitalize on the old tradition and the brand-name awareness. At that time (1985), plastic and metal luggage trunks for motorcycles suddenly became fashionable. R-Z decided to jump at the opportunity and to be the first in the market. The rush didn't pay off. Because of financial problems, the first series of the new product was manufactured with primitive and costly technology. At the same time, Bella and some other manufacturers flooded the market with much better and cheaper products. The founder and original owner of R-Z decided to sell off his share, and 80 percent of equipment was sold to cover the losses.

The new R-Z had a difficult start. A return to the motorcycle accessories and spare parts market was practically impossible because of competition and their weak financial position. In order to survive, the new owners decided to become subcontractors for big state-owned enterprises. After a careful analysis of newspaper ads and of the firm's expertise, capabilities, and equipment, the new management decided to produce mechanical components for manufacturers of electronic equipment (e.g., measurement instruments, industrial control systems, radios). The first contracts called for the use of the client's materials and equipment; this enabled R-Z to enter the market with a very limited capital involvement. Such a contract was attractive for state-owned enterprises because it enabled them to overcome the manpower barrier (due to the wasteful use and low productivity of labor typical of communist enterprises). Profitable orders poured in, and by the end 1985 the firm's survival was secured. Machines, equipment, and materials related to the new specialization were acquired, and employment increased from four to nine. Sales volume and profits were more than tripled in one year.

Between 1986 and 1990, R-Z considerably strengthened its position as a subcontractor in the electronics industry. Modern imported equipment was installed in such areas as metal processing and painting. R-Z also employed engineers who designed new products in close cooperation with the client. Different forms of promotion and active search for new orders, including television advertising, were developed. Surprisingly, for the kind of product offered by R-Z, television advertising proved to be extremely efficient. Television ads were still rather unusual in the '80s. They were cheap and could easily reach the target audience. Managers of the state-owned enterprises, for example, always watched the news on television at 7:30 p.m.

The firm's business, however, proved to be highly dependent upon fluctuations in the Polish electronics industry. In 1985 and 1986, 70 percent of the orders came from medium-sized manufactures who did not have their own production capabilities in mechanical components area, and 20 percent came from medium-sized manufacturers who had their own mechanical components production, but were insufficient—either unable to produce some specific elements or turn out sufficient quantities. R-Z management consciously avoided contracts from huge mass manufacturers, because that would mean total dependence on big state-owned enterprises whose futures already did not look so bright in 1986.

In 1987 and 1988, a new type of client emerged. Most of these were private manufacturers of highly sophisticated electronic devices of unique design, produced in short series or even as single units. In 1990, such clients (mainly producers of measurement devices, industrial processes control systems, medical equipment, etc.) were already responsible for 94 percent of the orders. Such a shift was due to the collapse—or at least considerable production volume reduction—of the state-owned enterprises when the Balcerowicz stabilization plan was introduced.

In 1990 market analysis indicated that the Polish electronics industry, no longer protected by tariff barriers and exposed to the foreign competition (due to internal convertibility of the currency), had no chance to survive. Only manufacturers of highly specialized and unique, highly sophisticated products were able to survive. These products were very expensive abroad because they were designed for particular clients' needs. R-Z had to adjust its structure and its equipment to serve this new type of client. It required development of design capabilities and high flexibility in production scheduling, as well as high quality. To serve some clients, R-Z also became a general contractor, organizing the whole network of subcontractors for a particular order. It enabled it to play the role of leader for a group of small privately owned enterprises and to buy into some of them for example, by supplying them with more advanced equipment.

A new line of products emerged from this cooperation alarm systems for individual houses and apartments were manufactured and marketed jointly with two other firms.

In the middle of 1990 the owner and general manager of R-Z, Mr. Rogojski, was absolutely convinced that he had to make a new strategic move that would secure in the future an optimum fit between his firm and the rapidly changing business environment in Poland. Probably, MBA courses taken at the International Business School in Warsaw helped him to realize that goal. He had two options:

- Further specialization in the design and manufacturing of mechanical components for electronic devices

- Diversification

Further specialization required considerable upgrading of the technological level of the firm and, more precisely, the acquisition of an automated, computerized machining center specially adjusted for the production of high-quality mechanical components for electronic devices. Rogojski asked for an offer from a Swiss manufacturer, Baltic—one of the few, and presumably the best, of the European producers of such centers—and calculated that the needed investment was worth $1.2 million. Rogojski realized that even if some financing could be obtained, he couldn't take such a risk, considering the high degree of specialization of the equipment and the dangerous fluctuations of the Polish electronics industry. Diversification remained a viable option.

The diversification option called for the further development of an alarm systems production, as well as the development and manufacturing of high-quality door locks, and the development and production of high-quality front doors for individual houses and apartments. These new complimentary product lines would enable R-Z to offer a full range of products and services to home and apartment owners. The demand for such products and services is constantly on the rise because of rising criminality and the emergence of a middle class increasingly interested in the security of their homes. R-Z engineers have developed a new door lock (unique in Poland) which is comparable with the best Western European products.

This diversification strategy was implemented at the end of 1990. New lines of products were added to the existing ones (mechanical components for electronic devices). At the end of 1990, R-Z employed 40 people and had nearly $300,000 worth of sales volume, and reported nearly $80,000 in net profits.

Using Mintzberg's terminology and perspective, one can easily discover that R-Z did not really have any binding long-range plan. It always reacted to changing market conditions, with better or worse results. The last strategic choice, in 1990, involved some planning in terms of setting a sequence of goals, but it was also intended to enable the firm to keep its maneuvering space and to react quickly to the challenges of a turbulent environment. Buying a highly specialized machining center would tie the firm to one line of business and make it unable to switch rapidly. Strategy as pattern in R-Z's behaviour could be formulated as flexibility, enabling quick reactions to market signals. The essence of strategy as perspective is minimizing exposure through quick adjustment. R-Z is certainly a survivor.

A & D is a small construction firm[7] that was founded after the fall of communism in Poland in 1990 as a limited liability partnership in an industrial town, C, in central Poland. The firm's initial capital was only the equivalent of $60. The founders of the company and partners were the owners of two other small businesses in the region who decided to diversify their investment portfolio in order to minimize the risk during recessionary times. Mr. Wronski is managing director of the firm, and one of the partners.

Wronski was a construction engineer with extensive experience in construction and civil engineering in state-owned companies. Over the years (he started in 1970, after graduating from a local technical university), Wronski built his reputation on high professionalism and integrity and developed an impressive network of valuable business contacts. The newly founded company has taken over a team of 10 construction workers along with a contract originally signed by another firm controlled by one of the owners.

In 1990 competition between construction firms in the region was very intensive. Many small private firms and migrant teams of builders competed for a limited number of contracts, mainly from private clients building individual houses, from expanding private businesses, or from state-owned firms adjusting to the new market conditions and developing new lines of business. Contracts for individual houses were relatively easy and lucrative, but the volume from each contract was low, and competition was fierce—because both capital investment and risk were low. Such contracts did not require highly qualified workers. Business clients offered much higher sales volumes, but required high quality and precise timing.

Wronski decided to shoot for the higher end of the market: business clients. In order to do so, he needed highly qualified workers and engineers. He attracted some people from the big state-owned construction enterprises. These enterprises were losing clients because of the recession and were not able to maintain an adequate pay scale. It enabled the company to build up its production capabilities up to four gangs of highly qualified workers employing over 60 people, including five experienced engineers. Because of four smaller contracts, including individual home, commercial building and subcontracting for bigger firms and serving big business clients (automotive factory and steel works), A & D was able to pay 20 percent to 40 percent higher wages than state-owned construction firms in the C region.

Using his apartment and his car as collateral, Wronski got the equivalent of $15,000 in bank loans to buy the most needed equipment and tools. He also applied to local authorities for a low-interest loan to finance the creation of 20 new jobs for the unemployed. Formalities took nearly six months. Finally, he got the equivalent of only $12,000 for the creation of only nine jobs. The decrease was due to the extremely difficult financial situation of the local government. This new loan was also spent to purchase new equipment and tools, some of them from liquidated state-owned enterprises.

In the middle of 1990, A & D decided to expand its activities in the construction business. Tempted by high margins, they also decided to diversify into retailing and fast food. Wronski took part in bids to build telephone lines (underground cable lines), and to rebuild a small portion of railway track. He lost the first telephone line bid because of the lack of specialized equipment. Equipment was purchased, and A & D won the next bid. A decision was made to invest further in the telephone line business and to make the necessary investment to adjust to the more technologically advanced contracts (e.g., telephone systems based on fibre optics). This approach paid off. The regional telephone company, impressed with A & D's attitude, awarded it a bigger ($200,000) contract. The railway track bid was won, and generated some cash during the summer of 1990, but management decided not to continue this low value-added line of business.

To start the retail and fast food businesses, A & D bought a small store (110 square meters of selling space), which they rebuilt and modernized. The store was divided into two parts: a grocery store and a small fast food outlet selling hamburgers, hot dogs, etc. Management realized, however, that it lacked the expertise in both new lines of business and that building up inventory would freeze much of the firm's needed capital. On these grounds, a decision was made to lease the store.

In June of 1990, the first big contract was signed with the big state-owned manufacturer of synthetic fibres. In recessionary times, this enterprise decided to mobilize all its remaining assets and to launch a completely new product unknown in Eastern Europe: fabric for disposable clothing (used, for example, by hospitals) and for a wide range of technological processes. An entirely new technology had to be installed, and A & D was given a contract for adaptation of already existing buildings for this purpose. This contract was worth $100,000 in 1990 (first stage), and that amount would more than doubled in 1991 if the client was satisfied with the first stage. This contract had a potential of building A & D's reputation among industrial enterprises in the region, but it was extremely demanding in terms of quality and precise timing. Starting mass production as soon as possible had crucial importance for the client, who counted on the new product line to beef up his slugging sales.

In spite of the difficulties (Wronski had to fire his closest friend, who was given the site manager's job and didn't perform up to the expectations), the contract was completed on time and the client was completely satisfied. As a result, the contract for the second stage (finishing of the new facility after the start-up operation) was also given to A & D.

The contract with the synthetic fabric manufacturer gave the newly created firm, for the first time, an opportunity to play the role of "general contractor" subcontracting certain (less lucrative or too difficult, too specialized) jobs to other firms, but assuming total responsibility and control. Wronski thought this might be an opportunity to develop more stable business contacts, and eventually to buy into such firms in order to create a whole group of enterprises offering a full range of construction services to industrial clients.

The first nine month of A & D's existence were quite positive: over $250,000 worth of sales and nearly $30,000 net profit, which was entirely re-invested into the firm's further development. Most important, however, was the reputation of the firm, its growing capabilities, and its growing network of business contacts among industrial enterprises of the region.

Using Mintzberg's terminology and approach to strategy, one can easily discover that there is little planning in A & D's activities. The firm is looking into many different opportunities, trying and selecting them. Strategy as pattern can be inferred from the firm's behaviour: It is constantly scanning the environment for opportunities and testing them. By doing so, it avoids financial exposure and the freezing of scarce capital. A & D is clearly able to withdraw from the business lines it does not find promising. Wronski wants to take advantage of his personal experience, reputation, and network of business contacts, and to position his firm as highly reputable and trustworthy contractor offering a full range of construction services to large industrial clients, public utilities, and municipalities. In the process, he wants to take control of other firms through subcontracting and eventually buying into them. He wants to reserve the most lucrative parts of the contracts for A & D. The firm's perspective is clearly dominated by specific features of its business environment, including recession, unemployment, and difficult and expensive credit. A rather cautious trial-and-error approach to business opportunities results from this perception of the business environment.

Some common or dominating features of the strategies of post-communist small enterprises can be outlined as follows:

1. Most of the "mom and pop" shops have to rely on self-financing or, more precisely on the personal savings of their owners. Bank credit is too expensive and too difficult for them to get. A survey, conducted among small private enterprises in the Gdansk region of Poland in 1991, indicates that only 18 percent of the entrepreneurs used bank credit as a source of initial capital. The predominant (73 percent) sources of capital were personal savings and personal loans from family and friends (Kreft 1991).

2. In order to protect their investment in a highly turbulent environment badly hit by recession, small private entrepreneurs diversify their investment, thus avoiding deep and capital-intensive specialization.

3. In order to provide clients with more complete lines of products and services, small enterprises often form alliances, partnerships, and different kinds of networks. This trend may be considered the beginning of a spontaneous restructuring and consolidation of highly fragmented industries on the regional or city level.

4. In the most cases "mom and pop" shops rely on personal expertise, experience, reputation, and the business contacts of their owners-managers.

5. As economic reforms introducing a monetary market economy (including convertible currency and free prices) progress, small businesses in post-communist economies are becoming more legitimate. The close ties with the second economy, under communism, gradually loosen and disappear. This process, however, may be stopped, and even reversed, by excessive taxation and prohibitively high capital costs, which result from highly restrictive monetary policies. Such policies push private entrepreneurs back to the underground economy, and force them to reveal only a part of their activities to the authorities. This phenomenon could be observed in Poland, Hungary, and to a lesser extent, in Czechoslovakia in 1991 and 1992.

Shark Strategies

The term "sharks," used here to describe large, privately owned enterprises, may be slightly misleading, because it covers both classic, very legitimate businesses as well as murky conglomerates and shady holdings growing visibly too fast for "normal" business standards. The cases presented below will discuss strategies of both types of sharks. It has also to be noted that sharks are more complex and more difficult to study. They are less transparent than other types of enterprises.

The biggest and most aggressive sharks seem to have one common feature. They are always somehow related to finance and money circulation, foreign currency exchange, or the banking system. This is where market imperfections are most clearly visible, and where the business environment in post-communist countries—with the exception of Hungary, where foreign commercial banks have operated since 1988—have not been adjusted to market economy requirements until the end of 1992.

For example, in 1991 the biggest private operation in the USSR was Menatep Banking Group, composed of the Commercial Innovation Bank of Scientific and Technological Progress, Menatep Trade House, and Menatep Invest Joint Stock Society. In early January 1991, Menatep offered shares to the public worth 1,3 billion rubles. It also organized its own stock exchange, buying back and selling its own stock directly and through brokers. (Loktiev 1991: 3; Kukushkin 1991: 9).

Strategies of big privately owned enterprises will be shown by the following examples:

- The Hungarian microelectronic firm, Muszertechnika

- The Polish "Polonia enterprise," Beta (clothing)

- Aleksander Gawronik enterprises, headquartered in Poznan, Poland

- The Polish holding, Art B International

Muszertechnika is believed to be one of the biggest private enterprises in Hungary. Its founder and majority shareholder is Mr. Gabor Szeles, age 46, an electrical engineer from Budapest (Fijalkowski 1991). In 1981, when the Hungarian communist government accelerated economic reforms, Szeles founded a small cooperative group leasing equipment from the state-owned enterprise and producing some simple electronic devices for special orders on the third shift (at night). Muszertechnika was founded in 1985. In 1990, it had $80 million worth of sales volume and in 1991, over $100 million. In December 1991, Szeles acquired Videoton, the biggest Hungarian TV manufacturer.

The initial business concept of Muszertechnika was to manufacture electrical instruments in Hungary, taking advantage of the high quality and cheap (by Western standards) engineering skills and workmanship. After accumulating some business experience, he switched to the more advanced and more profitable field of microelectronics. Mr. Szeles soon discovered that the best way to get the most attractive special orders from Western clients was to establish sales representative offices in the Triad countries. These would house teams of engineers and designers to work directly with the clients.

Muszertechnika was the first large private Hungarian enterprise to expand abroad. In 1991, it had over a dozen of foreign branches and sales representations in the U.S., Switzerland, Germany, Russia, Italy, Kuwait, and other countries. The biggest U.S. branch employs over 70 engineers on a permanent basis. This Hungarian multinational has obtained quite a few prestigious contracts such as electronic display tables in the stadiums of the soccer World Cup in Italy in 1990, or display tables in international airports. Muszertechnika cooperates closely with such electronic giants as Ericsson, Siemens, and ABB. Jointly with Ericsson, Szeles's firm is modernizing the Hungarian telephone network.

In 1989, when Soviet Prime Minister Rizhkov visited Hungary, he was shown the Muszertechnika factory and was impressed by Hungarian private enterprise. That is how cooperation with the U.S.S.R. started. Muszertechnika has a joint venture in Kazakhstan with a big under-utilized and outdated tractor factory. Eighty engineers and technicians from Muszertechnika helped to transform it into an electrical appliances and video equipment manufacturer. The deal is based on barter principles and involves deliveries of highly priced (on the international markets) manganese from Kazakhstan. Szeles has shown a lot of political intuition. Somehow, he anticipated the political decomposition of the USSR and negotiated a deal with the government of the Kazakhstan republic.

Szeles has a reputation of skillfully using political connections and visibility to enhance his business. At the end of the '80s, while Hungary was still under communist rule, an outspoken promoter of Hungarian capitalism—U.S. ambassador to Budapest Mark Palmer—helped Szeles to participate in a one-month management development course at Harvard, and to start the U.S. branch of his firm. Szeles is a high-ranking member of the Democratic Forum, the ruling party in Hungary since the 1989 election. As president of the Hungarian Industrial Association, a group private or privatizing companies, he participates in the formulation of his country's industrial policy.

Using Mintzberg's framework, it is not evident whether Muszertechnika has a strategy as an overall plan. The firm seems rather to have a number of programs organizing different streams of its activities. A ploy element seems to be present in the Hungarian multinational's strategy. Szeles wants his firm, and himself, to be treated as symbols and pioneers of the emerging Hungarian capitalism. Such an exceptional position certainly helps in business. A consistent behavioral pattern can be inferred from Muszertechnika's activities. It clearly wants to take advantage of the high skills of Hungarian engineers and designers, and to use the opportunities existing on the core markets as well as on the ex-COMECON markets. Muszertechnika has positioned itself as an intermediary or bridge between Central and Eastern Europe and the West in the area of the electromechanical and electronics industries. Muszertechnika's strategy can be also presented as perspective. The Hungarian multinational clearly perceives its environment in terms of transition from the communist to a market economy, and from an isolated, local business to an international and global business.

Beta[8] was founded in May 1982 (shortly after martial law was imposed in Poland in December 1981 by the communist military) as "polonia enterprise." The Polonia Enterprise Act enabled foreign investors of Polish origin to set up businesses in Poland and gave them certain privileges, such as three-year tax holidays. Initially, Beta was located in a little town near Tarnow in southern Poland. It produced leather and textile ladies handbags in a small rented workshop. The whole operation was inefficiently run and the owner, a Dutch citizen of Polish descent, decided to hire a new plenipotentiary and managing director, Stefan Kotowski.

Kotowski, age 43 in 1982, and holding degrees in mechanical engineering and in economics, can be certainly categorized as one of the communist *nomenklatura*. For a couple of years (in the '70's), he headed the economic section of the local Communist Party committee, and later was nominated managing director of the biggest and most important enterprise in the region (mechanical industry). In the '70s, he got a nationwide reputation as an excellent manager of the big state-owned enterprise, able to develop new products and new technologies (based on western licenses, know-how and equipment), and to produce products exported to the most demanding Triad markets. He was often quoted in the official press as an "exemplary socialist manager," rewarded and decorated. His enterprise was visited several times by Mr. Gierek, First Secretary of the Polish Communist Party, and by foreign dignitaries. The vice minister's position in Warsaw was easily within his reach, but he preferred to remain a local celebrity, enjoying all the privileges of the local communist elite.

In 1980 and 1981, he became a target of violent attacks of the newly born Solidarity trade union, both on the factory and town level, and in the fall of 1981, he was literally chased away from the factory he helped to build and develop (and considered as his own). When martial law was declared, he could have returned to the factory and had his revenge, but he promptly refused and decided to start again from scratch in the private sector.

Kotowski took his new job in November 1982. He realized quickly that nine months out of the three year tax holiday had been lost, and that he quickly had to find a new highly profitable product. In January 1983, he moved the few sewing machines Beta had to Tarnow, and started manufacturing work gloves, employing 30 unskilled workers (mainly women). Work gloves were badly needed by big state-owned enterprises in the region, and were chronically in short supply. Using his old contacts, he easily obtained a few big clients and very favorable prices. Already in 1983, Beta was making quite a good profit without any new investment. The foreign owner gained confidence in his new managing director and was willing to invest more money to develop the new product.

Work gloves were a low value-added product, certainly not exportable, and easy to imitate. Actually, many firms in the region, seeing Beta's success, started to produce work gloves. At that time, only those polonia enterprises that could export to hard currency markets could really prosper. In spite of the fact that only 45 percent of hard currency earnings could be officially retained (mainly for imports of raw materials, components, etc.), such things as tacit agreements with foreign partners and skillful transfer pricing could considerably increase un-declared and non-taxable profits in hard currency. When the average salary in Poland was $30 to $40 at the free market exchange rate (in the early '80s), such additional income ploughed back into the business enabled rapid growth and accelerated ever-growing returns.

Kotowski made several trips to West Berlin and to West Germany to study the biggest, closest, and most profitable market. He decided that Beta would specialize in "cut, make, trim" (CMT) contracts in garment production for big German retailers. He decided to specialize in men's sports jackets, trousers, and shirts made from materials primarily provided by the clients, and using clients' models and patterns. Because work gloves could still function as a cash cow in 1984, that year was used for careful preparation for the new line of business. A new factory building was purchased in Tarnow, which was capable of housing up to 600 workers. Industrial sewing machines, made in Poland and Czechoslovakia were acquired. To keep the amount of investment as low as possible, some of them were second hand and rebuilt. They were carefully checked and installed. Four engineers experienced in garment production were hired and sent for additional training in Germany. Kotowski decided to employ mainly unskilled women because of the low cost. In addition, he would provide meticulous, productivity-oriented work organization and elaborate quality control at each production stage.

The first contract was signed and the first series of garments delivered in late 1984. High quality, precise timing of delivery, and the low price convinced an initially hesitatant German client to place several bigger orders. Others big clients followed. In 1990, Beta's sales volume (nearly exclusively exports to Germany on CMT contracts) was worth over $15 million. The enterprise employed 1,400 people in seven different locations, mainly small towns around Tarnow where female unskilled labor was abundant. The company also owns its own fleet of trucks, providing a shuttle connection between Tarnow and Germany. The trucks transported finished products one way, and materials the other. This is certainly a cost-saving arrangement. In 1990, when polonia enterprises were able to change their legal status, Beta was transformed into "normal" joint stock company, with Kotowski as the majority shareholder and his sons as partners. The original Dutch owner retained 15 percent of the shares.

Since 1985, Kotowski has concentrated his efforts on reducing costs. Such items as new Japanese and German sewing machines, pressing systems, and computer-controlled cutters were purchased. New equipment enabled the company to reduce material and energy costs by over 15 percent. Until 1987, all foreign trade—both exports and imports—were handled exclusively by the monopolistic state-owned foreign trade enterprises, who charged a high commissions even if the deal was in fact negotiated by the manufacturer. The administration banned manufacturing enterprises (both state-owned and private) from foreign trade.

In 1987, the communist government started to give enterprises licenses for foreign trade activities. At the beginning, they were difficult to get, but probably because of Kotowski's old connections, Beta was among the first private enterprises to get one. Kotowski, who was clearly anticipating new regulations, had hired and trained two people able to carry out Beta's foreign trade business. Since 1988, nearly all foreign trade has been done directly, without costly intermediaries. This enabled a reduction of export costs—commission previously paid to foreign trade companies—by 5 percent to 7 percent and import costs (commission plus higher discounts) by nearly 20 percent. High productivity and good organization of the whole operation, combined with low labor costs (about $1.50 per hour), enabled Beta to compete successfully with other enterprises specializing in CMT contracts.

In 1991, however, Beta's situation became more difficult. Stable exchange rates (maintained from January 1990 to May 1991), combined with the nearly 260 percent inflation in 1990 made exports less attractive and triggered the wave of cost increases. Kotowski has to consider new strategic options such as becoming an independent producer offering original products based on his own design, independently purchased fabric, using his own technology, paying more attention to domestic and Eastern European market, and diversifying exports to other EEC countries.

Using Mintzberg's terminology, Beta clearly has strategy as a plan (probably more than any other previously discussed cases), understood as a consciously intended course of action, a guideline. Its status as a polonia enterprise was certainly a ploy, up to a point, enabling accelerated accumulation of capital in abnormal market conditions (from the enterprise point of view) existing in Poland prior to 1990 (restricted entry and non-convertible currency). Strategy as a pattern is also clear: one line of business, one market, focus on quality and cost reduction. Beta positioned itself as an intermediary, selling low-cost Polish labor on the German garment market. Beta perceives Poland as a low-cost labor periphery of the EEC, dominated by Germany.

Aleksander Gawronik[9] belongs to handful of about 50 new Polish millionaires, whose personal fortunes are estimated by the media to be counted in the tens of millions of dollars. Similar groups emerge and play an increasingly important role in other post-communist countries, including Hungary, Czechoslovakia, and Russia. For example in 1991 the Russian multi-millionaire Herman Sterligov, whose building materials firm has a sales volume of over 150 million rubles a year, founded in then communist-ruled Moscow, a Club of Young Millionaires. This club represents and defends the interests of new entrepreneurs. Only people conducting legitimate businesses can be accepted as members of this club.

Poland, however, seems to be the country where the number of new millionaires is the highest, and where the largest personal fortunes can be found. A unique combination of several factors contributed to that. The most important among them are the following:

- Because of the large Polish "diaspora" in the West and the close ties emigrants maintained with the old country despite the communist system, Poland receives a constant hard currency inflow in the form of direct transfers to private individuals. Earnings of Poles working legally and illegally abroad also have to be added. These officially registered transfers amount to over $2.5 billion per year, plus unknown amount of unregistered ("in the pockets") transfers. As a result, accumulated hard currency savings in Polish banks (over $7 billion in 1990), redistributed through second-economy channels, have made possible the accumulation of private fortunes in the underground economy. Widespread and long-tolerated by the communist authorities, the black currency market was the most important of these channels.

- Poland has had predominantly (close to 90%) private agriculture since 1957. Private agriculture has become fertile soil for small and gradually growing rural private entrepreneurs (small craftsmen, builders, retailers, etc.), accumulating capital over the years.

- Since 1987, severe economic crisis (shortages), political turbulence, and administrative measures (rationing of consumption items such as gasoline and meat) introduced under martial law accelerated the process of wealth accumulation in the second economy.

- Many second economy fortunes had legitimate "facades" or "fronts" in the form of small businesses (never completely eliminated by communists), polonia enterprises, etc. These "fronts" were able to grow very rapidly after the collapse of communism. The C.I.S. seems likely to follow the same pattern.

- Poland has the longest tradition of symbiosis between government structures, the political establishment, and private business. This tradition was started under communism and continued after its collapse. Poland is also characterized by the weakest public administration. This administration is rapidly disintegrating under transition conditions. This situation—in such areas as foreign trade, privatization, and banking—was conducive to large financial scandals involving the newly emerging big businesses and the accelerating accumulation of capital in a few private hands. This pattern might be also repeated in Russia, the Ukraine, and other ex-Soviet republics.

Aleksander Gawronik (born in 1948) graduated from the Law School of Poznan University. During his studies, he worked as manual worker. After graduation, he worked as an employee in the state-controlled cooperative and became its managing director. In 1976, Gawronik resigned from the Communist Party and was dismissed. He admits to being employed by Polish security services for 25 days. He started activities in the private sector in the late '70s. At different times he owned among other things, a chicken farm, a car repair shop, a clothing shop, and a legal counsels office. Gawronik switched from one business to another. He also represented three foreign companies in Poland.

Gawronik's rise to big business started in March 1988, when the Polish government legalized black currency market, allowing private individuals to operate official money exchange windows—selling and buying currency at the free market exchange rate, which they decided by themselves. Gawronik was the first to get a license for the whole network of such money exchange shops. In 1988 and 1989, this line of business was extremely profitable, due to political and economic instability. Gawronik still operates his network, among many other businesses, and intends to transform them into branches of his bank. He has a license to open a bank, Poznan Bank AG SA. This bank was already registered in 1990, but it was not yet operating. As of the end of 1991, Gawronik was still waiting for more precise government regulation of the banking industry.

In the meantime, the millionaire from Poznan started many new business lines. He is the biggest private importer in Poland of oil products and owns a 50 percent share in a joint venture with Exxon represented in Poland by its German branch, Esso AG, from Hamburg. In 1990, Gawronik imported 50,000 tons of gasoline into Poland, and when the higher duty on gasoline was imposed, he started to import crude oil and to process it in Polish refineries. To sell his oil products, Gawronik opened a network of gas stations in northern Poland. Gawronik is the Polish representative of a German firm, Tax Free, which reimburses the 24 percent German turnover tax to foreigners who buy in Germany and export purchased goods to other countries. Polish citizens buy a lot in Germany, and are reimbursed in Gawronik's money exchange shops. In December 1991, Gawronik became an official agent for John Deer tractors in Poland. Gawronik also sells insurance and delivers packages on Polish territory. In early 1991, the declared monthly sales volume of Gawronik enterprises were at the level of $20 million, and are rapidly rising. By the end of 1991, sales were expected to reach $100 million.

In the summer of 1991, when famous financial scandal involving holding "Art B" erupted, Gawronik was asked to manage it for private bank in Katowice that took over Art B. Gawronik accepted. His compensation for managing Art B was set at $600,000 per month. A couple of weeks prior to that, rumours were circulating that Art B owners were negotiating the sale of their holding company to Gawronik. The asking price was rumoured to be at the level of $500 million. After a month, Gawronik resigned from managing Art B and was replaced by Dr. Robert Rzadca, vice president of the International Business School, who also resigned after two months.

Using Mintzberg's framework, one easily discovers that there are no elements of rigid planning in Gawronik's strategy. He is just looking for opportunities, selects them and exploits them to the fullest extent. The ploy element is certainly present in Gawronik's strategy. His deals are often secretive and certainly interconnected. Details are very difficult to get. A pattern can be inferred from Gawronik's behaviour: he is looking for opportunities enabling accelerated circulation of huge sums of money and currency exchange, probably including currency arbitrage. He positions himself as a banker, providing capital financing for a large number of small transactions such as currency exchange, insurance, tax returns, and gasoline purchases. These transactions generate a huge and accelerated cash flow. Gawronik's perspective is difficult to infer from what is known about his business dealings. He seems to perceive the business environment in Poland primarily in terms of international cash flow, and clearly wants to control some of it.

The Art B story[10] is the best known Polish business sagas, because it involves a financial scandal of international dimensions. Art B's founder and president, Boguslaw Bagsik, was born in 1963 as a Jewish orphan, and was adopted by Protestant (Baptist) parents in the small town of Cieszyn on the Polish Czech boarder (where a small Protestant minority lives). He was a rock musician and musical instruments salesman. In 1988, he was given a two-year suspended sentenced for the "appropriation of funds" belonging to the Musical Instruments Cooperative in Cieszyn, where he was employed. In 1989, with two partners—a medical doctor and the lawyer, who had been his defense attorney—he founded Art B limited, as a limited liability company licensed for wide range of commercial and industrial activities. Initial stock issue was valued at 100,000 zlotys ($10).

In 1989, Art B started importing cheap foodstuffs and clothing from Germany. For 1989, the declared profit was $1,200. In 1990, the company started a period of unprecedented growth when, with the help of economists and computer scientists from the Wroclaw Academy of Economics, Bagsik and his partners developed a computer model showing the oscillating acceleration of capital. The main idea behind it was to pass funds as quickly as possible through as many interest-bearing checking accounts as possible, in order to maximize the number of days for which interest was paid. In doing so, Art B was taking advantage of the loopholes and weaknesses of the Polish banking system.

One of these weaknesses was the positive interest rate philosophy practiced by the Central Bank as an anti-inflationary measure. As a result of this, checking accounts are interest bearing, yielding 1 percent monthly.

A second weakness was that inter-bank communications are relatively slow and not computerized. Therefore, although certified checks are treated as cash deposits, clearing a check takes up to two weeks. No clearing house for inter-bank transactions exists.

Under such conditions, it was enough to make one substantial deposit, draw a certified check on it, deposit it in another town, and before the check was sent to the first bank, interest was paid twice on the same deposit. This operation could be repeated many times. According to the Art B's computer model, a $50 million initial deposit can bring over $820 million within a year, assuming five operations a day in 22 working days per month. Investigating prosecutors assumed that the first certified check was really without provision, because the bank's employee was bribed. It was also possible to use commercial credits (for six months, for example) accorded for imports of foreign goods (the original activity of the company) for acceleration.

Capital generated through acceleration was invested quickly in many different lines of business. Art B started a Goldstar TV set assembly factory in Walbrzych, employing over 1,500 people, acquired one of the largest milk processing factories in Poland, a poultry processing and packing factory, as well as dozens of other plants for food processing, textile production, electronic and medical equipment, its own small airline, a retailing chain, and many others unrelated businesses. Art B negotiated the sale of 200 tanks made in Poland, and contracted the entire production of the giant Ursus tractor factory (300 tractors per month). Art B was the first to start large-scale trade with Israel, and Boguslaw Bagsik acquired Israeli citizenship. In the summer of 1991, Art B directly controlled 200 companies, including some abroad, for example, in Israel and in England, and indirectly controlled (through other companies) 2,000. The sales volume in 1990 was over $300 million, and the company employed over 15,000 people.

Bagsik and his partners gave a lot to charities, organized Christian art festivals, gave press interviews, and were considered the rising stars of Polish private big business. For longer business trips, the company helicopter or private executive jet with an American crew, were used. Bagsik was elected council member of the city of Cieszyn and twice gave the city $10,000 donations from his personal account. Rumors circulated and were reported by the press that Bagsik intended to run for senator in the October 1991 parliamentary election.

The rise of Art B, and its presumed involvement in such sensitive areas as arms deals, became so conspicuous, that the State Security Bureau and Banking Commission started an investigation. On August 6, search warrants were issued and all of Art B official documents and books were seized. Several bank employees were arrested and the President of the National Bank of Poland was dismissed by the President. A few weeks later, he was arrested on the grounds of inadequate supervision of the banking system. In Poland, the President of the Banking Commission reports to the President of the National Bank of Poland. All Art B accounts were frozen. A couple of days after the arrest, an order was issued for Bagsik—but by that time, he and his family were already in Israel, as was the second biggest shareholder of Art B, Mr. Gasiorowski, who also applied for Israeli citizenship and was granted it in 1993 and his family. Poland does not have an extradition treaty with Israel.

In Israel, Bagsik bought a luxurious villa in a Tel Aviv suburb. In July, it was announced that he was buying a 50 percent share in the biggest Israeli oil company, Paz (controlling some of strategic Israeli oil reserves) from the Australian millionaire Mr. Lieberman. The price was $85 million. At the last moment, the deal was vetoed by the Israeli energy minister, Youval Neeman. Bagsik and Gasiorowski also approached the big Israeli bank, Hapoalim, proposing cooperation, but all contracts were frozen when they declined to present credentials and to explain the sources of the huge cash deposits they were making in the Israeli banks. The Israeli popular press reported the sensational news about Art B's jet bringing suitcases full of US dollars from Warsaw. In an interview given to the Polish press, Bagsik and Gasiorowski claimed the reason the scandal was played up was due to Art B's huge contract for the sale of $500 million worth of Polish steel to Egypt. They also declared their intention to stay in Israel, while the Polish government used diplomatic channels to bring Bagsik back to Poland for trial. It is estimated that because of the Art B "capital acceleration" scheme, the Polish banking system lost over $400 million, nearly all of it transferred illegally abroad.

In the meantime, it was announced in Poland that Bagsik and Gasiorowski had transferred their shares in Art B to the private bank of Credit and Commerce in Katowice, presumably in exchange for their debts to the bank. The bank declined to make any further comments, and hired Aleksander Gawronik to manage the assets of Art B. Gawronik declared his intention to restructure the holdings with the help of foreign management experts, and did not exclude the possibility of buying it himself.

The Art B story can be certainly perceived as a hit-and-run operation on an unusually large scale. As such, it cannot be analyzed in Mintzberg's terms designed for "normal" strategies of "normal" business firms. It seems to be, however, an interesting and significant anecdote, illustrating the issue of big business growth strategies in post-communist countries.

5
Post-Communist Organizational Cultures

Organizational Culture

This book is about the change taking place in post-communist enterprises in Central and Eastern Europe. The cases presented in preceding chapters clearly show that organizational culture plays a crucial role in the change process, both positive—when promoting and accelerating change—and negative—when stopping, slowing down and distorting the change process. The positive role of organizational cultures is probably most clearly exemplified by the newly created private enterprises such as the Hungarian firm, Muszertechnika, or the Polish company A D, described in the previous chapter. In such enterprises, the new entrepreneurial spirit imposes new rules of the game on the participants. Examples of the negative role of organizational culture can be easily taken from the experiences of dinosaurs, such as Rainbow, and unsuccessful pretenders, where the adjustment process is hampered and distorted by old behavioral patterns, norms, values, and social structures. Similar lessons can also be learned from aborted or failing joint ventures, such as PUT or Elfur. Understanding the dynamics of organizational culture seems to be the key to understanding of the whole process of change.

Schein (1990: 6) quotes six most commonly accepted meanings of organizational culture:

1. Observed behavioral regularities such as the language and rituals around deference and demeanour.

2. The norms evolving in the working groups, such as the norm "a fair days work for a fair days pay."

3. Dominant values espoused by an organization such as "product quality", "price leadership", and "technological leadership".

4. A philosophy that guides an organizational policy toward employees and/or customers.

5. The rules of the game for getting along in the organization and "the ropes" that a newcomer must learn to become an accepted member.

6. The feeling and climate that is conveyed in an organization to the members and outsiders by the physical layout, behavioral patterns etc.

Culture as a "learned product of group experience" is analyzed by Schein on three levels: articrafts and creations, values indicating what ought to be as opposed to what is, and basic underlying assumptions, sometimes called philosophies, such as famous McGregor's Theory X and Theory Y. Underlying assumptions cover such issues as the organization's relationship to the environment, human nature, relationships, and motivations. Such assumptions are often unconscious (Schein 1990: 14–19).

Culture changes are closely linked to the organizational changes. Change is possible only if culture is ready to change accordingly. Organizations with "frozen" cultures are also unable to adjust to turbulent environments and by consequence are likely to fail.

Schein (1990: 271–272) points out at different cultural change mechanisms at different stages of the organizational life cycle:

1. The birth and early growth stage involves such change mechanisms as natural evolution, self guided evolution through organizational therapy, managed evolution through hybrids (joint ventures, partnerships, etc.), and managed revolutions through outsiders (mergers, acquisitions etc.).

2. The organizational midlife stage involves, incrementalism, planned change and organization development, as well as technological seduction.

3. The organizational maturity stage is linked to such change mechanisms as coercive persuasion, turnaround, reorganization, destruction and rebirth.

The changes in organizational culture taking place in post-communist enterprises seem to fit Schein's general framework. The newly created private enterprises, as well as the new foreign enterprises and the new joint ventures exhibit characteristics of the early stage of organizational development. Most pretenders fit the description of the midlife stages. Dinosaurs seem to be at the maturity stage, if not beyond.

Leadership is undeniably one of the most important ingredients of the organizational culture. Some authors even believe that "the unique and essential function of management is manipulation of culture" (Schein 1990: 317). Leaders promote organizational change by promoting cultural change. In order to do so, leaders need a vision of the organizational future as well as the ability to articulate and enforce it. They have to be able to visualize a relationship between organizational change and organizational culture and to make desired thing happen. They need to influence organization through culture. Leaders have to act as intermediaries between the changing environment, organization, and its culture in order to secure optimum fit—or at least equilibrium—enabling organization to survive in a turbulent environment.

Managers of post-communist enterprises have to assume this leadership role in the milieu of sudden discontinuity and dramatic change. They are the only ones potentially capable of translating changes in the macroeconomic environment into corresponding microeconomic behaviour of the firms. Otherwise, transformation to a market economy will not happen. Managers have to change organizational cultures in order to implement successful strategies enabling survival in the new market environment. If a sufficiently large number of the total population of enterprises do not adjust quickly enough, massive recession will undermine the whole transformation process. The change of organizational cultures conditions such adjustment. Managers as leaders have a key role to play in it.

In order to assess the scope of the change, the communist legacy in organizational culture and managerial leadership will be presented in the following pages. New, emerging organizational culture and management style of a private enterprise will be demonstrated in order to show the gap between the communist legacy and the new, modern market-oriented organizational cultures. Different approaches and strategies of bridging the gap will be discussed at the occasion of presentation of managers as the change agents. Different types of change agents will be portrayed, such as: ''populist politicians'', ''new technocrats'', ''new entrepreneurs'' and ''foreign crusaders.'' In the conclusion of this analysis, some basic questions will have to be tackled: ''Are differences between management in the East and in the West vanishing? Are they going to be reduced to the differences between national cultures and levels of the economic development? How fast?''.

The Communist Legacy

Since the first years after the revolution in the USSR, the new type of management corresponding with the socialist character of the enterprise has been constantly debated and analyzed. As early as 1924, one of the Soviet authors addressed the issue in the following way: ''We feel we are walking on the edge. From one side production process requires unconditional unity of command and efficient use of labour at every stage of production process. On the other side many experts and engineers, even unconditionally devoted to the Soviet power, are not able to approach the workers and to gain their trust'' (Golcman 1924: 10). Another early Soviet management writer indicated basic differences between Soviet and western enterprises: "The situation of the Soviet enterprises is basically different from Western European both from the point of view of their social character and material potential. We have all the reasons to talk about much greater autonomy of our production units. In the West factory or plant are fully subordinated to the will or even caprice of the manager. In the Soviet Union we have the possibility to eliminate all the accidental expressions of the will of particular people using extensively control by participants of production process themselves (party organization, trade union organization, workers meetings). (Grossman 1923: 16). In other words, the basic dilemma of the communist management was the conciliation between the requirements of the unity of control and technical expertise with workers involvement and participation in the management process.

American researchers studying Soviet managerial behaviour in 1987 and 1988 were confronted with exactly the same dilemma. They thoroughly described the solutions related to power distribution and decision making. (Vlachoutsicos & Lawrence 1990).

The core of the Soviet hierarchy and power distribution system is a strange form to the Western observer which Vlachoutsicos and Lawrence call the Structural Task Unit, or STU. An STU can be any group charged with performing a specific task. "Soviet enterprises are themselves STUs and each contains as many administrative, service and production STUs as are necessary to carry out its mission. The smallest production STU is the brigade, which may have as few as three or four individual members, while the greatest STU of which its is a part may have more than a hundred thousand'' (Vlachoutsikos & Lawrence 1990: 51).

At least three attributes are key characteristics of the Soviet STUs

First, in their relations with the outside world, members of the STU consider themselves "we" and demonstrate loyalty to the leader and cohesiveness. They defend themselves against gaining strangers access to any information related to the STU's internal affairs. Unwritten norms prevent members unauthorized by the leader from cooperating or exchanging information with members of other STUs. It results in giving absolute priority to their own parochial interests at the expense of the interests of the organization as a whole. It also makes horizontal and interdepartmental cooperation and information exchanges extremely difficult and in some cases, virtually impossible.

Secondly, each STU leader has direct authority over all subordinate STUs, their leaders, and their members. It means that the leader can bypass subordinate managers and interfere directly with the work of any group or individual situated below him in the firm's hierarchy (sometimes even several layers below) for any length of time he sees fit. Bosses can assume direct authority over any of their subordinates even without consulting intermediary levels.

Finally, subordinates from all levels have the right of direct access to the STU's leaders and to bypass their direct and indirect superiors. Such direct contact between all levels of hierarchy can improve information in incidental (urgent and high priority) matters but in large organizations, it blocks communication channels and makes information flows disorderly.

Dilemmas between centralization and decentralization and unity of command and employees participation (collegiality) are solved by simultaneous use of centralized and decentralized forms of leadership and more precisely, by alternating the centralized and decentralized phases of the decision making process. The following phases of this process are described by the researchers (Vlachoutsikos & Lawrence 1990: 1958):

- *Phase One:* Setting Goals. The leader of the STU specifies to subordinates the general policy guidelines and goals to be attained.

- *Phase Two:* Deliberation. The lower levels of the STU participate in a general discussion aimed at the formulation of objectives and policies proposed by the lower levels to the STU's leadership.

- *Phase Three:* Bottom Up. Lower levels submit their proposal to the leadership.

- *Phase Four:* Deliberation. Leadership reviews and considers the proposal.

- *Phase Five:* Top Down. The STU's leader makes a clear decision, issues precise instructions, and communicates them to the subordinates.

- *Phase Six:* Implementation. The STU as a whole takes unified action following instructions precisely.

This picture of a combination of centralization and decentralization with unity of command and collectivism in Soviet managerial decision making is somewhat idealized and has to be supplemented.

In centrally planned economies, enterprises were not the biggest STUs, and remained very strongly vertically integrated with the organization of the national economy. Often, they were perceived as one huge super-organization or super-enterprise. This giant entity administrated the allocation of resources and tasks to be fulfilled by bigger and smaller units. Unions of enterprises, comprised of providers of relatively homogenous groups of products and services, and even ministries coordinating whole sectors of the national economy, clearly exhibit exactly the same characteristics as STUs described by American researchers.

Already in the '60s, Soviet economists such as Onika, Trapeznikov, and Lieberman, noticed that especially in relations between enterprises and higher levels, Phase Four is often followed by sending top-down a new, revised set of objectives and instructions. These are debated again, and the new proposals are sent to the leadership. The whole decision-making process takes on the character of bargaining, where lower and upper levels represent opposite interests. Upper levels favor ambitious objectives and limited allocation of resources, while lower levels want the opposite: objectives easy to accomplish and abundant resources. Once the compromise is reached between two levels, they become unified against the next upper level, because of the evidently common interest. Management culture and decision-making process in communist enterprises cannot be separated from the structure of the economy and the logic of administrative allocation of resources within the framework of a formal planning process. The elimination of such structures and processes does not automatically change the culture, especially since it is deeply entrenched in people's mentality, rituals, behavioral patterns, and organizational structures within the enterprises and in the outside world (mainly in government bureaucracies). This is due to the fact that for many decades, enterprises replicated the overall economic environment. Even the smallest STUs were structurally and behaviorally identical—or nearly identical—to the bigger and even the biggest ones. For example, every STU had its own planning unit and its own unit responsible for rationing resources. Such structures could be seen at the top level of the government bureaucracy down to the smallest workshop. In this way the bureaucracy and bureaucratic patterns of management completely penetrated the enterprises down to the smallest STU. This explains why tens of millions of people in the USSR were involved in the bureaucratic management of the economy. In other communist countries, the proportions were similar.

Vlachoutsikos and Lawrence explain the STU's characteristic decision-making process of combining centralized and decentralized phases by the characteristic features of the Russian national culture. This seems at best a partial explanation, since economic organizations in other communist countries—such as Hungary, Poland, and Czechoslovakia—which are culturally very different from Russia have developed very similar characteristics (Kozminski 1976; Buravoy & Lukacs 1985; Kovari & Sziracki 1885). Most of the existing cultural characteristics of the communist enterprises should rather be attributed to the overall socio-economic and political system shaping these enterprises strongly for so many decades.

The Work Culture

Cultures of communist enterprises can be described using Schein's three-level model.

On the articrafts and creations level, a distinction has to be made between the physical work environment, organizational rituals, and visible behavioral patterns. It might seem a prejudiced stereotype, but all the communist and most post-communist factories are ugly, poorly maintained, and dirty. As one of the interviewed Polish managers explains, "We have enough problems enforcing basic work functions and negligence in the maintenance has to be tolerated." Workers themselves do not feel responsible for the cleanliness and aesthetic looks of the work environment and do not do anything about it even if they complain. This can be explained by the fact that most of the workers are of peasant origins, and Central and Eastern European peasants are accustomed to dirt and a messy work environment. Traditionally, they accepted this as inevitably associated with their social position. (Doktor 1975: 57–70). In most cases, managers' offices are also rather modest. Managers seem to be afraid of workers reproaching them for luxurious work conditions contrasting with specific type of democracy dominating in the STUs and the egalitarian mood of the workforce.

To the contrary, rituals and ceremonies were abundant and rich. Often, meetings were called officially, to discuss the matters of production but in practice, serving to prove peoples' loyalty to the system and submission to the rules imposed by the party. Countless other similar events can identified festive ceremonies commemorating such events as revolution anniversaries, May Day, the Army Days, parades, election meetings, visits of foreign dignitaries to the factories, and "voluntary" work for the community. All of these events were organized by the companies on company time. All such events had carefully designed scenarios indicating a balance between the political and administrative hierarchy (selection of the people sitting on the top of table: in presidium), precisely indicating order of the speakers, content of the speeches and even "spontaneous" questions. The purpose of such rituals was to internalize the values of "the socialist work culture."

Visible behavioral patterns have been described above. The most important of them regulate behavior of the STUs leaders and members and relations between STUs in the process of decision-making. These behavioral patterns secured an acceptable compromise between centralization and decentralization, unity of control and workers' participation. Such a compromise was needed for ideological, political, as well as purely practical reasons.

In his original study of the Soviet style in management, Leites precisely indicates a set of values underlying communist organizational cultures (Leites 1985). They do not seem to be bound by the specificity of the Russian national culture. Instead, much they seem more strongly bound by the communist system.

The backbone of this value system is that political leadership for every level of economic activity is assumed by the communist party. Leading the economy is considered to be the most important of the Party's activities. In order to fulfil this role, the party had to penetrate down to the smallest units of the economy, such as brigades. Penetration of planning and the rationing bureaucracy mentioned above, parallels political penetration by the party. Communist enterprises were filled with people who did not perform any productive functions and people got accustomed to that for decades.

Within the enterprise, the party had to perform organizational, ideological, and educational roles. Unconditional submission to the party's leading role was the key value of the communist organizational culture. Can it disappear completely with the elimination of the party? Or, will it be transformed somehow into some other form of political leadership?

Constant stimulation of activity and maintaining the level of economic activism as the highest possible level seems to be an extremely important value in itself. "The more you produce better you are" assumption is deeply rooted in the economy of shortage. Taut, overly ambitious plan targets as well as the strong pressure to over-invest were among the consequences of this value. It has to be noted, however, that the maximization of production value is closely associated with the belief that whatever is produced will be sold, and that costs of production are irrelevant, both in human and material terms. Probably that's why marketing and cost accounting remain the weakest points of post-communist enterprises, even in deep recession, such as in Poland in 1991 and 1992.

High motivation, constant willingness of the individual to increase his or her involvement and to work more and harder (even at the expense of the private life; family, vacation etc) were considered instrumental values enabling the maximization of production at any cost. Pictures of the "socialist work heroes" were ever present on the walls of the factories and in the mass media. This high motivation was one of the main values of the official organizational cultures of communist enterprises.

Discipline, responsibility, and accountability were rightly considered to be another set of values enabling the fulfilment of ambitious production plans. Accountability went only bottom up; subordinates were accountable to their superiors. Everybody was accountable to the party.

The basic assumptions of communist work cultures can be derived from two previously described "more visible" levels (articrafts and values). They can be formulated as the following statements:

1. Industrial activity carried out by big production units was perceived as the key factor of progress.

2. Present life quality should be sacrificed for the sake of the future.

3. Enterprise was not an autonomous unit, it was a part of the bigger system, therefore it should not be authorized to make autonomous decisions and its interests should be subordinated to the interests of the larger system.

4. The same applied to the individual; interests of the individual should be subordinated to the interests of the group and the society.

5. These interests were fully represented by the party, therefore the party had the right and responsibility to interfere with the management process at every stage, every level, and every moment.

6. People were perceived as unable to fully understand the nature of the economic and social processes. They had to be led, inspired, directed, controlled, and coerced if necessary by higher political and administrative authorities.

7. Both natural and social environment were perceived as obstacles to the "socialist transformation." These obstacles had to be actively overcome and fought.

Contrary to Vlachoutsikos & Lawrence, I am persuaded that such organizational cultures are not viable ones under "normal" conditions of a market economy. This is due to the inherent contradiction between ideologically imposed overall objectives of the abstract society (represented by the party) and interests of real "flesh and blood" individuals and groups. The system can survive only as long as this contradiction can be resolved by "abnormal" measures. There are three groups of such measures: coercion and massive use of terror; compensation of inefficiency by centrally allocated resources; the development of an organizational "counter-culture," which enables people to pretend that the official culture is being observed. At the same time, however, they can reach some form of compromise, with the real interests of individuals and groups.

All three types of measures have been widely used at the enterprise level since the inception of the communist system. Under Stalin, terror was the dominating way of solving the contradiction (even in the extreme form of massive use of slave labor by "normal" enterprises). Since early '60s, however, two other groups of measures were gaining importance. Compensation of inefficiency was made possible by the extensive exploitation of natural resources and foreign debt. Development of "counterculture" became possible because of gradual relaxation of terror, liberalization, and consecutive waves of partial economic and political reforms. In 1989, all these resources were visibly exhausted and the system started to disintegrate, culminating in the dissolution of the USSR in 1991.

From the point of view of the present and the future of postcommunist societies "counter-culture" seems to be the most important. It was and still is based on three pillars:

1. Manipulation of workers' organizations and democratic processes,

2. Tolerance of poor performance and permissive work quality standards,

3. A "second economy," and especially private use of public resources within the state owned enterprises.

Manipulation has always been the modus operandi of the communist parties. Elections of all kinds, including workers' councils, trade unions, and local party committees have been in reality replaced by appointments within the party *nomenkaltura* system. Within the framework of this system privileges "elected" officials enjoyed were exchanged for absolute compliance with the party line, and in practice, loyalty to the clique or network, which had a decisive say in the appointment ("election").

Such practices made trade unions completely unable to defend workers' interests and even to represent the workers in general. As researchers in the '80s who studied a Hungarian factory namd Banki point out: "At Banki the union was too weak and collaborative to enforce rules that would defend workers against management" (Buravoy & Lukacs 1985: 734). The same statements can be made about any communist factory in any country of the socialist block. Existing regulations related to such issues as protection against accidents or health hazards were very permissive to the management and in any case, not enforced. Polish free trade unions, which played such a decisive role in the abolition of communism, were born out of workers disillusionment with the "official" unions so skilfully manipulated by the party.

Studies of the workers' self management organs introduced in Poland after 1956, show how quickly they became subjects of manipulation and tight party control (Hirszowicz & Morawski 1967). Manipulation made legitimate representation of the workers' interests virtually impossible. It is less evident, however, but still true, that it also made possible management's job. The primitive, populist formula of industrial democracy underlying the communist system from its beginnings in the USSR (management by meetings and by popular vote) could successfully block all managerial decisions. At the same time, development of more mature forms of industrial democracy (involving independent trade unions) was not possible under communist regimes, since it would automatically undermine the communist party's monopoly. The populist formula was the only one acceptable for ideological reasons, but it was impossible from the managerial point of view.

Tolerance of poor performance and permissive work quality standards resulted from strict administrative procedures of manpower planning and wage limitations due to the shortage of skilled labour. Calculation methods based on scientific norms were just a ploy to convince higher authorities that an effort was being made to improve efficiency, or even more likely, to provide them with an alibi vis à vis their higher authorities. In reality, easily fulfilled norms and lax work standards were and still are offered to workers (especially skilled workers) in exchange for their limited compliance and minimum effort. Loose norms are substitutes for monetary incentives which management was not allowed to offer under the central planning system.

Sociological research conducted in 1984 in a Hungarian mechanical industry enterprise employing about 1,000 people demonstrated that the scientific norming process is just for show. In reality, industrial engineers decide by guess work where the loosest rates should be applied. "Proposals for norm change are than sent to the department heads, who consult with foremen, union officials, and finally the operators themselves. Then there is a discussion as to whose jobs and which norms should be cut. Operators are thus actively involved in cutting their own rates, with two consequences. First the looser rates tend to get cut. Second, workers who have less power in the enterprise might face tougher norm cuts. Thus the norms on jobs done by women and Gypsies tend to be tougher than those of the more skilled male workers" (Buravoy & Lukacs 1985: 728). The acceptance rate of norm cuts by the workers is on average around 50 percent (ibidem).

The process of norms negotiations presented above is still quite civilized and quite sophisticated for a communist enterprise. In most cases, norms were not even set and tolerance of poor performance was an integral part of the tacit agreement between workers and management.

Such negotiated agreements based on the principles of "parasitic reciprocity" or "exchange of favors" regulated the majority of transactions concerning the allocation of resources among or inside communist enterprises. Such key decisions as the allocation of investment funds, research and development funds, hard currency, promotions, and foreign travel were affected (Kozminski & Tropea 1982; Kozminski & Zawislak 1982; Kozminski & Obloj eds. 1983).

This negotiated allocation of resources clearly resulted from the absence of market mechanisms. It enabled the lower levels of the hierarchy (enterprises, factories, brigades) to cope successfully with the excessive pressure from above, following the culturally bound principle of ambitious, taut plan targets and the accommodation of aspirations and interests of individuals and groups. Such a work culture, based on negotiated tolerance and permissiveness was parasitic in the sense that it allowed social problems to be solved at the expense of economic efficiency.

Because this "counter-culture" was a way of life for many decades, people learned to cope with it as reality. As such, it became socially sanctioned and acceptable. The emerging market mechanism certainly will not be able to immediately annihilate it. The new organizational cultures will certainly absorb elements of existing ones (especially in the big state owned "dinosaurs").

The second economy, often perceived in the West as "pathological" or even criminal, was for the people inside the communist enterprises not only a perfectly acceptable way of life, but in many cases the only possible way to cope with the absurd business environment created by the economic and political (party) bureaucracy. Let us examine briefly the most common forms of the second economy at the enterprise level:

- Information distortion and falsification

- Manipulation of pay regulations

- Barter exchanges between enterprises

- Private production on company equipment and on company time

- Access to scarce goods and services (often at a lower price) in exchange for "help" and compliance

- Exchange of "services" between enterprises

• Corrupt interface between state-owned and private enterprises

Knowing the culturally bound pressure of the upper levels of the hierarchy for the highest possible production volumes, ambitious plan targets, information distortion, and falsification seemed the only natural way to cope with such pressures. Enterprises had to hide their real production capabilities and to ask for many more resources than they really needed. They also had to falsify output data. For example, the Hungarian Tungsram electric bulbs factory put rocks into the boxes of electric bulbs (Greenhouse 1990; Tully 1990) and the Polish coal mines mixed coal with the rocks and sand. These practices were generally accepted. Such tricks served the management through bonuses and promotions and also served the workers through better pay. This mental set did not vanish after collapse of communism. When restrictive monetary policies were introduced after the fall of communism, state-owned enterprises quickly realized that taxes and other payments to the state in such cases are difficult to collect. Many simply do not pay. Unpaid taxes became a new source of financing for state enterprises. For example, in Poland during the first half of 1991, the state received only 20 percent of the due payments of the dividend (tax on the fixed capital assets), 20 percent of the income tax and slightly over 30 percent of turnover tax. (Misiak 1991b).

In order to control employment and wage funds, communist planners used detailed pay scales and administrative limitations of the aggregated wage funds or limits of the average wage growth rates. Similar instruments are also used by post-communist governments to control inflation. For example, the Balcerowicz plan imposed administrative limitations on the average wage growth rates by punitive taxation of excessive wage increases (above 60 percent of the inflation rate) Enterprises dodged these rules with tricks that had worked in the past. They employed "dead souls" (no work) at the minimum wage rates in order to push down the average and still be able to pay relatively good wages to the core employees. In Hungary Gypsies often accept this role. Another trick was to employ a secretary in the position of "chief specialist" or procurement personnel in foremen positions.

Barter exchanges between enterprises were widespread and extremely useful under conditions of the economy of shortage and soft budget constrains enabling enterprises to accumulate stocks of the products unrelated to their specialization in the hope of exchanging them for something useful (deficitary). During the transition to a market economy, tight monetary policies force enterprises to use a similar approach to the credit issue. By delaying payments, they try to avoid the trap of expensive and difficult credit. Accounts receivable of the post-communist state-owned enterprises reach astronomical figures.

Private production on company time—often with the company equipment, energy, and materials—is practised on a small scale by moonlighting workers, and generally tolerated under the assumption that workers are underpaid. In some cases, in Russia and some other ex-USSR republics, these activities take rocket dimensions. A large percentage of the output of the state-owned enterprises are mafia controlled.[1]

Access to scarce goods and services has always been an attractive incentive under conditions of the economy of shortage. Power elite and people having something to offer in exchange, did not have to wait in lines and were often given discount prices (first quality sold at the price of second or third). In Hungary, Poland and Czechoslovakia, where market reforms are the most advanced and everything became easily available for a price, these communist rituals have been replaced by ''normal'' bribes. In other post-communist countries, where the economy of shortage still prevails, they still play their usual role.

The exchange of services between enterprises such as waiver of penalties for delayed deliveries or low quality in exchange for better access to the scarce products in the future or ''lending'' workers in exchange for a secured contract to acquire the product, were common under communism. A market economy seems to gradually eliminate such practices, but out of court settlements of disputes seem still more popular than in the Triad countries (especially in the US and Western Europe).

Criminal exploitation of the interface between state-owned and private companies is certainly one of the characteristic features of the transition period. The most visible profiteers of this opportunity are the members of the old communist *nomenklatura* still occupying managerial positions in many state-owned companies and trying to illegally transfer some of the state-owned assets to privately-owned companies where they, members of their families, or their cronies own the shares. It is accomplished through the formation of joint stock companies jointly owned by the state-owned companies and private people and usually specializing in the same line of business as the state-owned company. As a result, costs are incurred by the state-owned company and profits go to private pockets. It takes such forms as low-cost leasing of state-owned space, equipment, and other resources or skillful partitioning of jointly performed jobs (the private company getting the most lucrative parts of the job). (Levitas & Strzalkowski 1990).

The culturally acceptable rules of theft were observed by the author during a visit to one of the Soviet meat processing factories in the '70s. The factory guard checking the passes of personnel entering and exiting was driving a brand-new Volga worth several years his official monthly wages. The guard's job was not only to check the passes but also to prevent theft and to check people's bags and packages. The rules were simple: people carrying a "normal" load of the stolen meat (1–2 kg.) were supposed to give the guard 1 ruble bill when leaving the factory. If the load was unusually big (3–5 kg.), 5 rubles were due. The guard thoroughly checked the people who did not pay him. If anything was found, he denounced them to the authorities. It helped to keep at the acceptable level his "discovery rate".

The guard was a respected person because he provided security to the people at a fair price. To the contrary, practices of the management of the company were condemned by the people with whom I talked. Managers drove their cars into the factory grounds and could leave carrying trunks full of meat of the best quality without being checked and without paying anything to anyone in the factory. Local dignitaries did the same when "visiting" the factory. Such "visits" enabled factory managers to operate freely. To compensate for stolen meat, water and paper pulp were added to the product (in order to keep required weight).

Certainly it is difficult to draw the line between acceptable and unacceptable theft in the work place. Such distinction is strongly influenced not only by national, but also by local and individual company cultures (to the extent they existed under communism). Sociological research does not give satisfactory answers. The only certain thing is that a surprisingly wide range of unlawful activities is socially acceptable and legitimized in communist and post-communist enterprises.

The most convincing explanation was given to me by an employee of the Soviet meat processing factory presented above: "people accept when everybody takes advantage of the skim and when managers do it for themselves but also for others, when managers do it for themselves only and do not share its unacceptable". This opinion was confirmed by the Polish experiences of 1980 and 1981, when the newly-born Solidarity was fighting management corruption. They focused on cases in which managers did it for themselves only, such as in building individual homes with building materials acquired from the enterprise at a fraction of the price and erected by the enterprise building team often for free or for a token price.

Elements of organizational culture and counter-culture inherited from communism are certainly counter-productive from the point of view of transition to a market economy. But they will certainly not vanish overnight. Culture is by definition slow to change, and the existing norms, values, behavioral patterns, rituals, and basic assumptions will have to be subject to the long process of transformation and adaptation to the new conditions. The process has already begun. For example, in Poland some local Solidarity organizations at the factory level assume the role of party organizations and the old communist rituals are being repainted as patriotic and religious demonstrations. It is quite natural, the vacuum left by the communist system has to be filled somehow. It is also evident that in a democratic society and market economy, the old culture will gradually change its meaning and its functions, but only gradually . . .

The Roles of Managers

Management has a key role to play in such a cultural transformation. To understand it, it seems necessary to assess the role of the manager in the communist enterprise.

In 1977, the Soviet Academy of Sciences prepared a special set of requirements which a communist manager should meet. These requirements were supposed to serve as guidelines for selection, evaluation of performance, promotion, training, and development of "socialist managers". (Akademia Nauk SSSR 1977). Six such requirements were formulated:

1. Full devotion to the communist ideology, and absolute loyalty to the Communist Party

2. Ability to organize the work of others, and maintain authority and social responsibility

3. Practical technical knowledge in the fields of technology, management and administration

4. Ability to educate people

5. Ability to forecast the future development of science and technology, and to develop new ways of solving problems

6. Political, party, state, legal, and moral responsibility for actions taken by the manager

Other communist authors formulate similar requirements.

Kozminski (1976) studied the pragmatic content of the role of the communist managers and identified its two major components: participation in plan formulation and plan implementation. Participation in the plan formulation process required diplomatic and "gamesmanship" qualities enabling the manager to persuade higher levels that plan targets should not be too high and an allocation of resources generous enough to allow further development of the enterprise. Such outcome was highly desirable from the enterprise point of view and obviously damaging from the overall economic efficiency point of view. Plan implementation required such management actions as:

- Redistribution of planned tasks among different departments of the enterprise

- Setting the norms to which execution of the plan targets should correspond

- Building of an information network and monitoring information processes

- Distribution of material inputs and energy within the enterprise

- Selection of personnel for the execution of particular tasks and monitoring their performance

- Use of punishments and rewards (incentives) associated with different performance levels

Kozminski (1976) has indicated the existence of inter-role and intra-role conflicts associated with the positions of communist managers. Inter-role conflicts resulted from the extensive role sets of communist managers. In order to protect themselves from multiple pressures and to keep all options and communication channels open, they had to be active party members participating in the party organs. They often became elected local officials, parliament members, and officers of professional organizations (engineers, accountants', economists' etc). Such extensive role sets created conflicts, but enabled them to achieve synergistic effect of sorts: to promote the manager's role and to become more successful negotiators through high prestige and high visibility in other fields.

Intra-role conflicts resulted from the existence of multiple and influential groups of role senders articulating sanctioned expectations related directly to the manager's role performance. The most important among these groups were administrative and political authorities directly supervising the enterprise, workers and workers' organizations, suppliers, clients, banks, and local governments. The "counter-culture" (manipulation, negotiated compromise, second economy "tricks") enabled managers to cope with conflicting external expectations and resulting role conflicts.

Kozminski and Tropea (1982) have clearly demonstrated that bureaucratic structuring of communist industry—characterized by hierarchical bureaucracies that are subject to political pressures—inevitably created informal parasitic networks and coalitions. Such informal networks are able to subvert intentions in applying performance criteria and in meeting operationalized goals—which usually take the form of economic plans presumably imposed on the enterprises from above, but which in fact are subject to negotiations and bargaining. Using such networks enables managers to circumvent legal controls from above and transform even engineering issues into bargaining phenomena. In this way bureaucratic structures loose their only presumed advantage, that is, monolithic controls enabling them to achieve selected objectives at any price. Because of negotiations, bargaining and reciprocation ground rules regulating relations between such actors as managers of state owned enterprises and administrators from the government agencies supervising those enterprises, party "apparatchiks" (functionaries), trade unions etc. Because of these networks, communist economic system were for many years consistently unable to achieve their objectives on the enterprise level. Informal structural coalitions and unwritten ground rules became a source of the "negative power" of the managers, enabling them to win the games with the upper levels of bureaucracy and to achieve their own personal goals as well as the goals of subordinated personnel at the expense of economic rationality and efficiency.

Empirical research on innovations in the communist enterprises (Kozminski & Obloj eds. 1983) shows that only initiatives supported by a winning coalition of managers using game strategies well suited to the environment could be successful. The following strategies were identified:

- Strategy of redundant promotion of the idea, through parallel vertical channels such as the administrative channel (ministry), political channel (party), trade union channel, professional association channel (engineers), and the regional lobby channel.

- Strategy of promoting innovation consistent with the actual themes of the political campaign, in which the party was involved. This would include for example, "anti-import" production or promotion of certain types of industries such as mechanical, chemical, and electronic and presenting it as "exceptional" chance to achieve politically determined objectives.

- Strategy of pushing decision upward as high as possible (up to the level of party leadership) in order to secure sufficient political clout for the initiative and its promoters.

- Strategy of fuzzy responsibility, in which large numbers of unnecessary individuals were involved in the decision-making process.

They were then skilfully manipulated by a group or individual. Such a crowd serves as a ''protective shield'' for innovation promoters.

• Strategy of avoiding open conflict politically damaging for all concerned participants and benevolent submission to arbitration by the upper levels of political (party) or administrative (ministry) hierarchy. (Kozminski & Obloj 1884)

It is hard to imagine how such management strategies could be erased without a trace from the organizational cultures of post-communist enterprises. Strong political pressures from ''dying dinosaurs'' clearly confirm this hypothesis. Political games and coalitions based on reciprocity are still being practiced. They will probably gradually become more similar to lobbies and pressure groups found in modern democratic and pluralistic societies.

Empirical studies (Zvorykin & Geliuta 1977; Kohout 1970) showed that in practice, the role requirements of communist managers were composed of three groups of elements: technical skills, managerial ''diplomatic'' skills (mainly the ability to negotiate with the outside world and to protect the enterprise from excessive pressures), and interpersonal skills enabling them to avoid tensions and conflicts inside the enterprise. Among such managers' qualities viewed as positive by Soviet respondents, the most important ones were the following (Zvorykin & Geliuta 1977: 527):

1. Fair, does not patronize anyone

2. Follows orders, but regards them critically

3. Consults with subordinates in making decisions

4. Combines persistence and demands with tact

5. Listens attentively to requests

6. Informs subordinates of higher management decisions

7. Sincere, states opinions in a straight-forward manner

8. Always willing to lend a hand on the job

9. Is not afraid to assume responsibility

The communist managers' role did not contain three elements considered as key factors in market economies: entrepreneurship, strategy, innovation, and leading change. The essence of the communist managers' role was passive, a defensive response to conflicting pressures. A study of Soviet managers conducted in the '70s by Zvorykin and Gieluta (A. A. Zvorykin & A. M. Geliuta 1977: 516) indicates the following hierarchy of managers' objectives stimulated by special incentives (bonuses, promotions):

1. Over-fulfillment of plan

2. Improvement of labor productivity

3. Organization of rhythmic work

4. Economizing of supplies

5. Reduction of costs

6. Improvement of product quality

7. Introduction of new technology

8. Modernization of equipment

Only two items at the end of the list have anything to do with innovation and change. Elements of entrepreneurship and strategy are conspicuously absent. As the latest studies available indicate, despite all the attempted reforms, this basically passive character did not change in the "communist bloc" until the end of communism. For example, in 1988 in the Polish fruit and vegetable industry, an association was created to serve the industry through strategic planning and the promotion of innovation. Contrary to this idea, managers used the association exclusively for short term problem solving. An empirical study reveals that managers believed that this was the only right way to operate. That is how they perceived their role (Obloj & Davis 1991).

Are the organizational cultures and the contents of managers roles changing now, after the collapse of communism? In the case of dinosaurs, this process is strongly influenced by the renaissance of the populist version of industrial democracy. Recent history of the biggest Polish steel mill, Huta Katowice, illustrates this argument (Dziadul 1991).

Huta Katowice was designed and built in the '70s as the biggest steel mill in Europe. The mill, which was never completed, employs over 16,000 people. Under communism, Huta Katowice was considered one of the key industrial enterprises and privileged as such. It was given cheap, subsidized energy and raw materials, a generous allocations of investment funds, higher wages and managers' salaries, and benefits. 1989 and the first half of 1990 were good for Huta Katowice. The rapid decrease of the home market demand caused nearly 70 percent of the output to be exported. These exports were very profitable because raw materials and energy were still subsidized and the exchange rate introduced on January 1, 1990—9,500 zlotys for one U.S. dollar—was extremely advantageous. This exchange rate was also used for revaluation of the hard currency reserves and payments for 1989 sales. Pretty soon, however, subsidies were eliminated, costs increased because of inflation (260 percent in 1990), and the exchange rate stabilized, making exports much less interesting. 1990 profitability was only 5 percent, and the last quarter brought $8 million deficit. The first 4 months of 1991 generated nearly $18 million of net loss. Competition became much more difficult. The domestic market deteriorated further, and it was suddenly discovered that because of backward technology, production costs of one ton of steel were $40 higher at Huta Katowice than in Western Europe, although it was the most cost effective of all Polish steel manufacturers. Exports started to create losses which had to be absorbed. To make things worse on domestic and foreign markets, Huta Katowice had to face Soviet and Czechoslovak competition in 1990 and 1991 still backed by subsidized energy and raw materials exactly the same way Huta Katowice was in 1989.

At the beginning of 1990, when the crisis was already apparent, competition for the general manager's position was announced, in accordance with the 1981 law of state-owned enterprises. Mr. Emil Wasacz, an engineer, who couple of months earlier had become the president of the local Solidarity trade union chapter, won the competition. Mr. Wasacz was selected (in January 1991) based on the convincing restructuring program he presented. He argued that technologically, Huta Katowice was not complete and in order to become competitive on the European market, it still needed a $500 million investment in modern equipment to enable so-called continuous casting technology.

Modernization can be completed by 1995 without state budget subvention. Huta Katowice will only need government financial guarantees in order to start close cooperation with German steel manufacturers who expressed serious interest in buying into it. In order to start the whole process, however, the legal status of Huta Katowice has to be changed into a joint stock company. In the first stage, it will be wholly owned by the State Treasury. The treasury would then sell its shares to domestic and foreign investors. Mr. Wasacz's program was approved by Prime Minister Mr. Bielecki, who visited Huta Katowice in May 1991. The Prime Minister has promised to speed up Huta's transformation into a stock company. Such a transformation means that the company loses its legal status as a state-owned company, which means that workers' self management is automatically eliminated. This point was strongly contested by a handful of vocal trade union activities organized in a dissident Solidarity 80 trade union.

This conflict, which could eventually kill Huta Katowice, is extremely interesting from the organizational culture point of view and calls for an explanation.

There are five different trade unions in Huta Katowice: the communist SNZZ trade union is still the biggest—7,500 members, Solidarity—3,500 members, autonomous trade union—250 members, young workers' trade union—250 members, and dissident Solidarity 80—number of members unknown (June 1991).

Communist trade unions founded by the military and party authorities in 1981 to replace the banned Solidarity, were expected to collapse completely after the collapse of communism in 1989. These expectations did not materialize, because when it was legalized again in 1989, Solidarity was too busy with political matters and neglected purely trade union activities. Communist trade unions, fighting for survival, concentrated on defending workers' interests and gained some credibility. As a result, nationwide, they still outnumber Solidarity.

Solidarity was very active in Huta Katowice in 1980 and 1981. When martial law was declared in December 1981, Solidarity leaders were arrested and the union itself went underground. Mr. Cieslicki was the underground Solidarity leader who led the union through the 1988 and 1989 strikes which resulted in the final collapse of communism. He was one of the legends. In spite of his glorious past, in the fall of 1989, he was voted out of office by the members who criticized his high level of political activism. He was replaced by the pragmatic engineer, Mr. Wasacz, who did not participate in the union's underground activities.

It is widely believed that being president of the Solidarity organization helped Mr. Wasacz to win the election competition and become Huta's general manager. Presumably, the old (communist party) *nomenklatura* system was replaced by the new one (Solidarity's). Mr. Wasacz strongly denies this. He cites his restructuring program as proof. However, people do not believe him. Cieslicki and his followers, scandalized by the harmonious cooperation between Solidarity and management, were especially distrustful. For them, Solidarity has assumed the role of the communist party on the shop floor level as well as on the national level (with Walesa elected president of the country) and became the official "facade" political organization. That is why they decided to secede and to start the new independent "real" trade union defending the old ideals of "Solidarity" initiated in 1980 in Gdansk. Nationwide, "Solidarity 80" was officially registered under the leadership of Mr. Jurczyk, one of Walesa's early "companion in arms" from the underground.

In Huta Katowice, Solidarity 80 was determined to fight Wasacz's restructuring plan, particularly the transformation of the state-owned company into a stock company and the resultant elimination of the workers' council and other self-management organs. Mr. Cieslicki could consider a temporary alliance with yesterday's deadly enemy—communist trade unions—but not with the treacherous "official" Solidarity, which according to them took the place of the old communist party and the "new *nomenklatura* management. Asked what is going to happen with Huta Katowice, they say it is the government's responsibility to rescue state-owned enterprises. In the meantime, foreign investors started to feel uneasy. Finally, Huta Katowice was transformed into a joint stock company but the lack of an overall industrial policy in the steel industry prevented the foreign partners from entering serious negotiations until mid 1992.

The Huta Katowice case demonstrated how deeply the organizational culture inherited from communism is entrenched in the mentality of the same people who were the most active in fighting and eliminating the communist system. It should be remembered that many underground workers' activists fighting communism, new revolutionaries, in reality, deeply cherish the early communist ideas of the populist version of industrial democracy. For them, contemporary capitalism is as unacceptable as the late, corrupt communism of Brezhnev or Gierek. This mental set seems to be present in the big dinosaurs and especially in two countries, Poland and the C.I.S., where workers' movements played a decisive role in abolishing communism.

The new, emerging organizational cultures are much more likely to be found in the private sector, in enterprises created by the new breed of post-communist entrepreneurs. It does not mean, however, that the old mentality is not present even there, in one form or another.

6

Changing Organizational Cultures

New Emerging Organizational Cultures of Private Enterprises

The phenomenon of new, emerging organizational cultures is closely linked to the new type of business leaders, entrepreneurs and managers who create, develop, and cultivate such new cultures in the process of building up their enterprises and adjusting them to the specific conditions of the post-communist economies. Management cultures will be presented below as creations of business leaders:

- Krzysztof Horodecki, president of Ekolog, a private company specializing in waste water treatment installations

- Vladimir Vinigradov, chairman of the largest and one of the Soviet Union's first non-state banks, the Moscow Innovation Bank, Mosiknombank

- Three friends (partners), who founded a private cooperative enterprise specializing in decorative and medicinal plants in Novosibirsk, Russia (Siberia)

Krzysztof Horodecki[1] was born in 1953 in Walcz, in northern Poland. His family was rather poor. In high school, he was mainly interested in sports. His ambitions and expectations were not very high, which is still typical for inhabitants of small towns in Poland. He was not even sure whether he wanted to get a university education (free of charge in communist Poland) but as an outdoor enthusiast, he became seriously interested in ecology and in 1972, applied for admission and passed the exams to Poznan Polytechnic School of Environmental Engineering. Horodecki states that he received a solid and up-to-date engineering education. He decided to specialize in waste water treatment systems. During his university years, Horodecki visited Western Europe (France, Germany, Austria, Italy) on a tourist visa, but in fact, worked occasionally on farms and in the restaurants. This was very important for the young man. He realized how far his country lagged behind and how different the work culture in the West was.

After graduating from Poznan Polytechnic in 1978, Horodecki was offered a job in the state-owned civil engineering firm Investprojekt. The firm offered him an apartment which was and still is, quite an incentive in Poland, which has a severe housing shortage. The young engineer was given important and independent assignments in designing municipal waste water treatment facilities, water treatment plants, boilers, and water distribution systems for housing developments. He enjoyed the job and found working with a young team of well-educated engineers was both fun and a valuable professional experience.

In 1981, Horodecki applied for a leave without pay and decided to visit the US in order to gain some experience, make some money, and see the country. His wife and then 6 year old son remained in Poland. In December 1981, the declaration of martial law caught Horodecki in the US. In spite of the fact that he was offered an attractive job in an environmental engineering firm in Texas and could possibly bring his family to the US in the future, he decided to return to Poland. He explains his decision: ''What I knew about what was happening in Poland was really scary: tanks on the streets, partisans in the forests, who knows—maybe a civil war or stalinist terror? But I thought of my family and about other things as well. I decided go to home.'' After his return in early 1982, he learned that he was fired from Investprojekt although his trip was perfectly legal and he was officially granted a one year leave of absence without pay. Times were not inviting to contest such decisions on legal grounds. In June of 1982, he found a new job in another state-owned civil engineering firm, but the work for the paralyzed state owned company, which was rapidly deteriorating under military rule did not satisfy him in any way. Even the pay was very low. After a series of frustrating incidents, he decided to leave the company and start a business of his own. In this way, Ekolog was born in 1983, under the name of Environmental Protection Engineering Institute, which was owned solely by Mr. Horodecki.

In 1983, the attitude of the Polish communist government and local authorities toward private entrepreneurship was ambivalent and could even be called schizophrenic. The old communist dogma of the superiority of the socialized forms of ownership of the means of production and extreme suspicion of the individual entrepreneurship of private citizens were still cultivated in the communist power elite and the communist propaganda. Such hostile attitudes often resulted in punitive actions such as constant fiscal controls and excessive taxation, cancellation of orders from the state sector, and other discriminatory practices. At the same time, however, many important changes took place.

Economic reform designed in 1981 and implemented in 1982 under the exceptional conditions of the newly declared martial law gave the "green light" to small private enterprises already considered to be an important supplement to the insufficient and inadequate production of the state sector. In some regions, the private sector was already responsible for nearly 25 percent of the goods and services offered to individual consumers (Kozminski 1988). Special privileges were granted to foreign private investors of Polish descent ("Polonia enterprises"). Through its attitude toward private entrepreneurship, the military communist regime wanted to show its willingness to promote radical economic reforms and to persuade the West to lift economic sanctions imposed after martial law was declared in December 1981. Many communist officials, especially at the local level, got unofficially involved in private business deals.

Horodecki experienced this ambivalence during the first years of the firm's activities. His one-man (during the first months) company was licensed to provide services in the field of design, maintenance, and implementation of environmental protection systems. The company's first orders were the ones rejected by competing state-owned enterprises because they were not the most lucrative ones. As soon as Mr. Horodecki confirmed his willingness to take an order, some of the powerful state-owned enterprises immediately took it over, even though they had formerly rejected it. After struggling alone for some time, he was joined by two of his colleagues from his previous job. Eventually, they got their first order: the renovation of a waste water purification plant: The plant was not operating and was in very bad condition. They took the job although it was by no means the job they were dreaming of. It consisted mainly of tough physical labor of cleaning the plant. The equipment has been visibly neglected by its owner—a state-owned enterprise. As usual, the company had forgotten about preventive maintenance. Mr. Horodecki summarizes his first experiences as private entrepreneur in the following way: "But we have learned something from this experience and it was humility. Maybe we needed that: we highly educated hopeful professionals".

In July of 1983, martial law was lifted and some parts of the communist establishment were trying to promote private entrepreneurship. However, the legal and political environment was still dominated by a rigid and corrupt bureaucracy. Mr. Horodecki's honesty got him into serious trouble with the local communist elite. They wanted him to provide an alibi for a politically influential manager of the big state owned farm, in exchange for a "fat contract and no real work." The manager was a major polluter. Horodecki refused and offered to fix the problem, and even started to work without a contract. Afraid of exposing their negligence, the farm management refused to sign the contract on Horodecki's terms. When Horodecki insisted, the whole local bureaucracy went after him. They even managed to take him to court on the pretext that by hiring one part timer he was breaking an absurd formal regulation limiting the number of people he was allowed to employ as a private entrepreneur. He was forced to seek protection from the Central Craftsman Association in Warsaw but eventually was absolved from the absurd accusations. He proved that he was able to stick to his principles of professionalism and morality and survive even in the most unfriendly environment.

Horodecki's fight with the local communist elite and his victory—which was highly unlikely in 1984—brought him an unexpected gain: a reputation of uncompromising professional excellence. It helped him to get new orders from municipalities who were becoming increasingly sensitive to local public opinion. In 1984, he got a big project to design and construct the waste water treatment system for a medium-sized Polish city, Inowroclaw. In 1985, other bigger projects followed for such cities as Znin, Dobrzyn, and finally Kolobrzeg, which is a big port city and vacation resort.

Because each project was completed successfully, professionally, and within the strict limits of the agreed budget, the firm's reputation grew. The real breakthrough did not come, however until 1986. This was the first year in which the firm could afford not to get credit for current operation (to supplement its working capital). In 1987, the company employed 15 people and offered a broad range of services from design to construction, start-ups, and maintenance of waste water treatment systems. It also started to manufacture compact biological waste water treatment units of different sizes under its own license. These were called Ela, to honour his wife Elizabeth (abbreviated in Polish as Ela). These units have an excellent reputation for simplicity, reliability, and energy efficiency. The firm also licensed a few other inventions, mainly in nitrogen and phosphorus removal technologies installed in bigger plants of the FOSFO-KIAR type.

In 1987, within the framework of the "last hour" communist reforms, a new law was passed in Poland, the law of innovation and implementation enterprises. This new regulation provided for more favourable treatment of small and medium-sized enterprises (mainly private) active in technological innovation such as generation, promotion, and implementation. More favourable treatment included tax breaks, preferential credits, and the right to employ more people by private entrepreneurs. Horodecki applied for this privileged status, and in 1988, was recognized officially as an Innovation Enterprise and granted resulting privileges. These privileges enabled the accelerated growth of the company, which reached an employment level of over 200 people in 1989. When communism was abolished in Poland after the June 1989 election, the company was ready for further expansion. In 1990, it was renamed Ekolog, and new branches in Poznan, Szczecin, Zielona Gora, and Bydgoszcz—all located in North

Western Poland—were opened. Cooperation with American, Danish, and Finnish companies was also started.

Ekolog has high quality standards which are comparable to Western European firms. It services not only for the entire Polish market but the international market as well. Horodecki especially foresees his company's participation in the clean up of Eastern provinces of Germany and of Czechoslovakia. In 1991, Ekolog won an American contest for the best environmental project. The project will be financed by the American government. The $700 thousand grant consists of four regional projects of waste purification for Warsaw, Krakow, Lodz and Katowice. These are the biggest Polish cities, where until recently, Ekolog was not active. Recently, a European Phare program for industrial waste neutralization in Eastern Europe has been started. Ekolog hopes to be included in the project, since the company has accumulated know-how and experience in the area.

In June 1991, Horodecki felt that his company was approaching another turning point in its history. Employment was rising rapidly, growing from 250 to 400 people. 40 percent of them were highly qualified designers and engineers. This is due to the fact the substitution of mechanical, chemical, and electrochemical methods of industrial waste water neutralization by the biological treatment methods is gradually becoming the new focus of Ekolog's R & D activities, requiring the hiring of more staff and closer cooperation with foreign technological leaders.

The company is moving rapidly—it expanded from a local to a regional to a national and even international firm. It requires decentralization and redesigning of the actual rather unclear organizational structure. At the moment, three principles of building the structure are applied simultaneously (by product, by location and by function) and where informal relations are still more important than formal structure. The inflow of new management talent is needed. As far as top management is concerned, Horodecki has a strong preference for young well educated engineers. Out of 16 top management people, only four are over the age of 40. Such people, however, require additional training in management. Horodecki is aware of that and sends his people to Polish and foreign business schools.

The new management team and the structure have to be fit for joint ventures and temporary partnerships which may be established with foreign partners for specific large contracts, such as construction of big and complex sewage treatment facilities or the manufacturing of specific types of equipment in Poland and abroad. Such partnerships according to Horodecki precondition successful penetration of foreign markets by Ekolog.

In 1989, Horodecki himself applied for admission and was accepted to the International Business School (an off-spring of Warsaw University), the only institution in Poland offering a full-fledged American type executive MBA program. The program is taught partially in Polish and partially in English by Polish and foreign professors. Horodecki took special interest in business strategy, finance, and marketing courses and liked the physical fitness program very much. The program is run in sessions: every month participants spend one week together in a training center 40 km. outside Warsaw. Horodecki enjoyed the company very much and developed quite a network of useful business contacts, enabling him to penetrate the central provinces of Poland and the new industries such as metal surface treatment factories, where effluent from galvanizing and pickling processes are highly toxic, aggressive, and contain heavy metals.

In 1990, the US Embassy in Warsaw offered the International Business School three six-month scholarships to the US. Horodecki won the competition and completed a six month management education program in California, under the Alexander Hamilton Fellows Program. The program included three month internship in an environmental engineering firm. He feels that he has learned a lot and Ekolog is now cooperating with the American partners such as Post, Buckley, Schuh and Jerningan Inc., International Technology, Eckenfelder Inc., and Killam.

Since 1983, Horodecki has been able to forge a strong and distinctive organizational culture of his company. Using Schein's framework, it can be summarized in the following points:

On the level of artifacts and creations, Ekolog is clearly a high-tech company attaching enormous importance to technological transition (from chemical and electromechanical to bio-technology) to R&D. It is also an innovation driven company, where engineers and designers are encouraged or even forced to innovate. Horodecki himself sets an example: Ela, the compact waste water treatment unit, is his creation. The company's culture seems to be built on the cult of innovation and modernity. Even offices and design labs are furnished and decorated in a modern way consciously carrying a message of this "cult".

Ekolog is certainly not overly formalized; to the contrary, communication channels bottom-up as well as horizontal are always opened and informal relations play an important role. Horodecki practices "hands on" and wandering around" management style. He believes that his people, including managers and engineers, should be able to perform a wide range of functions and tasks—including physical labor if needed. He seems to be rather reluctant to delegate and to decentralize. He knows that he has to do this as the company grows but he "wants to oversee important things by himself." Although still an outdoor enthusiast fascinated by sports and an exemplary family man, he is nonetheless a workaholic, putting in 12 hour days, six days a week. Similar level of effort and work intensity is expected from Horodecki's subordinates, especially the managers.

On the level of values, Horodecki was able to promote the image of the company and its stable growth and development as key elements of Ekolog's organizational culture. He wants his people to believe that they belong to an exclusive company. That is why Horodecki carefully avoided all business deals or even contacts with the companies of doubtful reputation. For example, in 1990 Ekolog was invited to participate in the creation of a regional trade center. Horodecki liked the idea very much. However, when he learned that a company involved in imports of alcohol and suspected of wrongdoing (later confirmed) was also involved in the project, he flatly refused to participate. As one of the Ekolog's executives puts it: "He did not want to risk Ekolog's good name: neither just for today nor for the long run". Horodecki wants people to be proud of working for Ekolog and to attract the best people on these grounds. He pays well, but he wants moral incentives such as the company's reputation and opportunities for personal growth and self-realization, to be the most important factors.

In spite of his extremely busy schedule due to the ambitious programs for developing Ekolog, Horodecki decided to actively participate in the political life of the newly emerging democracy. In the first fully democratic parliamentary election in Poland in October 1991, he was elected to the Senate.

Growth of the company as a value is clearly visible in Mr. Horodecki's behaviour. He does not consume what he earns but reinvests every penny in the company. Horodecki's personal fortune is certainly worth well over $10 million but he does not show-off. He is unlike others belonging to the new breed of Polish entrepreneurs who are crazy about such things as big ranchos and houses, the most expensive models of Mercedeses and BMWs and safaris. His employees respect him for that. Says Mr. Trojnarski his deputy "Since he reinvests every penny, we see it this way: we are working hard for the company, for our future". The company's future growth and development are becoming a value for its employees.

The basic assumptions level of the organizational culture is the most difficult to penetrate. Ekolog's culture seems to be built on three pillars:

1. An uncompromising belief in technological capabilities to clean the environment

2. A strong belief in individual private entrepreneurship and its role in promoting progress in post-communist countries like Poland (Ekolog was born out of its owners' frustrations with the state-owned enterprises. Other employees had similar experiences.)

3. A conviction that Polish managers, engineers, and workers are not inferior, that they can catch up with foreigners, compete with them, and eventually win

Horodecki certainly played a key role in forging Ekolog's distinctive organizational culture. He seems to possess all the characteristics of an ideal leader in a mature organization identified by Schein (1990: 322–325): perception and insight, motivation and skill, emotional strength, ability to change cultural assumptions, creation of involvement and participation, and depth of vision.

Horodecki's co-workers perceive him as a man with a mission and a vision. His mission is ecology and the company. His managerial vision and intuition have proven accurate many times, sometimes against the evidence. For example, in 1987 he started to hire more people than he was allowed, anticipating innovation and implementation unit status. In 1988, he planned to double employment and profits in two years. Once again, it was accomplished. Such a reputation contributes to his charisma and his legend, thus helping him to build organizational culture of the company.

Vladimir Vinogradov[2] was born in 1955 in Ufa, the Soviet capital of the aviation industry. He studied at Ufa Aviation Institute and because of exceptionally high grades, he won the prestigious Lenin scholarship, which enabled him to enroll in the famous Moscow Aviation Institute. In 1979, he graduated with honors as a specialist in "electrical missile and nuclear space propulsion unit".

After graduation, Vinogradov went to Volgodonsk to work for Atommash on the construction of a giant factory designed to manufacture machinery and equipment for the whole nuclear industry in the USSR and in other "brother countries" COMECON members. Unfortunately, improperly tested soil caused the whole structure to sink in the construction process.

This experience induced the frustrated young engineer to become a career functionary of The Young Communist League (Komsomol—equivalent of the communist party in the youth movement) for a while. He was earmarked for promotions and privileges and was even promised a transfer to Moscow to the Young Communist League headquarters. But after less than a year, he got completely disgusted with that kind of career and exited the communist career fast-track.

After leaving his political career behind, Vinigradov wanted to get a job with the Foreign Trade Academy. This option was blocked by the KGB, who presumably didn't like and couldn't recruit the young rebel engineer. Vinogradov decided then to join the Postgraduate School of Economics and to specialize in "economics of industrial branches." He had to live on a scholarship which was not enough to support his family. In search of additional income, he took a job as an economist with the Promstroibank, one of the brances of the state-owned bank financing industry. The salary he received was twice as high as his scholarship. Although promotion was in sight, Vinogradov once again wanted to change his life. In 1987, taking advantage of the new cooperative law, he and a group of friends decided to establish their own private company.

The prospective partners considered starting a joint stock company to finance a small businesses in the field of new technology. One fateful day, they came across the document which seemed to authorize the establishment of non-state commercial banks. Confesses Vinogradov: "I knew too well from my previous experience that once you decide something and do not start implementing it within a short time, it will never come to life". Vinogradov seized the moment and registered his bank immediately after the new law was made public. The shareholders meeting elected Vinogradov chairman of the board. A day after registration, the ceiling of the office collapsed, but business continued nevertheless.

At the beginning, the meager R4.5 million capital did not provide for the salaries of the bank founders, who were also its only employees. A small firm was established to produce a research book on the alternative economy and its tiny profits were used to pay modest wages for interior decoration. Business opportunities, however, were abundant and Vinogradov took advantage of them.

The planned economy regime was rapidly deteriorating but still in existence as late as 1992. Under this system, enterprises experience money shortages at the end of each year and are dying for loans they can repay with a large amount of interest at the beginning of the next year, when government subsidies start to pour in again. What makes non-state owned commercial banks especially attractive to the enterprises is the fact that they are not part of bureaucratic structure of the state mono-bank used as an additional instrument of control of the enterprise performance against detailed plan targets and formal regulations. Access to independent source of credit gives enterprises some degree of autonomy. Even without any publicity, the bank's entire money was on loan when first credits were offered. Vinogradov believes that demand is three to four times higher than his bank's lending capacity. Mosinkombank can afford to be choosy about its clients. It invests in ventures which seem to be both the most profitable and the most promising in the long run. As a result, the bank's own assets increased from R4,5 million to R1,2 billion in two years. By a comfortable margin, it has become the biggest among non-state-owned commercial banks in Moscow.

By 1990, Vinogradov's salary was nearly equal to the Prime Minister of the USSR's (R.1 200 per month officially). This fact was often exploited by conservatives attacking institutions of the emerging alternative economy. Vinogradov believes that he can afford not to pay too much attention to such attacks. He strongly believes in the victory of a democratic system and market economy in Russia.

Until 1990, Mosinkombank did not have permission to conduct foreign operations, but it established working relationships with the foreign banks and foreign firms and provided some intermediary services for them.

During the short time between late 1987 and 1990, Mosinkombank developed a distinctive organizational culture visibly based on the assumption that the Russian economy is doomed to become a market driven one, where commercial banks will play a key role. They want to be the forerunners, to be ready before the others and to take full advantage of early entrant privileges.

Vinogradov and his colleagues know that nothing comes for free and that they have to support political forces which will eventually bring the long-awaited market economy. That is why they have donated equipment to the representatives of the Democratic Russia Bloc, actively supported Boris Yeltsin, and provided interest-free credit to the commercial press. Vinogradov skilfully invests in advertising and sponsorship. He wants the name of his bank to become a symbol of the emerging free Russia. For example, the bank invested R100,000 in Mstislav Rstropovithc's (the famous Russian violinist and composer who left Russia in early '70s and was officially stripped of Soviet citizenship) tour of the USSR in the spring of 1990. Such political activism is not uncommon among the emerging Russian capitalist class. The author has been told by a high-ranking member of the Russian parliament that during the attempted military coup in August 1991, the "new entrepreneurs" were over 30 percent of the 15,000 people defending the parliament building.

Independence from the state apparatus, and pride in being an independent economic agent paving the way for the future, seem to be the most important features of the Mosinkombank's organizational culture. This is due to the fact that the bank emerged from its founders deep dissatisfaction with the Soviet way of life in a broad sense, not limited to the economy and banking.

The story of a private cooperative in Siberia (Novosibirsk)[4] illustrates negative effect of the enterprise's inability to develop a distinctive organizational culture capable of providing a conflict resolution platform. The story begins in 1988, shortly after the Soviet Parliament passed the Cooperative Law, enabling the creation of small privately-owned enterprises intended as family businesses with a very limited number of employees. Many of the more active Soviet citizens (especially intelligentsia) started such enterprises as second jobs. Many such cooperatives developed in symbiosis with the state-owned enterprises using their resources at considerably undervalued prices. For obvious reasons, more influential members of the communist *nomenklatura* had easier access to such resources. That is why cooperatives were often attacked from both sides of the Soviet political spectrum, the orthodox communists attacked them as evil elements of capitalism, and radical liberals attacked them as parasitic creations of the *nomenklatura*. Similar phenomena could be also observed in other countries in transition from communism to a market economy.

The cooperative was founded in Novosibirsk by three friends. The first was an economist, working for a research institute and well-connected in the local government and business community (including the shadow economy and newly emerging cooperative movement). The second was an agronomist, working as the deputy director of a state-owned farm specializing in production of clippings and root cuttings of decorative and medicinal plants. The third was in charge of procurement in a big construction cooperative (very important function in the economy of shortage where buying is difficult, sometimes nearly impossible and selling easy).

The families of the partners had long been friendly and were involved in the cooperative. The business concept of the cooperative was rather simple and ingenious: production and distribution of cuttings from decorative trees such as silver fir and spruce, and root cuttings of medicinal plants. The Novosibirsk region specialized in such production and demand from municipalities and medical supply companies from all over the USSR was practically unlimited and remained mostly unsatisfied.

The agronomist was able to hire part-time workers and lease equipment and land from the state-owned farm. Since the decorative trees (the dominating product line) required three years of investment before the first cuttings could be sold and the partners had very limited private resources, credit was needed. Regular bank credit was very difficult to get because of the lack of collateral. The economist obtained the needed credit for three years from one of the new production cooperatives. The cooperative committed itself to extend R40,000 a year of credit in exchange for 50 percent of the cooperative's net profit for the first three consecutive years of profit starting from the first year of sales.

In 1988, 40,000 rubles was a considerable amount of money, considering at that time, the price of a tractor was 5,000 rubles and a medium-sized truck cost 3,000 rubles. The provider took responsibility for procuring necessary materials, but the economist took initiative this time. He used his personal contacts to secure purchase of a large batch of seeds from rare medicinal plants (with detailed know-how) from a research institute specializing in medicinal plants.

The agronomist's wife was also an agronomist and got actively involved in the activities of the cooperative. The economist's wife, who was a certified accountant, took care of book keeping and accounting. In short, all the conditions for success seemed to be fulfilled. Unfortunately, conflicts between cooperative members quickly undermined its very existence.

The first conflict resulted from the aportioning of salaries between cooperative members. During a meeting, the three families decided that the agronomist, who would leave his position at the state owned farm, would receive 600 rubles per month. The economist, who would keep his job at the Institute but still because of his flexible schedule be able to do all the required work in financial and strategic matters would receive 400 rubles. His wife would receive the cooperative's 150 rubles as accountant. The provider, who would also keep his job at construction cooperative would receive 300 rubles per month. The traditional Soviet (marxist) work culture attaches the highest value to direct production, while neglecting managerial and financial functions. This attitude is clearly visible in this solution. All three partners considered themselves equal; nobody was personally in charge of the whole operation.

The economist felt undervalued because the whole idea of starting a cooperative was his. He secured a loan enabling the whole venture to take off, he arranged for the purchase of the seeds, he did all the paperwork, and he took care of all the legal details connected with registration of the cooperative. Additionally, he was the one who assumed the role of strategist and leader. Pretty soon, the economist and the agronomist realized that the provider's services were not really needed because all the purchases were secured by them. The provider's salary was an unnecessary burden on the cooperatives' finances. The issue was raised at the meeting, and the economist proposed to substitute the provider's monthly salary with occasional payments linked to precisely determined services rendered to the cooperative. The provider and his wife considered this a personal attack, motivated by the Economist's greed who presumably wanted to increase his salary. Deeply offended, he left the cooperative and broke friendly relations with two other families.

Because of constant shortages, the importance of procurement is very deeply internalized in Soviet organizational cultures as is the tendency to believe that if someone is important in one organization, he should have the same importance in others. This belief results from the old tradition of a strict hierarchy of social status of individuals, involving many formally independent organizations such as the party, the government administration, and the scientific community etc. The provider was certainly very important in the large construction cooperative where he was a vice president. He was responsible for all purchases of building materials critical to the functioning of the enterprise.

Work and management styles were another source of conflict. The economist wanted to impose weekly meetings devoted to such things as strategic and financial planning of operations, coordination of activities, review and assessment of the current situation, and legislative changes. The provider opposed such meetings, because he believed that only "doing something" on a practical level, like planting the seeds or watering the plantation was worth his time. The agronomist was also against the meetings, saying that he wanted to get away from planning and all the bureaucracy. The economist did not have any formal authority to impose his views. He tried to use friendly persuasion, but he did not succeed. Planning and coordination meetings were abandoned.

The cooperative received its final blow from the conflict between the economist and the agronomist. When the provider left, the economist recruited a specialist in medicinal plants. The specialist worked in a research institute, from which he acquired a batch of seeds. This connection might have had a crucial role for further development of the cooperative. The institute was very successful in developing unique highly valued medicinal plants, but it was not allowed to sell its products commercially and its employees were constantly looking for forms of additional income. Cooperation or an informal partnership between the Institute and the cooperative could eventually provide for such an opportunity. The cooperative could eventually become a selling agent for the most attractive of the Institute's products. Such an arrangement, however, would require strong informal ties between the agronomist and the people from the Institute. In order to secure them, the economist—with the help of the institute employees recruited by the cooperative—arranged for the agronomist to take a job with the research institute. He became a foreman responsible for planting the most valuable medicinal plants.

Unfortunately, the agronomist completely misunderstood his role. Instead of mixing and socializing with the people from the Institute and developing useful contacts, he went to work once a week with five members of his family and performed physical labour himself. He considered such a solution honest and more convenient for him, because he wanted to devote more time to the small garden around his house. People from the Institute were dissatisfied and angry because he was never available for consultation or help. After three months, they fired him for not showing up for work. The person who had recommended him was also very seriously reprimanded and got angry both with the economist and the agronomist and left the cooperative. The economist was mad at the agronomist, and the cooperative was dissolved after less than two years of existence. The long time friendship also dissolved.

When the cooperative disbanded, only 40,000 rubles of debt was left. The economist who arranged for a loan and was personally responsible for it had to pay it entirely from his own personal money. He was able to pay it off, because he was quite successful in some other cooperative business ventures. The provider was also quite successful in charge of procurement in a construction cooperative. The agronomist acquired land and became an independent farmer.

Small private enterprises are mushrooming in Central and Eastern Europe. Many of them are failures. Inability to create distinctive, coherent and pro-efficiency organizational cultures is certainly among the reasons for such failures. Since surveys and comparative data do not exist, it is difficult to generalize and make comparisons between countries. One might, however, suspect that in Hungary, Poland, Eastern Germany, where private firms have survived under communism such organizational cultures are more likely to emerge. Szelenyi (1988) in his in-depth study of rural entrepreneurship in Hungary, has demonstrated how entrepreneurial culture has not only survived but even developed under communism in the rural areas of Hungary. This is certainly not the case in the ex-USSR republics and other more ideologically rigid communist countries such as Rumania, Bulgaria, Albania, where legal private ownership of enterprises—and even small farms—was not tolerated. Czechoslovakia is a special case. Until 1948, it had highly developed market economy and afterwards a highly repressive and rigid communist regime which survived until "velvet revolution" of November 1989.

The case of the cooperative in Russia demonstrates the difficulties in creating organizational culture conducive to private entrepreneurship in an environment where legal private enterprises have been non-existent since the late 20-ties. It is striking that such differences between postcommunist countries do not result from differences in national cultures, but rather to much greater extent from systemic differences between previous communist regimes.

Communism was an attempt to impose forcefully an artificial culture on the existing, living one. It massacred and crippled the culture, creating a strange mixture of systemic communist, national, and local elements. The Communist elements dominated in these mixtures and that is why very similar organizational cultures can be found in the countries of very different national cultures such as Russia, Poland, Hungary, and Czechoslovakia. In this sense, the label of the "communist bloc" reflected reality. The transition to a market economy is dominated by the process of liberation of national and local cultures and subcultures from the constraints imposed by the monstrous communist shell. This process, roughly common to all post-communist countries, will dominate their organizational subcultures for some time before natural national and local cultural differences come into play on the common grounds of the market economy. This will certainly not happen overnight. The focus of this analysis is on the dominating systemic factors that shape organizational cultures. That is why the issue of national cultures was not really addressed here. This issue, however, will become increasingly important for organizational cultures and management styles in the years to come.

The Change Agents

Undoubtedly, entrepreneurs and entrepreneur-managers play a key role in the process of forming the new organizational cultures. But the role of professional managers (not necessarily owners of the enterprises) should not be underestimated. At least the following types of managerial roles in the process of cultural change can be identified:

- The *populist politician,* turning around enterprises with the help of workers' support (and such organizations as) self management organs and trade unions

- The *new technocrat,* restructuring enterprises using "traditional" technical and managerial knowledge as well as traditional sources of organizational power linked with top management positions in state-owned or privatized companies

- The *foreign crusader,* helping to restructure or turn around post-communist enterprises as manager of joint ventures, co-owner, hired management expert, or volunteer.

All three types of managerial roles call for more detailed presentation within the general framework of cultural change.

Populist politicians can be found mainly in dinosaurs, where the old traditional behavioral patterns of workers' activism and populist industrial democracy developed during the last years of communism and the first stages of the transition. In the new business environment dominated by restrictive monetary policies and recession, inefficient "dinosaurs" had to fight for survival. The organizational cultures were used by the managers for this purpose.

Poland in 1992, provided plenty of examples of this understanding of the managerial roles. The restrictive, anti-inflationary monetary policies of 1990 and 1991, triggered a dramatic drop of domestic demand, aggravated by the loss of the Soviet and ex-COMECON markets. Severe recession—close to a 40 percent decrease in industrial production volume between 1989 and 1991—was combined with a lack of industrial policy and the opening of the Polish market to foreign competition (low tariff barriers). These factors resulted in the dramatically worsening financial situation especially of the big state-owned enterprises. This situation was clearly visible in many industries: the automotive, machine industry, agricultural machines (due to rapidly growing agricultural surplus and sluggish demand), light industry, and many linkage industries.

Stomil, located in Sroda (in Western Poland)[4], is one of the enterprises in such industries. It is Poland's only producer of valves for tire tubes, armoured hoses, piston gas rings, and other accessories combining rubber and metal elements for the automotive, tractor, and machine industries. The company is relatively modern. Its plant was completed by the end of the '70s as part of the ambitious program of developing the tractor and automotive industries. Its financial situation is worsened by a tax on fixed assets, which state-owned enterprises are obliged to pay is high, due to the high value and low depreciation of these assets.

Stanislav Szczot is the general manager of the company selected in the competition process required by the law of state-owned enterprises passed in 1981. Under this law, trade unions and workers' council representatives have a say in the selection process. Szczot was selected in October 1990. He describes the situation of the company as extremely difficult. During the first months of 1990, Stomil was working on three shifts and the market could still have absorbed more. In the second quarter of 1990, the volume of orders started to drop. In the second half of 1990, production volume stabilized at the level of 50 percent capacity. In the last months of 1990, something moved for while and orders increased slightly. Anticipating an improvement announced by the government, Stomil kept its employment at the usual level of over 500 people. In 1990, sales volume was about $3.3 million worth, but $850,000 worth of profits were completely eaten by taxes (on fixed assets and income) and nothing was left for development. The average wage of $63 per month, was well below the industry average.

People hoped 1991 would be better. 1991, however, turned out to be worse than the worst predictions. Orders reached a record low level: the equivalent of $220,000 per month. Revaluation (inflation adjustment) of fixed assets in January 1991, considerably increased the fixed assets tax (by the equivalent of $70,000) and already in January, the gross profit was not high enough to cover taxes. Debt started to accumulate and by the end of April, reached a level of equivalent of $280,000. The bank refused further credit and Stomil could not finance its current operations any more. It could not even afford layoffs because Polish labour laws call for special compensation of economic layoffs (6 months salary) paid by the company.

In such a situation, privatization through liquidation seemed to be the only solution. This would allow the sale of the existing production facilities to the highest bidder (including foreign investors), liquidation of the debt burden, and continuation of the operation of the company after downsizing and restructuring. Such a complicated process, however, takes time for such things as for legal procedures, evaluation of assets, identification of prospective buyers, and negotiations. First of all, however, the Ministry of Industry has to make a decision.

The workers of Stomil could not wait: their wages were hardly on subsistence level and unemployment in their town was rising dramatically because other state-owned enterprises were rapidly approaching bankruptcy. In order to put pressure on the authorities to accelerate the process, Mr. Szczot and the trade unions together with the workers' self management organs, organized a series of strikes and demonstrations demanding the acceleration of the liquidation process and some kind of solution to Stomil's problems.

From the cultural change point of view, such a joint effort involves two aspects. First, it requires the promotion of a new solidarity between workers and management based on the assumption that only workers and management together can solve the company's problems. It also requires a psychological adjustment to the new market conditions where nothing comes for free. (Companies can survive and prosper only when they successfully adjust to market conditions, including restructuring and eliminating over-employment.)

Skilfully playing the company's internal politics, Szczot was preparing the way for the new rules of the game in the new privatized Stomil, which would eventually emerge from the liquidation and privatization process. He was also trying to save the existing industrial facilities.

Similar strategies are often used by the managers of state-owned dinosaurs. For example, in the Ursus Tractor Works and in the Starachowice Truck Factory (Wrobel 1991), similar workers' actions supported or even inspired by the management, led to more radical restructuring programs enabling these enterprises to survive. It remains to be seen to what extent such pressures lead to the occasional patronizing of the ailing enterprises by the state, and to what extent they induce an overall industrial policy conducted in accordance with the principles of the market economy. What counts, is the resultant cultural change engineered or skilfully orchestrated by managers who have mastered the game of politics of the populist industrial democracy. This game will certainly persist for some time in the post-communist dinosaurs. The agents of change cannot ignore existing cultural mechanism inherited from the communist system. They have to use it in order to promote change.

New technocrats are practicing cultural change strategies attributed by Schein to the "organizational midlife" growth stage: planned change and organization development, technological seduction, and incrementalism. Quite often, they also use "managed revolution through outsiders". The "New Technocrats" are younger, well-educated engineers promoted to the top from middle management ranks after the end of communism. Mr. Skawinski, managing Mera Pnefal (presented in Chapter 4), precisely corresponds to that description. The Mera case illustrates planned change combined with technological seduction and incrementalism.

Since November 1989 Jozef Kowalczyk, age 36, has been managing Bumar Warynski Works in Warsaw,[5] manufacturing excavators and power hydraulic systems for earth moving equipment. He is another example of a manager and agent of change using the strategy of "revolution through outsiders". Under communism, Bumar Warynski was one of the leading Polish enterprises closely connected to Soviet market. In fact, 60 percent of production volume was exported to the USSR. As a result of the collapse of the Soviet market and severe recession in Poland in 1990, sales were 76 percent lower than in 1989. Warynski was facing imminent bankruptcy.

Under such an extreme and imminent threat, a restructuring plan was prepared by one of the US leading consulting firms Booz, Allen and Hamilton Inc. The plan was approved by the World Bank Mission in Warsaw, which committed itself to help finance it. The plan is composed of three stages:

- *Stage One*. Technical transformation of the state-owned company into a joint stock company (and elimination of the workers self management council) is linked to the settlement of the firm's outstanding debt amounting to the equivalent of $8 million. The government-sponsored financial institution, the Agency of Industrial Development SA. offered a credit of that amount in exchange for debt to equity swap option when the company became privatized.

- *Stage Two*. Restructuring of the company involves a change in the production profile into manufacturing of parts and components of excavators and other earth-moving equipment, and subcontracting for major western manufacturers. At this stage, necessary modernization expenses for imported equipment will be covered by the World Bank credit. The restructuring program at this stage calls for deep decentralization and breaking the company into three independent but technologically linked companies specializing in distinctive product lines and together forming a holding structure.

- *Stage Three*. Privatization of these companies is achieved through the offering of shares to domestic and foreign investors (especially foreign buyers of Warynski's products).

Such a restructuring program calls for a dramatic change in the organizational culture of the company. These changes would include high work discipline and high quality regimes, decentralization and creation of an organizational climate conducive to the initiative and assuming of responsibility by middle management, streamlining of the company and reducing of employment by at least 7 percent, and new compensation systems linking compensation with productivity and allowing for more differentiated pay scales. The most sensitive issue of the restructuring program was the elimination of the pillar of the "populist industrial democracy" workers' council.

This restructuring program was a rather classic and standard one. It is hard to imagine that Mr. Kowalczyk, brilliant and a well-travelled engineer would not be able to come up with a similar program using his own staff and Polish management consultants. It may seem that Booz, Allen and Hamilton played no necessary role. However, it played a key role in Kowalczyk's cultural change strategy.

Foreign consultants legitimized the program vis à vis external financing agencies: The Polish Agency of Industrial Development and the World Bank. Without them, the restructuring program could not be financed so easily. Additionally, foreign consultants played a similar role of a legitimizing, unbiased and presumably objective arbiter vis a vis the workers of the company. Workers had to accept the hard to swallow medicine under the threat of massive layoffs.

In this way, foreign consultants certainly helped to start the process of transforming the organizational culture of the company. Similar strategies are common for "New Technocrats" turning around around post-communist enterprises, especially more technologically advanced ones and ones that export to the West. Technological and managerial expertise rubber stamped by foreign consultants gives "New Technocrats" the leverage necessary to trigger the long process of cultural change. Without such support, they risk being suspected of promoting their own interests, especially when eliminating the influence of self management and the workers' organizations.

Foreign crusaders are usually somehow emotionally motivated to get involved in Eastern Europe. As such, they should be distinguished from foreign "mercenaries." Mercenaries come to Central and Eastern Europe in search of a "quick buck" and profit from the funds offered to local governments and other institutions from different Western sources. "Mercenaries" are mainly highly paid management consultants and educators low-ranking in their own countries, who are in the business of selling standardized Western management techniques in simplified versions to Eastern and Central Europe. They do not take into consideration such things as local context, or cultural differences. They work on the assumption that "we know better".

Precisely because of this assumption "mercenaries" usually do not have any positive impact. Their activities might be exemplified by standardized mail-order distant learning packages poorly translated into Polish, Hungarian or Czech and offered to local students without explanation or $300,000 a piece "sectorial studies" prepared for a small fraction of the fee by some "whiz kid" assistant professor from the local university supplemented with some published in the West data and sold under more or less prestigious western name as "technical aid" to Poland, Hungary or Czech republic. When taken seriously, such studies might be of interest for Western competitors of the local industries in such industries as for example coal mining in Poland or oil industry in Russia. In Poland "mercenaries" are known under the nickname of the "Mariott brigade." In other countries, they have similar labels, ironically reflecting the predatory character of their activities.

Crusaders have different motivations and different types of sensitivity. Says David Chase, the Jewish-American millionaire and Holocaust survivor who is investing $20 million in a cable television network in Poland: "I have gotten some flack from my own people, especially the survivors, who say: 'Why do you want to go back to Poland? Is money that important to you?' It's not a question of money. I guess deep down I always wanted to go back. Deep down part of me will always be in Poland and never left Poland" (Wandycz 1991: 170).

George F. Varga who returned to Hungary after 30 years of exile to head the GE-Tungsram joint venture puts it in the following way: "Sometimes I am amazed. I left here as a kid. Now I am whisked around town by a chauffeur and call the ministers by their first names. This isn't a job, it's a crusade" (Tully 1990: 142). He admits that it takes "a bit of a missionary zeal to do this right,'' to mesh two cultures and to make that culture clash pay off.[7]

Joseph W. Karoly is a retired RCA executive who served three months in Poland as an IESC (International Executive Service Corps) volunteer, helping to restructure Polkolar, a color television tube manufacturer. He talks about his motivations in the following way:

> "Since leaving RCA, I had spent most of my days improving my golf handicap. But the offer from IESC—in effect, to be part of the economic revolution sweeping Eastern Europe was a challenge I could not resist. My wife Ruth was also a part of the package. Her project was to put together a manual about Poland to help familiarize future IESC volunteers and their spouses with the culture. (The fact that Ruth happens to be of Polish descent made her enthusiastic, but was of little practical value, she did not know a word of the language)" (Karoly 1990: 31).

Crusaders promote cultural change in three ways as exemplified by the activities of the three people presented above:

- They offer new types of products and services, and create new types of organizations;

- They manage cultural clashes;

- They provide and implement new tools and new management techniques.

David Chase has launched a Warsaw based wholly owned subsidiary, Chase International in Poland, run by his son-in-law. Chase International operates a cable TV network in the Gdansk region. Plans call for it to expand into a fiber optic telephone system. A commercial and investment bank, Solidarity Chase Bank, has been opened in Gdansk. Solidarity has given Chase its famous logo for 99 years in return for 51 percent of the equity. Chase puts up capital and expertise and has 49 percent of the equity. An insurance company is in the making. Chase believes in starting his companies from scratch in Poland, in order to avoid the consequences of the cultural heritage of communism. Says Chase: "If I were to make a deal with one of the privatizing banks I would have to take over the practices of the last 45 years. Rather than take a person and change his or her habits we would rather train a person from the ground up" (Wandycz 1991: 170). It is worth noting that all the businesses initiated by Chase are offering new products in Poland (including commercial and investment banking offering home mortgages unknown under communism and competitive commercial insurance). Chase's business in Poland are all somewhat related: cable television is regarded as a vehicle to promote the telephone network as well as banking and insurance services. Such an innovative business concept is being translated into a new type of organizational culture in the newly created organization.

Varga's mission is turning around Tungsram, the Hungarian state-owned electric bulb factory. A characteristic feature of his strategy is using as agents of change seasoned American executives required to show cultural sensitivity instead of GE's usual cockiness and arrogance (of the "young wolves"). Modern office equipment and flexible routines are supposed to eliminate bureaucrats and to introduce a new management style "by wandering around" gradually eliminating a barrier between workers and management inherited from communism. Says Varga: "The most difficult part is the human software. New ideas were discouraged and there was very little initiative and zero sense of ownership. Attitudes will be the most difficult to change. It's not a problem you just throw money at". (Greenhouse 1990). Varga believes that people should feel that Hungarian ways are still appreciated even when modified and changed according to Western standards. Respect shown to local culture should neutralize people's worries that Americans are trying to colonize. In short, Varga cushions cultural shock and manages it consciously. He tries to avoid too much change too quickly in order to make it easier to absorb.

It's worth noting that ABB turning around electrical turbines manufacturer Zamech in Poland, for example, is using a completely different strategy of accelerated change. ABB is using exclusively Polish managers assisted by experts from foreign subsidiaries and company headquarters in Zurich. Special attention is being paid to training and communication. Polish managers are supposed to meet the same performance standards as ABB managers all over the world (Taylor 1991).

Karoly was not a manager at Polkolor but as a change agent in the purest sense of the word: a volunteer helping the process of change. He was invited to help by the local management and his work was organized by management. He responded to the problems raised by management and management provided him with all the means to carry out his task. He worked on two projects: the restructuring of the organization in order to improve productivity and a quality control system and designing of a standard cost accounting system to calculate costs at different stages of the production process.

The organization was broken down into distinctive cost centers and a 14 page cost accounting manual was prepared and people were trained. Karoly made specific recommendations for quality and productivity improvement including the establishment of a preventive maintenance system and setting up a specific bonus program for meeting production quotas, improving quality etc. Recommendations were also made that targeted the elimination of the 20 percent over-employment rate inherited from the communist system.

Both reading Mr. Karoly's article in the *New York Times Magazine* and interviewing concerned people at Polkolor (my students in the executive MBA program), impressed upon the author how much could be accomplished in terms of cultural change by one person in such a short time. New behavioral patterns were set because Mr. Karoly had special credibility as a volunteer. He made an effort to find out what could be improved at the shop floor level. This form of consulting combined with the in-house training seems to be an especially effective way of promoting change in organizational cultures in the post-communist enterprises.

Western-type management education, training and management development certainly play an important role in promoting change in organizational cultures. Hundreds of independent initiatives in this field have emerged in Russia, Poland, Czech republic, Hungary and other countries. Some of them are assisted by Western aid funds and by respectable Western educational institutions.[7] Successful, high quality western-style management education institutions are the most likely to emerge in these countries, where western-style management education and research had already begun under communism in the '70s and where local management educators can play the role of linking pin between "foreign crusaders" and the local business community. Poland, Hungary, Estonia, Russia and Ukraine are on the top of the list of such countries.

For example in Hungary, the International Management Center was created. It offers a ten month MBA Program called The Young Manager Program (Magala ed. 1991: Appendix XXIII) and executive courses that last from two days to two weeks. IMC is supported by York University in Canada, INSEAD, IMD, and the University of Pittsburgh. The University of Pittsburgh is IMC's lead academic partner and provides extensive support for curriculum development and local faculty development. It has to be remembered, however, that the local Hungarian faculty of the IMC was trained in the '70s by Karl Marx University, which started western management education as well as faculty development in the US and in Western Europe relatively early. The first IMC dean Dan Fogel was "borrowed" from the University of Pittsburgh.[8] In 1991, Fogel and the University of Pittsburgh created a similar western management training and development institution in Czechoslovakia.

In Poland in 1989, the International Business School was created, offering a full-fledged four semester American-type executive MBA program (Magala ed. 1991: Appendix XX). IBS (mentioned several times in case descriptions presented above) is an off-spring of the Warsaw University School of Management created in 1972 and offering western-style management education on an undergraduate level. In the '70s and '80s several professors of the School were trained in the US and in Western Europe.

IBS is affiliated Warsaw University and offers its postgraduate degree. The program is bilingual in Polish and English. Courses are taught partially by Polish professors with extensive training and experience in the US and Western Europe and partially by foreign professors from Denmark (Copenhagen School of Management), the UK (Strathclyde University, London Business School, Oxford) and other western countries. The foreign professors' salaries are financed from funds allocated by Western governments for aid to Poland. IBS also offers such programs as short management development courses, in-house training, consulting services, and executive seminars.[9]

Without abandoning IBS, the same group of management educators started the International Postgraduate Management Center at Warsaw University in 1990. It offers joint degree MBA programs with Western partners. Three such programs are being run.

The MBA for Eastern Europe is organized with the Rotterdam School of Management (Erasmus University). The program gives a Rotterdam MBA degree and is run by three institutions in Eastern Europe: Warsaw University, Budapest University of Economics (Hungary), and Prague School of Economics (Czechoslovakia). Participants are recruited from these three countries.

The second MBA program is jointly run with the University of Illinois at Urbana Champaign. The program gives a joint degree. The University of Illinois provides assistance in curriculum and local faculty development and provides around 50 percent of the faculty.

A special program in entrepreneurship is run by Babson College in Massachusetts. This program offers seminars for entrepreneurs starting and developing small businesses.

All these programs are partially financed by the participants, partially by the Polish government and partially by different public and private western sources such as: a Dutch government grant, the US Information Agency, the Mellon Foundation, the Ford Foundation etc.[10]

Similar initiatives started in Russia as early as 1989. The Higher Commercial Management School in Moscow, connected with the Russian Ministry of Foreign Economic Relations, has opened 20 regional centers across Russia.

In Kiev, Ukraine BIZNEX, a business school for managers specializing in international trade was opened in 1989. Swiss IMD signed an agreement with Ukrainian Academy of Sciences to set up a management school offering full fledged 1 year executive MBA program.[12]

In Talinn, the private Estonian Business School was created in 1989. It offers a wide range of management development courses. It must be remembered, however, that in Estonia, management development centers using a western approach and western techniques (cases, games) have existed since the early '70s. The Management Development Center of the Ministry of Light Industry is a good example of such institution.[13]

It is too early for surveys, comparisons and general conclusions. One comment must be made. Nearly all the management education and development programs emerging in Central and Eastern Europe under the influence of the West and often assisted and financed from western sources focus on hard aspects of management: accounting, finance, marketing, and production management. Transformational leadership is not included among the skills, which seems the most needed both to the local people and to the western advisers. Such an approach might create some problems in promotion and acceleration of the change of culture on the enterprise level.

7

Lessons for Western Managers

Scenarios for the Future

The economic potential of Central and Eastern Europe seems undeniable, especially when compared with Third World countries. A number of factors substantiate this statement:

- Markets are large and per capita incomes, while low by Western European standards, are still much higher than in the third world and are often supplemented by unregistered economic activities (shadow economy), or by direct financial transfers from abroad.

- The educational level is high and the work force, although undisciplined and visibly lacking quality standards, can certainly handle modern technology and equipment.

- Large groups of well-educated engineers can competently manage modern production facilities and generate innovation within the framework of often highly developed R&D institutions (though these are seldom linked with the production processes).

- There are a few relatively highly developed industries and a handful of enterprises are relatively close to western standards in each country in the region. Example include Hungarian agriculture, the Russian and Czech armament industries, the Polish pharmaceutical and garment industries, and the Bulgarian fruit, vegetable and wine industries.

- A strong industrial tradition, dating from beginning of the century is still present in some countries and some industries in the area. Some examples of this can be seen in the mechanical and automotive industries in Czechoslovakia, the electrical industry in Hungary and the textile industry in Poland.

- High expectations and high consumption aspirations provide for high motivation and induce entrepreneurship.

- The transformation of Central and Eastern Europe has high visibility, and is able to mobilize different forms of humanitarian aid, financial help, and economic and technical assistance provided by western governments, supra-national organizations (such as the EEC) and financial institutions (such as the IMF or the World Bank).

Looking at the bright side of the picture, one might easily come to the conclusion that post-communist countries have a better starting point for accelerated development than other newly industrialized countries, such as South Korea or Taiwan had in the early 1960s. In light of their first years of experience in the European post-communist countries, such a statement clearly appears to be overly optimistic. They were not able to overcome recession and start economic growth. In 1992, only Hungary and Poland seemed to be approaching the end of recession and ready to promote export-led growth (Gabrish et al. 1992). Certainly some delay can be attributed to political turbulence of systemic transition, but a visible lack of any development vision and policy needs an explanation. Such explanation is closely related to the transition strategies adopted by the post-communist governments.

Transition strategy seems to be a key factor influencing growth perspectives of the post-communist countries. The choice of such strategy is a political act of the government. In other words, in the absence of a fully developed private sector, capital markets, banking system, and distribution channels, and where economic agents lack experience and expertise relative to the modern market economy, the government has to take a leadership role in shaping future economic development. East Asian governments, such as the Korean or Taiwanese, were extremely successful in promoting export-led growth of their countries. They consciously distorted prices (through government subsidies) in order to enhance investment and trade, and gradually to nurture world competitors in selected areas. Nationalized banks directed low-cost credit (often at negative real interest rates) toward industries that had shown high growth potential in other industrializing nations. Export subsidies, trade barriers, strong incentives pushing local enterprises toward global competition (high government decided export targets) and high selectivity in approving investment by foreign firms completed the list of economic development measures.

Cultural factors did not play a decisive role in the successful late industrialization of such countries as Korea or Taiwan. Consistent economic policies of the governments played a key role:

"The Taiwanese and South Korean states only became developmental pragmatically. Once they began not just to subsidize business but to impose performance standards on it (not least of all export targets), then growth increased. As growth increased, the state became more committed to economic development and allocated more resources to it, which increased development further. Thus the state transformed the process of economic development and, in turn, was transformed by it.'' (Amsden 1991: 286)

Some authors believe that a similar approach should be adopted by post-communist governments in Central and Eastern Europe (Amsden 1990).

Such a scenario, however, seems rather unlikely in the immediate future for most countries of the region. Implementation of the Asian plan of development requires a strong, politically stable government able to generate an ambitious vision and to work consistently toward realization of this vision over long periods of time. It also requires a stable and high-quality civil service able to carry out a development mission in a consistent way. Government decision makers should be knowledgeable of global competition conditions and market economy mechanisms and institutions. They should also know how to use direct government intervention when necessary, without compromising the market. Considerations of market competition should be balanced against economies of scale and global competition requirements in order to decide how many firms should operate in any given industry and to what extent foreign competition should be allowed. In order to enforce an Asian model of the late industrialization policy, the government must channel economic surplus resulting from productivity increases and a low standard of living into ''preferred'' sectors and enterprises nurtured as future global competitors (Amsden 1990).

Implementation of such a development policy also requires high negotiation skills. These skills are especially important in dealings with powerful international financial institutions such as the IMF. The primary interest of these institutions is to secure the financial solvency of debtor countries. This is achieved through such measures as budgetary austerity, convertibility of the currency, deregulation of prices, and low tariff barriers. In the process of complex negotiations, these objectives and these economic policy measures have to be reconciled with the country's economic development policies. The formulation and implementation of these policies, as well as negotiating the support of powerful international and foreign partners, is a prime responsibility of the government and its civil service.

Only Hungary seems to have a civil service approaching these requirements. But the Hungarian government, although more stable due to a more developed democratic multi-party system, does not seem to have an

Asian vision, nor to be able and willing to implement one. The Asian model of development is too close to socialist industrialization practiced for decades by the communist governments of the region, and which finally led to economic disaster. Such experiences makes it difficult to accept that a re-industrialization drive is needed and that, once again, the government has to play the role of chief architect of structural change. This time, such a program has to be inspired by global competition requirements. A rather primitive and naive vision of the market economy, espoused by the post-communist political leaders, makes it difficult for them to understand that a strong leadership role by the government (in order to promote growth and structural change) can remain in perfect harmony with the market mechanisms and private ownership. Post-communist elites are deeply committed to ''Reaganomics'' and ''Thatcherism.'' Economic progress in these countries depends on how soon they discover ''Asian tigers,'' Spanish industrial policy, the unprecedented Finnish economic miracle, and other models of successful economic policies practiced by countries trying to ''catch up'' with the core economies.

Textbook free-market solutions are naturally much easier to accept for the emerging elite in Central and Eastern Europe who neurotically reject all forms of government intervention, all trade barriers, and all forms of state ownership. Such tendencies are reinforced by foreign advisors to post-communist governments in the region who develop two-stage economic programs: a difficult and stormy accelerated transition through ''shock treatment'' therapy, followed by a self-regulating market economy that automatically provides for economic growth and prosperity. Such visions are also sold to the populations of the regions in political campaigns. Standard items on such agenda include:

- Elimination of the budget deficit and easy credit policies in order to eliminate shortages and halt inflation

- Elimination of all the subsidies and complete liberalization of prices in order to establish a demand and supply-driven price determination mechanism

- Establishment of free trade with the West by creating a convertible currency and the elimination of all restrictions on international trade, allowing post-communist economies to ''import'' the world price structure

- Rapid de-monopolization by dismantling the large state-owned enterprises and economic organizations (such as unions of enterprises which represent most enterprises of a given group of products)

- Accelerated privatization involving the whole state sector (Sachs & Lipton 1990: 55)

- Dismantling the communist welfare state

Such a credo of post-communist reformers seems far from the Asian Plan and other successful economic development policies. Shock treatment therapy, as a starting point for transition seems, at least psychologically, inevitable in all the post-communist countries except for Hungary. Hungary was the only country which started a transition toward a market economy under communism in the late '60s. It was able to maintain these policies until 1989, in spite of all the political pressure from ''big brother'' and his faithful disciples. Because of this, the collapse of communism in Hungary did not bring the dramatic changes of economic policies, only acceleration and final liberation from political and ideological constraints. Even Hungary, however, does not seem to have a clear vision of a modern market economy.

In the case all other socialist countries, shock therapy is justified economically by strong inflationary pressures and a completely unrealistic price structure inherited from communism. The key question remains— what will happen after shock therapy, and how soon? For countries which have adopted shock therapy (Poland in 1990, Czechoslovakia in 1991 and partially Russia in 1992), three types of scenarios can be developed: a violent switch, a late switch, and an early switch.

A violent switch scenario is a result of too much shock therapy treatment, which results in the deepening of the recession (massive bankruptcies of viable enterprises), as well as rapidly growing unemployment, which results form constantly falling domestic demand, overly expensive credit, unfair foreign competition on the domestic market and the inability to sell on foreign markets. In the early post-communist countries, taxes from state-owned enterprises contribute over 80 percent of the total tax revenues. When these state-owned enterprises become unable to pay taxes, social services have to be drastically cut.

As a result of too much shock therapy, demand-driven inflation, typical for communist economies, gives way to the new type of cost-driven inflation. This cost-driven inflation results from such thing as low volumes, low productivity, the high cost of credit, low production volumes inhibiting economies of scale, and the inability to invest in modernization of technological processes. Restrictive monetary policies geared to counter demand-driven inflation, if applied for too long, can create recession and cost-driven inflation.

Such a situation, combined with the lack of a convincing anti-recession strategy is very likely to trigger massive popular dissatisfaction.

This was the case in Poland in late 1991 and early 1992. In the Polish parliamentary elections of October 1991, only slightly over 40 percent of the voters showed up at the polls and post-communist parties got nearly 20 percent of the vote. Also the extreme right parties were quite successful and scored close to 20 percent.[1]

If such a final warning is not heard and shock therapy is continued without serious qualitative adjustments, the chances of a late switch fade away, and a violent switch becomes the only logical consequence of the previous events. One might ask what the reasons are for the continuation of such policies in deep recession.

Shock treatment becomes a part of the political ideology for some of the new emerging and influential political forces, who want to be visibly anti-communist and differentiate themselves as much as possible from the previous (communist) economic policies. Reaganomics and Thatcherism are advertised as ideals of economic policies. All opinions advocating more state intervention, at least during the transition period, are easy to attack and to discredit on purely emotional grounds as having a socialist or communist flavor.

Eastern European politics can be very emotional, if not hysterical. Shock treatment is also simple, dramatic, and easy to grasp for the mass media. It has all the characteristics of a magic recipe facilitating emotional fixation—while the technical details of flexible, precise, and meticulous economic policy of the Asian type are dull, difficult to explain, and do not have emotional appeal.

Shock treatment is also fully backed by the IMF and other international financial institutions interested in monetary and fiscal discipline, including austerity programs as well as the country's ability to repay foreign debts. International business is also visibly interested in a quick and complete opening of the markets and elimination of subsidies. Even in mass employment industries such as textiles, unshielded Eastern European pretenders can not immediately compete against the productivity of western enterprises. The accelerated collapse of the post-communist enterprises means the elimination of potential competitors, opening of the large markets and eventually, an opportunity to acquire valuable assets at a low price.

If shock treatment is continued beyond the limits of social and political tolerance, a violent switch seems inevitable. Two possible scenarios of such policy shift can be envisioned.

Under the first scenario, shock treatment is simply canceled and the government gives in to the populist pressure. It means a return to the communist policies of printing ''empty money'' to satisfy all the demands, and to the government subsidizing non-viable enterprises without a comprehensive plan to phase them out. Such economic policies can easily materialize under the political banner of the xenophobic, anti-western extreme right. Regardless of the political label, such economic policies cancel all the positive effects of the early stages of shock treatment such as the elimination of shortages and convertibility of the currency, and antagonize western partners and investors. In practice, it means that the whole transition process is thrown into jeopardy.

The second scenario, a violent switch, provides for the forceful elimination of political forces opposing the continuation of the shock treatment, suppression of the newly born democracy, and imposition of an authoritarian form of the government. Such a change complicates relations with western democracies, and carries the risk of the continuation of shock treatment policies without any alternative. It means a permanent depression with all the economic, social and political consequences.

A late switch implicates radical, but rationally controlled economic policy changes involving:

- Comprehensive tax reform providing for stable and secure budget income base (Taking into consideration the disarray of public administration, a taxation system has to be extremely simple and easy to enforce.)

- Tolerance of controlled budget deficits and restoration of some subsidies aimed at softening the social consequences of the transition (as for example housing subsidies), or to promote economic growth and the expansion of selected groups of enterprises (e.g., export subsidies, local development subsidies)

- An anti-inflationary program based simultaneously on money supply and cost reduction policies

- A program to resolve the enterprise's indebtness,

- Controlling the growth of unemployment both on a national and regional level

- Some forms of price control, adopted selectively (e.g., on energy and basic raw materials)

- Selective trade barriers introduced in order to provide local industries with some protection against foreign competition

- Restrictions on de-monopolization policies, imposed selectively in order to create globally competitive economic entities

- Privatization of state-owned enterprises following restructuring, strong support (e.g., credit and tax incentives) of private enterprises and job creation in small businesses

- A comprehensive plan of phasing out non-viable enterprises, restructuring all key industries and raising them gradually to the international competition requirements

- A plan for attracting maximum foreign investment

An early switch can be qualified as softer than a late switch because of the less dramatic character of policy change. Shock treatment policies are not yet set in stone, and negative (recessionary) results have not yet accumulated. In such a situation, a swift policy change permits taking full advantage of the positive results of the shock treatment and prevents too deep a recession. The policy changes are the same as in the case of a late switch but because they are introduced earlier, they are softer on the economy. They allow more gradual phasing in. For example, different forms of export subsidies can be tested in different sectors of the economy. Countries which are starting the transition process (mainly ex-Soviet states) are the prime candidates for such a rational transition path, following the phases indicated in the introduction: political, early marketization, inflation control, institutions building, anti-recession, and growth.

Both an early and a late switch contain the positive effects of a gradual approach. A violent switch carries the risk of blind continuation of shock therapy. It also carries the risk of the forceful creation of some form of a collectivist or rather populist economic and political system (radically opposed to an open, capitalist, market regulated economy) backed with the leftist or rightist ideology. Ideological flavor is not important; in both cases the positive results of shock treatment—paid for with considerable social cost—are likely to be wasted.

A gradual transition strategy could be tested only in Hungary, because of the uniqueness of the Hungarian experiences under communism. It will probably produce more aggressive growth and structural policies of the government, which will in turn attract more foreign capital and stimulate more growth. The probability of such an optimistic scenario remains relatively high, since the gradual transition approach provides for political stability, enabling the consistent continuation of the transformation process. It provides room to accommodate political pressures both to accelerate and to slow down within a democratic framework. A tense, overambitious shock treatment program does not leave such a possibility, and remains politically vulnerable.

Rumania, Bulgaria, Yugoslavia, Albania, and all the ex-USSR republics did not really start their transition toward a market economy until
1992. All these countries have some common characteristics:

- Highly oppressive communist regimes which, in the past, successfully prevented the formation of non-communist political elite

- Market economy traditions that are nonexistent or completely
forgotten

- High potential for violent conflict between ethnic groups

- Hard-line communist *nomenklatura* (under a different label) that remains influential in the civil service, in local authorities, and in the
army and the police

- Absence of realistic transition programs with sufficient political
backing

Transition programs in these countries cannot really start before conflicts are resolved either through negotiations, limited conflict as occurred
until 1992 between the slavic ex-USSR republics (Russia, Ukraine, Be-
lorussia), or through violent civil war as in Yugoslavia or parts of the ex-
USSR. In the former Soviet republics—and especially in Russia—the
aborted military coup attempt in August 1991 allowed the conflict to be
resolved by eliminating communist hard liners from influential positions,
and, allowing the formation of a political platform for negotiating and
reaching compromise on a transition program. As a result, in November
1992, the Russian parliament voted to rescind prices and wages controls
which were to have taken effect in December 1991, and were then post-
poned until January 1992. A similar move in 1989 by the last Polish communist government triggered hyper-inflation, which provided the starting
point for a shock treatment program. Similar transition paths can be en-
visaged for other post-communist countries which have not yet started
their journeys toward a market economy.

Viable Strategies of Western Enterprises

According to Rumelt (1988), a viable enterprise strategy should meet
the following criteria: consistency, consonance, advantage and feasibility
(Rumelt 1988, 51). This list can be applied to the strategies of western
enterprises operating in the post-communist countries.

Consistency requirement means that strategy used in Eastern and Central Europe should be consistent with the firm's overall strategy. It should help to accomplish general strategic objectives. Going to post-communist countries for the sake of it, or in the hope of discovering some unknown opportunities or designing a special unrelated strategy for such a venture might be a very costly mistake. As the "Special Report" on Eastern Europe published by *Mergers & Acquisitions* puts it: "The company must determine where and how Eastern Europe fits into its plan to compete strongly on an international basis".[2]

Let us examine some basic, generic strategic goals which might be pursued in Eastern and Central Europe:

- "Maintain your presence, and prepare a head-start position for the penetration of larger market."

- "Reduce your costs through the use of local resources."

- "Take advantage of the uniqueness of your location."

Preparation for a larger market strategy can be inspired by four future scenarios that are not mutually exclusive:

1. Closer association of Central Europe with the EEC, and the eventual membership of some countries

2. Formation of regional market(s) in Central and Eastern Europe

3. Changes in life-styles and consumption patterns

4. Ending the recession in Eastern and Central Europe, thereby bringing increased investment and consumer spending

All four scenarios will probably materialize some day. For the time being, however, nobody dares to guess when. The western entrants' dilemma is how to secure the heard-start advantage and not to lose money while waiting. Here are a few clues:

Tapping the existing hard currency reserves in post-communist countries (both in the official and second economy circuits) can help to cover operating expenses and even generate modest profits. Poland, with its huge hard currency reserves in private hands, is obviously the best place to practice this approach. It is being practiced there by the Japanese and recently, also by Korean car and consumer electronics manufacturers. The same approach can also be practiced to a different extent in other countries.

Firms can offer expertise and services, which are not available in Central and Eastern Europe to cover operating expenses while waiting for market opportunities. For example, Citibank had a representative office in Warsaw until the end of 1991, although it hesitated to open a branch office. In the meantime to cover expenses, the bank provided consulting and financial services to its Western clients operating in Poland. Large auditing firms operating in central and Eastern Europe take similar approach.

Production capabilities can be very carefully built to serve a fraction of the potential market at the beginning, and to be expanded when the market has been tested and a profit repatriation mechanism put in place. This an approach has been taken by Coca-Cola in Poland, McDonald's in Russia, and by ComputerLand and MicroAge stores in Moscow. Such an approach is much easier to take in Poland, Hungary, and Czech republic, where some degree of convertibility of the currency exists. When this is not possible, barter agreements or a decision to re-invest all the profits are the alternatives. Barter agreements however, can only be considered temporary solutions. Business concepts build around barter are too vulnerable to such changes as the stabilization plan introduced in Poland in 1990. The Elfur case discussed in Chapter 4 illustrates this argument.

Reducing cost through the use of local resources requires the use of unskilled and skilled labor as well as brain power, natural resources and existing facilities. The Sovmav case presented in Chapter 2 illustrates the use of cheap Soviet unskilled labor. It must be remembered, however, that highly skilled labor and creative talents in science, technology, art, and liberal professions are in Eastern and Central Europe cheaper, relatively speaking, than unskilled labor. This is due to relatively good educational systems and low differentiation of wages with much more of bargaining power on the side of blue collar workers. Taking into consideration complicated labor relations, militant trade unions, and the low work ethic of blue collar workers, using Eastern and Central European skills and brain power makes more sense for western enterprises.

Using natural resources at relatively low cost presents another set of opportunities. Western enterprises can get access to such cheap resources in exchange for badly needed capital investment and technology. Russian oil deals exemplify this approach the best. The experiences of Occidental Petroleum or Chevron clearly indicate, however, that such big deals are difficult to negotiate and implement. Russians are suspicious of foreigners trying to take advantage of them.

Some industrial enterprises in Central and Eastern Europe do have valuable facilities requiring modernization, which western partners can use. ABB's acquisitions in Poland or Volkswagen's big deal with the Czech Skoda, involving over $6.6 billion, are examples of the use of such opportunities by western investors. An American contractor who built in the 70-ties a meat processing factory designated for the US market is now negotiating a "buy-back" deal.

In all three cases, major manufacturers position themselves in Eastern Europe in order to increase market penetration and to lower costs by using existing facilities, brand names, and an existing client base. The move is as good as its suitability to the overall strategy of the firm.

Taking advantage of the uniqueness of the location requires participation in servicing the movement of people, goods, money, information, skills, and ideas mainly between Eastern and Western Europe. The parts of the same continent have been separated by cold war politics; now they come together again. Such an increased intensity of movement requires new providers of related services. It is a well-known fact that Eastern and Central Europe do not have such providers and is unable to develop them quickly.

Opportunities in hotels, transportation, construction of highways, ports and airports, and modernization of railways are well known and often taken advantage of by such businesses as hotel chains (Mariott, Holiday Inn, Hilton, Novotel, CBC France, to name the few), builders and contractors (Ilbau), and transportation firms (Swedish Railways, which is modernizing the Polish railway system).

Similar opportunities do exist in the area of the movement of information. This area was purposefully neglected by the communist regimes, which restrict access to information. Eastern European telephones are notorious. US West is helping to modernize telephone systems in Czech republic and Spanish Telefonica and French Alcatel are working in Poland. But even in these two countries, there is still room for many more western suppliers and providers of services. Developing financial services, banks, stock exchanges, and insurance industry, modern taxation systems as well as hotels, airlines, and railway systems will require computer networks. The process of designing and implementing such systems has hardly begun. For example, French Bull is helping to computerize the Polish taxation system and adjust it to a major tax reform (individual income tax).

Post-communist countries are also facing privatization of their media. For example in Hungary, not even one daily newspaper is in Hungarian hands. In 1990 and 1991 Hungary became a battleground for two western press magnates: the late Robert Maxwell, and Rupert Murdoch. The same two giants joined the German firm Springer in the fight for the East German press market. Cable television and video markets are likely to become the next attractive targets for western entrepreneurs. It is already happening. For example, the American David Chase is starting a cable television network in Poland. Private television stations are also coming along, but they seem less attractive at the earlier stages of transition to the market economy because of the huge initial investment needed and the relatively low price of TV advertising.

Transfer of knowledge and skills also offers an attractive business opportunity for consulting and accounting firms, as well as educational institutions such as business schools and management training centers. For the time being, big accounting firms such as Ernst & Young, Arthur Andersen, and Price Waterhouse are leading the way to having offices in Russia, Hungary, and Poland.

Strategies related to the uniqueness of location have one common characteristic distinctive from the two other categories discussed above. They are often tied to aid offered to Eastern European governments by western governments or the EEC, and take the form of government contracts. Additionally, business opportunities result from the governments releasing control over previously strict government monopolies of information. Few governments can resist the temptation to maintain some degree of control over the media. The issue is highly political, as is the issue of big government contracts financed by foreign grants. This political undertone makes the difference.

As Rumelt points out, consonance of the strategy should be understood as the way in which business relates to its environment (Rumelt 1988, 52). When entering post-communist countries, western companies bet on change and are ready to assume the role of change agents. This means that passive adaptation to the existing environment, which is turbulent, unstable, and even unpredictable in the short run, is not advisable. The western entrant formulating and applying his strategy in Eastern and Central Europe has to answer a fundamental question: what kind of change are we going to promote? Using the broadest possible analytical categories, three types of change can be identified.

Technological change means not only the use of new production techniques, including equipment, technology and production management, but also putting in place new functional systems in such areas as distribution, banking, insurance, hospitality (hotels, restaurants), and logistics (transportation, storage). Such a broad understanding of technology helps the western firm grasp the hard aspect of the civilization gap between East and West.

Social and cultural change means not only new life-styles and consumption patterns, but also new work cultures and management styles. It has to do with both the inside and outside of the organization.

Economic change implies new market structures, and new patterns and mechanisms of financing economic activity and promoting economic growth.

Western entrants preparing strategies for Central and Eastern Europe have to be reasonably sure that the existing environment will accept the changes they are promoting.

The first group of factors to examine from this angle is the legal framework. Legal regulation of such things as foreign investment, property rights (especially real estate), intellectual property, monopolistic practices, banking, insurance, currency, and labor have to be carefully analyzed from the point of view of the strategy of the western entrant. This is obvious—and almost everybody does it better or worse. Proper assessment of the dynamics of the legal system is less obvious, but probably even more important. Eastern and Central Europe will remain politically unstable and turbulent for some time. It means that changes in the legal system are likely. Proper anticipation of such changes can strongly influence the strategy of a western company (Hertzfeld 1991, 82, 86).

Differences in legal culture and understanding of the law should be also taken into consideration. For example in Russia the law is (and for a long time will be) understood as an instrument of the ruling elites (sometimes even local elites). The 1991 cancellation of 100-ruble bills is good example of this way of understanding the law. Another example is even more striking. In 1987, the local authorities of Krementchug, a small town, forbade taking money out of town as cash, and enforced this rule with blockades and police searches. (Alimov 1987). In more "westernized" post-communist countries, something like this is much less likely to happen. But even in Hungary, a sale of a hotel chain to a Swedish investor was cancelled because the price was too low. For the same reason (officially), the Warsaw city council cancelled the sale of an office building to the Jewish Nissenbaum Foundation in 1990.

Political aspects of the strategy also merit attention. For a long time in Eastern Europe, there will still be "right" and "wrong" firms, and "right" and "wrong" people. Western enterprises operating in this region have to take that into consideration. The Labels different people and organizations wear, such as "communist," "catholic," "populist," and "self-management supporter," often seem more important than what they actually do. The selection of partners has to be consonant with the dominant political mood. The same rule applies to the rhetoric promoting the venture. The right key words—once again consonant with the dominant political mood—have to be chosen. Soviet *perestroika,* and to an even greater extent, the Russian revolution of 1992 is promoting such key words as "market economy," "collective property," "satisfaction of consumers' needs," "clean environment," and "opening." At the same time in Poland, the key words would be: "competition," "free market," "opening," and "becoming Europe again."

The principle of consonance of strategy also applies to the attitudes, opinions, motivations, and behavioral patterns of the people as consumers (or users) of the products and services provided by the company.

The issue of "exotic" Eastern and Central European consumers seems to be blown out of proportion. The ability to absorb foreign products seems to be much more a question of disposable income than anything else. Western goods and western life-styles have a special appeal for consumers in that part of the world. The unprecedented speed of the dissemination of VCRs and personal computers in such countries as Poland and Hungary seems to be the best proof of this. Mass media, and especially television, are becoming rapidly westernized—and, probably more precisely, Americanized. They play an important role in the promotion of new consumption patterns. Hard currency shops have played this role for a long time. In countries which were more open under communism, like Poland and Hungary, travel abroad and direct contact were even more important. A rapidly growing middle class quickly develops completely westernized tastes and life-styles. The younger generation wears the same type of clothes, listens to the same music, and watches the same TV shows.

Market potential results mainly from the amount of disposable income in different categories of consumers. In most cases, western goods are more expensive in Eastern Europe than in western countries, especially in the US. This is due to the inefficiency of distribution networks. Cheap mass distribution can considerably increase market potential.

In the case of capital goods, insular applications (isolated, without adequate support of interface industries: suppliers, subcontractors, buyers, wholesellers, retailers) of imported modern western technology were quite popular in the '70s. Communist leaders tried to modernize their economies through imports of technology and equipment. The results of such policies clearly confirm that Eastern European engineers, technicians, and workers can handle modern technology. The problem lies in the total "value chain" and the compatibility of the western production system with the systems of suppliers and users. Modern equipment requires standardized, timely input (materials, components, sometimes even air), transportation, storage and logistics in general. A modern product requires sophisticated users using appropriate equipment. Such compatible supplier and user structures often do not exist in Central and Eastern Europe. Building them might be very costly.

The same requirement of compatible structures in the environment also applies to consumer goods and services. For example, American Express' idea of installing automatic teller machines in Moscow in 1991 seems premature, considering the general underdevelopment of banking services and client reluctance to use them. Many consumer durables cannot be sold in larger quantities without consumer credit systems. The construction of American-type individual houses in larger numbers is not possible without a mortgage credit system. Many business activities are not possible without suitable (by western standards) insurance against business risk, such as interruption of business. Such compatible structures conditioning consonance of the business strategy can be technical, financial, or organizational. They have to be studied before the implementation of the strategy starts. Afterwards is too late. It may also be too late for managers who are accustomed to taking too many things for granted. That is why many experts advise Western companies operating in Central and Eastern Europe to use a vertical integration strategy. This strategy is shaped after McDonald's strategy in the Russia. McDonald's has its own sources of supply, processing, and storage, enabling it to control its own environment and to secure a sufficient degree of compatibility (Hertzfeld 1991). It is a very costly strategy, however, and can be only considered as temporary for some bigger players. It is also a copy of a strategy of a typical communist enterprise, maximizing its autonomy and self-sufficiency. Promoting suitable changes in the environment and bringing in western partners who might transform it, is a more ambitious alternative to the vertical integration strategy. But it is also much more difficult, because it requires the harmonious cooperation of different western enterprises in a turbulent foreign environment.

A viable strategy should provide for the creation and maintenance of a competitive advantage in the selected area of activity (Rumelt 1988, 51). Applied to the western company entering the post-communist environment, it means in most cases, achieving economies of experience—the transfer to the new environment of the skills, technologies, business philosophies, structures and systems that provide for the company's competitive advantage in the global or international arena. The same notion of a competitive advantage should be applied to the Eastern or Central European subsidiary as it is to the company as a whole. Obviously, being competitive in a local environment is not an advisable strategy for a serious western entrant.

ABB's approach to restructuring Zamech in Poland illustrates this argument perfectly. ABB's competitive advantage results from its unique combination of global orientation and global economies of scale, personalized by leaders in over 50 business areas who are responsible for groups of products worldwide, and a local orientation enforced by country managers and presidents of local companies. Such a structure enables it to share expertise, skills, engineering and managerial talents worldwide, without losing strong ties to its local customer base. The same logic was applied to ABB's Polish operation. It was reorganized into three discrete profit centers. A core group of local managers was identified as change agents, and given well-defined responsibilities, ambitious tasks, clear performance indicators, and high standards. At the same time, the transfer of management expertise and skills to the Polish subsidiary was assured (Taylor 1991).

Similarly, GE acquired the Hungarian firm Tungsram, in order to become competitive on the European market in general, especially the EEC market. The Hungarian acquisition resulted then, from the GE's global strategy and required quickly upgrading it to Western productivity standards (Greenhouse 1990).

Putting it in more general terms, at least the following conditions have to be met in order to extend to a post-communist country the same competitive advantage a company enjoys in broader western markets.

First of all, local managers must be carefully selected to turn around a Eastern or Central European wholly-owned or co-owned subsidiary. This should enable the company to maintain its national character and its management, and at the same time make it fully receptive to western management and the philosophy of the western parent company. Such managers or potential managers (in the most cases engineers) do exist in the post-communist world, although they may need a lot of additional training in business English, accounting, finance, and marketing and acculturation. Using them, and giving them responsibilities, seems to be a much better solution than to have Eastern European subsidiaries run by costly expatriates who will be quickly lost in local conditions. If company policy requires insiders to hold key positions in a major foreign subsidiary, at least people speaking the language and able to understand the local culture should be selected. This is the case with GE, where Varga runs GE's Hungarian operation.

The transfer of technology and shop-floor level production management seems to be the next condition for establishing and maintaining a competitive advantage. It usually requires considerable capital investment, not only in actual manufacturing, but quite often in creating a compatible infrastructure (transportation, storage, maintenance etc.) GE's operation in Hungary is a good example of such a basic transfer. GE engineers adjusted glass making temperatures, bulb thickness and pressure inside the bulbs as well as installed new quality control equipment (Greenhouse 1990).

Establishing an information system linking the Eastern European subsidiary with other parts of a multinational or global company seems to be the next precondition to achieving a competitive advantage. The link can be purely physical, as is the case of satellite communication between ABB's headquarters in Zurich and its Polish subsidiary. This type of link is especially important in a country where telephones do not work.

Or, it can be a social link, preventing the marginalization of the Eastern European "poor cousins" by getting them involved in the process of exchanging ideas, sharing experiences, and upgrading skills across national borders.

Establishing information links also requires the most basic thing: teaching people "business English." A marginalized Eastern European subsidiary can simply remain a source of problems and a cost center.

Adequate financing of a radical restructuring process and development of the Eastern or Central European subsidiary is also an important condition for creating and maintaining a competitive advantage. There are two reasons why this is especially important. First, there is a scarcity of capital in Eastern Europe. This is often aggravated during the transition period by restrictive monetary policies and high interest rates. Secondly, it is widely recognized that countries in the region are unable to increase productivity to western standards without considerable investment in modern equipment. For example, GE intends to spend over $60 million to upgrade the Tugsram factory in Hungary (Greenhouse 1990). To finance such an investment effort, GE can use its own powerful financial subsidiary GE Financial Services. This subsidiary holds over $91 billion in assets and produces 24 percent of the parent company's profits. Such financing is certainly abundant and cheap by Eastern and Central European standards (Fogel & Friedman 1990). Also European Bank of Reconstruction and Development founded in London to serve Central and Eastern Europe offers financing available to Western firms entering these markets.

All Eastern and Central European enterprises are seriously overstaffed—including the ones being overtaken by western companies. For example, GE's 18,000 lighting workers produce more than $2 billion worth of products, while Tugsram's work force (which is the same size) turns out only $300 million. Such over-employment inhibits a competitive advantage and has to be eliminated. It is not easy, considering rising unemployment and the militant trade unions in post-communist countries.

A competitive advantage requires a competitive product world-wide. A product of outdated design and technology, which is only competitive in Eastern and Central Europe, does not provide a large or stable enough market base to sustain development of a major organization. The inevitable opening of Eastern and Central European markets and the convertibility (at least internal convertibility) of the currency waiting down the transition road will inevitably eliminate outdated local products. Only a product which can be sold simultaneously on local and international markets can provide for a real and stable competitive advantage.

GE found such a product in Tungsram's light bulbs, as did Phillips, when it acquired the Polam bulb factory in Pila, Poland. Hunpump (described in Chapter 2) is facing serious difficulties because its product has become obsolete, and can be sold only on shrinking Hungarian market. Exactly as it is within the Triad, constant development and up-scaling of the product range (adding more high value-added, high-end products) seems to be the next precondition of a sustainable and stable competitive advantage worldwide. Both local and global resources of the company should be used for product development. Eastern and Central Europe has plenty of well-prepared and creative engineers. As cultural and language barriers are gradually overcome, they can blend nicely into the existing pool of engineering talent the company has internationally.

An emphasis on fully internationally competitive products does not exclude also carrying some local products and services in addition to the main product lines providing they generate additional sales and a reasonable return on investment. Spare parts for discontinued Eastern European automobiles and machines or modernization of the existing power plants (in fact proposed in 1990 to the Polish authorities by Westinghouse) are good examples of such additional product lines.

Feasibility is the last of Rumelt's strategy evaluation criteria. Applying this criteria to the strategy evaluation process basically means answering the question: can we really implement our strategy in local conditions? This general question can be broken into two more specific ones.

The first question is, has the organization demonstrated that it possesses the problem-solving abilities and/or special competencies required by the strategy (Rumelt 1988, 55)? Basically this is a question about the ability to create a fully competitive business unit integrated into the company's international structures and policies but at the same time able to function in local conditions in the post-communist country. Companies such as ABB, with extensive experience in successful international restructuring, can certainly answer that question affirmatively, on the basis of past experience. The question of ability to act within the specific conditions of Central and Eastern Europe remains open, however. This question can be approached from two angles: the selection of subsidiary management and headquarters staff overseeing Eastern or Central European operation, and the selection of adequate staff and consulting support.

The issue of subsidiary management has already been addressed. The issue of a selection of the headquarters person who has to act as intermediary, or linch pin, is less obvious and seldom addressed. Such a person has to meet two requirements. First he/she has to be a company insider able to enforce company policy and philosophy and to help rapidly acculturate local employees. Secondly, he/she has to be a person able to work closely with the locals and able to coach them. Such a person does not have to speak the language, but must be able to develop empathy and take pride in the success of his or her Eastern European "pupils." Depending on circumstances and personalities, different approaches might be taken from "drill sergeant" to "caring mother," but empathy and pride are essential.

While in the US in 1991, the author had an opportunity to listen to a talk given to MBA students by a German executive of a major international corporation. Asked about East Germany and Eastern Europe, he replied that East Germans can not employed by West German firms because they do not know how to work and Eastern Europeans are even worse. So, he concluded with ease, that part of Europe will remain poor and underdeveloped for a long time. He is certainly not a person to supervise Eastern European operation of his company, if he can supervise anything at all. Such ethnocentric attitudes and strong beliefs in the inherent inferiority of the "Osties" (a degrading name given to East Germans in West Germany and sometimes generalized to other Eastern and Central Europeans) are not unusual even among managers of international corporations.

The issue of adequate staff and consulting support is especially difficult and because of that, it feeds many predators and parasites both in the West and in the East. These are high priced consultants who pretend to know how western companies should do business in the East, while in fact, they do not know Western companies can not really check them. The harm they do costs much more than their fees, because they often mislead their clients. In 1990, the author met an American executive in Warsaw who was planning to bring large supplies of food and other consumers items to Warsaw to motivate the employees of a subsidiary he was opening in Poland. His US based consultants told him do so, because they did not realize that since the introduction of its stabilization plan in January 1990, Poland had food surpluses, and everything became easily available and cheap by American standards. They probably believed that the situation in the USSR could be safely generalized to other Eastern European countries. On another occasion, an American representing a major US corporation in Russia, told the author that he was "just about" to strike an extraordinary deal because, two weeks ago, his local "power broker" put him in touch (for a fee, obviously) with a powerful political figure. Unfortunately, he was unable to read Russian newspapers because on the same day this conversation took place, the resignation of the "powerful political figure'' was publicly announced. Hundreds of such examples can be quoted, some of them quite humorous. Warsaw, Budapest, Moscow, and Prague are full of business consultants offering their services to domestic and foreign enterprises. Only few of them are really trustworthy. In the West, the ranks of rather doubtful Eastern European experts and consultants are also growing rapidly, as businesses are moving East.

The ideal consultant should understand both local and international, western business. Unfortunately, such consultants are extremely rare. The only reasonable solution seems to be to use western consultants for the Western side of the operation, and eastern consultants for the eastern side, and occasionally bring them together. For example, ABB brings their top experts in functional areas such as finance and marketing (Taylor 1991) to Poland for short visits, and GE brought their production management specialist to reduce the 70 percent defect rate in halogen bulb production to a manageable 30 percent, or only 10 percent more than in the West (Greenhouse 1990). As far as selection of local consultants goes, the judgment of local managers seems to be the most important input, because they know local conditions and what is needed.

Such an approach requires, however, an extensive use of judgment by the headquarters person supervising and overseeing Eastern or Central European operations. Often, trips to the field are needed, as well as networking on his or her own, and building up contacts enabling better, deeper understanding, and a proper assessment of the local situation and performance of the local management team.

Secondly, has the organization demonstrated the degree of coordinative and integrative skill necessary to carry out the strategy (Rumelt 1988, 55)? The real issue here is dealing with diversity and complexity on the global scale. Some firms like ABB are very good at this, others, like Phillips, have experienced major difficulties because of their inability to cope with global complexity and diversity. Eastern European operation of an international or global company will certainly for quite some time stick out as an exotic addition to the corporate structure. The real challenge is to integrate it into the overall structure without losing its local character conditioning its ability to operate in a specific post-communist environment. It can be accomplished in two parallel ways: through acculturation, and through suitable a corporate structure.

Acculturation refers to the local managers and means a specific mixture of skills, attitudes, values, and behavioral patterns making up its specific character and specific strengths of the company on a world-wide scale. It is achieved through training, combined with a constant interaction and rotation of managers across national, functional, and product lines. Such a revolutionary change requires, however, strong leadership on the global scale and a clear vision of corporate culture. Both ABB's Barnevik and GE's Welch seem to have such a vision.

In the case of ABB, it is a culture of a multidomestic company, where global and local orientation peacefully co-exist and reinforce each other and people are willing and able to share information, expertise, experience, knowledge across all the formal borders within the company; both horizontally and vertically. Innovation is encouraged as a result of such cross-feeding. This approach is combined with a clear definition of tasks and responsibilities. High standards are expected of everyone and performance is constantly monitored (Taylor 1991).

In the case of GE, the new corporate culture (seen as an attempt to overcome traditional weaknesses of American management) is dominated by a similar theme of "integrated diversity" overcoming parochialism and particularism. It is supposed to be achieved through speaking out: promotion of candid evaluation of performance top-down and bottom-up as well as horizontally, across functional and product lines. Welch believes in blending hard issues such as down-sizing, reducing levels of management, and driving productivity, with the soft ones such as the values of compassion and securing a "soft landing" for redundant employees, participative management style, and innovative behavior (Quickel 1990).

In both companies, the dissemination of the new winning management cultures is being secured by constant team work mixing people together, and team training such as the legendary "work out" sessions in GE's Crotonville Management Development Institute in Ossining, New York or "Mini MBA" taught in Warsaw by INSEAD professors for ABB's Polish managers (Talor 1991; Greenhouse 1990).

The integration of an Eastern or Central European operation into the company structure depends to great extent upon the intensity of the participation of the local managers in such activities. Only such integration will enable the company as a whole to cope with the additional diversity created by a newly added operation in Central or Eastern Europe. As long as such an operation remains an exception in a class by itself it will be a costly and troublesome operation.

Formal structure also plays an important role in providing for the coordination of activities on a world-wide basis. Striking similarities between ABB and GE can be observed.

First, both companies are organized around strategic business units, over 50 in the case of ABB and 13 in the case of GE. These business units are responsible for world-wide competition in relatively homogeneous groups of products. Secondly, power and responsibility are decentralized downward so business units can be responsible for global competition requirements. Third, effective, open communication is established on a world-wide basis between business units, their sub-units and sub-sub-units. Finally, a company-wide system of monitoring productivity and financial performance is put in place.

These are the similarities between two leading global companies who seem to cope successfully with the coordination of their Eastern European operations within a global framework. There are obviously many differences, such as bigger and more complex business units at GE, or greater decentralization and a unique matrix structure at ABB. (Taylor 1991) The lesson for managing operations in the post-communist countries is simple: local management team should be given full responsibility and accountability for the operation as soon as possible. In some cases this will preserve the identity of the old firm such as with Tungsram. Full responsibility and accountability should come with the open communication channels, intensive training, and staff assistance in functional areas such as marketing, finance, accounting, and production management. Operating in such a structure may be shocking for people who for decades have been accustomed to living in stiff functional bureaucracies, where responsibilities and accountabilities were fuzzy. That is why in principle, new people, not those who previously occupied managerial positions, should fill new structures.

Dos and Don'ts

The number of unsuccessful or dormant foreign operations in Central and Eastern Europe is striking. Let us briefly examine the most common reasons for failure and try to formulate some positive lessons.

"Stick to the knitting" principle seems to be even more important in a turbulent foreign environment than in a well-known and well-functioning western environment. The example of a computer manufacturer getting into the furniture business in Poland (the Elfur case in Chapter IV) is especially instructive. When internal convertibility of the currency eliminated barter opportunities and electronic line of business became marginalized, the Western partner lost touch with core of the business operations and became only an obstructive factor. American Trade Consortium in Russia seems to be another negative example (Hertzfeld 1991, 88). It is a joint venture of five blue chip US companies: Chevron, Archer-Daniels-Midland, Eastman Kodak, RJR Nabisco and Johnson & Johnson led by the Mercator Corporation, an investment bank created especially to serve this particular venture. Ford, which had originally been involved, dropped out. The business concept behind the consortium was simple. The Soviets would give Chevron the rights to develop a rich oil field, on condition that all parties in the oil joint venture agree to share their hard currency earnings with a consumer goods joint ventures opening plants in Russia to serve the internal Soviet market. In such a way, companies like Nabisco and Johnson & Johnson find themselves in the completely unknown business of oil in a completely unknown and highly turbulent post-USSR environment. It is also evident that such a business concept will completely lose grounds when internal convertibility of the currency is introduced. This is exactly what happened. The whole deal fell apart after the dissolution of the USSR. In 1992, Chevron struck a deal with the government of Kazakhstan.

Belief that a company can do in Russia or in Poland something it did not try or it was not successful at in the US or in Germany, can become a very costly illusion. A competitive advantage results from the economies of experience and from the transfer of skills and knowledge.

Many failures result from local politics for at least the following reasons. First of all, the "wrong" political connections can bring the whole venture down. Dealing with the workers' elected representatives makes negotiations extremely difficult, complex and inconclusive (see the Rainbow example in chapter 1).

In addition, post-communist countries are facing a relatively long period of political instability and turbulence. A favorable political climate may suddenly change into an unfavorable one. A viable venture should therefore be based on a sound mutually profitable business concept instead of exceptional political favors, which may quickly and easily backfire. For example, the ATC consortium mentioned above, was able to get the ear of Gorbachev, who granted it special concessions such as five years loss carry forward privileges, which were included in a special decree of the Council of Ministers. Such privileges might not be respected by the government of independent Russia. In fact, Gorbachev's decrees have completely lost validity since the dissolution of the USSR.

A balanced network of political contacts, including all the major players as well as restraining from participation in local politics seems to be a sound policy. Extraordinary, exceptional deals granted because of political connections are revocable, especially when the political climate changes. This happened in Poland after presidential election of 1990. Examples of cancelled deals are quite abundant. A burned-out company has little chance to come back.

The author has noticed that many western managers have a strong tendency to perceive Central and Eastern Europe as similar to the third world countries, where corrupt and dictatorial regimes provide for the relative longevity of unilaterally profitable (for western companies) deals and enable "hit and run" operations. Even if some social and economic indicators are similar, the way that governments operate has to be different in recently liberated societies where the newly acquired freedoms of speech and press are especially cherished. This is true even if more authoritarian forms of government temporarily emerge. Such governments will have a populist tone, which automatically means a rather suspicious attitude toward foreign investors. Domestic second economy organizations and institutions are much deeper entrenched and integrated into the country's social and political fabric, and therefore will be better tolerated than violations of the post-communist national interests by "greedy foreigners".

In an extremely interesting interview given to the Russian daily "Business World," Mr. Surkov, a member of the board of directors of the private banking institution, Menatep, warns strongly against careless attitude toward foreign investment in Russia. (Miliukov 1991:6). He points out the dangers of selling off valuable assets for symbolic prices, of foreign companies totally owning Russian market (and inhibiting development of domestic private enterprises), and of moving dirty and ecologically unsafe industries to the ex-USSR republics. Surkov's main concern is that the Russian government structures, Soviet bureaucracy are unfit to handle serious negotiations with western investors. To support his point, he cites the "market illiteracy" of post-Soviet bureaucrats, the fact that they are really not accountable for decisions they make and their sensitivity to small bribes (travel abroad, gifts, etc.). According to Surkov, the Russian government is only able to pursue extreme policy vis a vis foreign capital: either to ban it entirely or to completely surrender and give everything away on the foreign investors' terms. Both policies are damaging. A balanced middle of the road approach is needed as well as skilful negotiations with foreign investors. He proposes that representatives of Russian private business should be included in such negotiations. He argues that they can be much better watch dogs of Russian national interests, being much more market conscious. Since they are financially accountable for their decisions. Additionally, because they are personally much more affluent, they are less vulnerable. The dissolution of the USSR in 1992 and creation of the independent states does not seem to change the validity of the remarks related to the Soviet bureaucracy.

Similar warnings related to foreign investment in Russia can also be found in the article published just a couple of day later in the same daily by Mr. Shishkine, director of the consulting center of the Ministry of Foreign Affairs, dealing with foreign investment. (Shishkine 1991: 5). He points out that the small size of the average Western investment (500,000 rubles in 1990), and their concentration in non-manufacturing sectors (for example only 7 percent of the total numbers of joint ventures in mechanical industry) and the low technical level of foreign investment.

He complains that managers of state-owned enterprises are not equal partners with their Western counterparts and because of this, they are likely to "give away".

Similar concerns are being raised all over Eastern Europe. In Poland, it was one of the major campaign themes of the independent presidential candidate, Canadian entrepreneur Mr. Tyminski, who challenged Mr. Walesa in the 1990 presidential election from the extreme right wing populist position. In Czech and Slovak republic, the still influential communist party, which has close to 15% of the popular vote, is warning against foreign capital. In Hungary, issues of the proper handling of foreign capital are included in the platform of the ruling Democratic Forum. Governments can not remain indifferent to such concerns.

The only reasonable response of foreign investors is the one which brought such a spectacular success to American firms operating in Western Europe after the World War II: to make a serious, long-term commitment and to become responsible and loyal corporate citizens of the host country, honestly contributing to its development, building up its manufacturing strength, and gradually developing its markets in exchange for a fair share of the profits. ABB in Poland and GE in Hungary are certainly among the pioneers of a healthy approach by western investors in the battered parts of Europe, but others are following such as Volkswagen in Czech republic, GM in Hungary, Phillips in Poland, and McDonald's in Russia. It is evident, however, that such examples are marginal and will remain marginal for some time. Foreign capital will certainly not rush in into recessionary and politically unstable economies. It can be a booster of the economic growth in these post-communist countries, enabling them to overcome political instability-recession-inflation syndrome typical for the region. Hungary, Poland and Czech republic are undoubtedly the first candidates that may do so.

The mind-set, attitudes, opinions and emotions of western managers penetrating the post-communist world seem to have an important role in the success or failures of business ventures initiated, managed, and developed by these managers. The biggest trap of all is disrespect for local personnel a belief in their inherent inferiority. Such attitudes are especially likely to develop in a very specific business environment created by disintegrating post-Soviet bureaucracy. Paul O'Brien, the food and beverage manager for US-Russian Hotel "Slavyanskaya" (an Introurist-Redisson joint venture), located near the Moscow-Kiev railway station told the Los Angeles *Times* reporter the "list of horrors" he has encountered in Moscow (Goldberg 1991: D.16). In order to get some china and glassware out of storage, five signatures and five stamps were needed according to "Intourist" regulations. Four days after the hotel signed a contract for telephone service to be paid in rubles, the lines were suddenly disconnected and hotel management was told that it must pay for the phones in hard currency and the lines remained dead for 10 days. In one of the few foreign hotels in Moscow, 40 percent of the dining room silverware was stolen within two weeks after opening. A truckload of breeding chicken was ordered by the manager of a US-Russian restaurant. The roads have been so rough between the farm and town, however, that most of the birds' necks were broken and the driver killed the rest, thinking he was doing his boss a favor.

In such an environment, which takes extreme forms in the ex-USSR but is somewhat similar in other post-communist countries, maintaining respect for the local people and trying to understand their motivations seems to be an especially difficult task. It is necessary, however, to conduct business on a regular basis. It takes people with special characteristics, such as cultural sensitivity and the ability to develop empathy (Harris & Moran 1987). It also requires some knowledge of the language and history, enabling them to understand behaviours and cultural patterns and a lot of patience. Mr. O'Brien says, "A lot of people have come over here and run into problems and said, 'Hey we can go somewhere else' But in the end I am real positive about what we are doing here, if I wasn't I wouldn't be here".

Local managers acculturated to the company corporate culture can certainly help to develop such understanding as well as iron out the problems. To accomplish this, they must be trusted and treated as partners. That is why careful process of screening, selection, monitoring, development, and training of local managers have such crucial importance. Some western companies, when exposed to this idea, raise doubts whether huge investments in local managers will really pay–off, since under the conditions of an extreme shortage of local managerial talents, they are likely to be lured by competitors. Examples are cited. Here once again the problem of exceptional treatment of Soviet or Eastern European operations returns. Every corporation in the US or Western Europe has to develop attractive packages of managerial compensation and career opportunities in order to keep and develop its best talents. If it fails to do so, it looses them.

The same principle applies to operations conducted in post-communist countries. Local managers treated on equal terms with other managers of the same qualifications, seniority etc. and offered pay and career opportunities within the world-wide company structure, are much more likely to stay with it than managers treated as "second class" or "third class" hired hands who should be happy to make $300 or $400 per month in a country where the average salary is $100, and who should "know their place". Playing the ambition of local managers seems to be the right approach to secure their performance and loyalty. ABB's Barbara Kux, overseeing operations in Poland explains: "We put in place a management team that lacked the standard business tools. They didn't know what cash flow was, they didn't understand much about marketing. But their ambition was incredible, you could feel their hunger to excel" (Taylor 1991: 103).

Informal and interpersonal relations play a much more important role in post-communist countries than in the orderly and highly structured business environment of most western firms. This is the heritage of the Stalinist system, where everybody had to make illegal (but not necessarily immoral) deals with other people in order to survive. Personal relationships and mutual trust are rightly considered to be preconditions of such deals. That is why, in the post-communist countries, telephone calls, official letters, and faxes (even when they come through) are much less acceptable substitutes for personal contact than they are in the West. Reliable, serious business partners have to be personally known and personally trusted. Building such relationships is a long-term investment.

Notes

Chapter 1

1. This case was developed on the basis of research done in Silesia, the coal mining region of Poland, by Professor Andrzej Matczewski of The Polish Academy of Sciences. Used with permission.

2. The SovTruck case study is based on an article published in *Harvard Business Review* (Vlachoutsikos & Lawrence 1990). The article resulted from a program of empirical investigation carried out by an international team of researchers in 1988–89.

3. *New York Times.* April 3, 1991: 3.

4. Author's interview with Polish negotiators of the contract, who prefer to remain anonymous.

5. Based on research conducted by Dr. W. Grudzinski, of Lodz University, and author. The company's name, and some of the data, have been changed.

6. Based on the author's own research conducted in Hungary in 1990. The company name has been disguised.

Chapter 2

1. Based on an unpublished case developed in 1990 by Prof. B. Millner from the Soviet Academy of Sciences in Moscow. Used with permission.

2. Based on a presentation by J. Menyhart President of the Joint Venture Club in the Hungarian Chamber of Commerce, International Management Center, Budapest, in June 1990. The names of the companies and details have been changed.

3. Polish weekly *Wprost* publishes a list of the 100 richest Poles. Sources of some of their fortunes indicate links to the second economy (List of 100 richest Poles 1991).

4. *Business Week*, April 14, 1991: 48.

5. Case description based on the article by E. Dyson (Dyson 1991).

6. The case was developed by the author. Names ahve been changed.

7. Case description is based on the article published by the Soviet economic and business weekly, *Commercant* (Vassilieff 1991).

8. *Business Week*, April 15, 1991: 50.

9. Developed on the basis of Kadiroff's story published in the Soviet press (Kadiroff 1991).

10. Interview with Dr. Alexander Shaposhnikoff of the Siberian Department (Novosibirsk) of the Soviet Academy of Sciences, May 23, 1991.

11. Case description based on author's research performed on two Polish "growing sharks." Their identity is not disclosed.

12. Developed on the basis of J. Rosenthal's article published in *New York Times* (Rosenthal 1991).

Chapter 3

1. Known to the author from his personal consulting experience and visits to the shipyards. See also Mareing 1990.

2. Based on materials published in the Polish economic weekly, *Zycie Gospodarcze* 1991, Nr. 33, 34, 41.

3. *Rzeczpospolita* 1991, Nr. 186 (2921), August 10–11: 3.

4. Case developed on the basis of the author's own research and interviews with Mera management. Background material was also provided by Henryk Skawinski, Mera's general manager and student of the second-year MBA program of the International Business School in Warsaw (1991), who prepared a written analysis of the firm. Used with permission. Some data have been changed.

5. Fictional case representing typical characteristics of the Czech luxury glassware industry. Based on the interviews with industry insiders who asked that their names not be disclosed.

Chapter 4

1. *Commersant* 1991, March 18: 6.

2. OPIC information leaflet.

3. *Rzeczpospolita* 1991, Nr. 186 (2921), August 10–11: 3.

4. Case researched and developed by the author. Identity of the company has been disguised. Background information was provided by Dr. J. Piotrowski, in 1990/1991 an MBA student of the International Business School in Warsaw.

5. Case researched and developed by the author. Names and identity of the company have been disguised. One of the earlier versions of the case has been co-authored by Prof. K. Obloj from Warsaw University.

6. The case was developed by the author on the basis of background information provided by Mr. W. Rogojski, a 2nd year MBA student of the International Business School in Warsaw. Used with permission.

7. The case was developed by the author. Identity of the company has been disguised.

8. Case researched and developed by the author. Identity of the company has been disguised.

9. Based on materials published in the Polish press in 1991: *Rzeczpospolita* Nr. 188 (2923), August 13: 3. *Gazeta Wyborcza* Nr. 188 (657): 2; *Wprost* Nr. 24 (447), June 18: 27–42.

10. Based on materials published in the Polish press. See among others: Markiewicz (1991), Papuzinska (1991) also numerous articles published in such daily newspapers as *Zycie Warszawy, Rzeczpospolita, Glob 24.*

Chapter 5

1. See analysis of the second economy in previous chapters.

Chapter 6

1. Case developed by the author with the considerable research help of Dr. Monika Kostera of Warsaw University, to whom the author wants to extend his thanks for her contribution. The case was originally developed for and sponsored by EFER (European Foundation for Entrepreneurship Research). A modified version of the case is presented here with the EFER's permission. The case has been also approved by Mr. Horodecki.

2. Based on the article published in the Soviet press (Podshivalov 1990).

3. Based on the interview with Dr. Alexander Shaposhnikov of the Soviet Academy of Sciences in Novosibirsk, May 17, 1991.

4. Based on the interview with Stanislav Szczot, general manager of Stomil, published in the Polish economic weekly *Zycie Gospodarcze* (Fronczak 1991).

5. Based on the interview with Jozef Kowalczyk, general manager of Bumar Warynski, published in *Zycie Gospodarcze* (Wieczorkowska 1991).

6. GE Carves out a Road East, *Business Week,* July 30, 1990: 33.

7. This is demonstrated by the initiatives of Group 247, created after President Bush's visits to Central and Eastern Europe (1989–1990) and to EEC headquarters in Brussels. Also the British, Dutch, Danish, American, French, and German governments have all stated that management education is a primary area that each of them will support in the post-communist countries. As early as 1989, British Prime Minister Margaret Thatcher created a Know-How Fund for Poland, targeting management education in particular. Similar initiatives were also originated by supra-national organizations such as the Economic Development Institute (EDI) of the World Bank and the EEC, which included Central and Eastern Europe in its educational programs, such as ERASMUS and PHARE.

8. Author visited IMC twice in 1990.

9. Author happens to be the President of IBS.

10. Author is director of the Warsaw University International Postgraduate Management Center.

11. Soviet Business School Teaches Ways of West, *Commerce Today,* April 11, 1989: 9.

12. Information provided by Dan Fogel in a lecture delivered at IMC in Budapest, June 4, 1990.

13. Author visited Estonian management training centers several times in the 1980s.

Chapter 7

1. *Rzeczpospolita*, 1990 Nr. 232 (2987) vol. X. October 28: 1.
2. *Mergers & Acquisitions*, 1991 March–April: 67–70.

Bibliography

ABB 1989. *Six-Month Report*. Zurich: ABB.

ABB 1991. *The Art of Being Local Worldwide*. Zurich: ABB Marketing Services.

Adam J. 1979. *Wage Control and Inflation in the Soviet Bloc Countries*. New York: Praeger.

Agthe K. E. 1990. "Managing the Mixed Marriage." *Business Horizons*, January–February: 37–43.

Akademia Nauk SSSR 1977. *Trud Rukovoditelia: Utchobnoe Possobie dlia Rukovodiashchikh Upravlencheskikh Kadrov*. (Work of the Manager: Manual for Managerial Personnel.) Moscow: Akademya Nauk SSSR.

Alimov G. 1987. "Dengi na Botchku." ("Money on the Side.") *Izvestia*, December 16: 5.

Amsden A. H. 1990. "An Asian Plan for East Europe." *New York Times* April 6: 7.

———. 1991. "Diffusion of Development: The Late Industrializing Model and Greater East Asia." *A.E.A. Papers and Proceedings* 2 (81.) May: 282–286.

Arbose J. 1988. "ABB–The New Energy Powerhouse." *International Management*, June: 24–30.

Aslund A. 1985. *Private Enterprises in Eastern Europe*. London: Macmillan

Atlas Z. 1947. *Denezhnoe Obrashchenie i Kredit w SSSR*. (Money Circulation and Credit in the USSR). Moscow: Ekonomika.

———. 1969. *Sotsialisticheskaia Denezhnaia Sistema*. (Socialist Monetary System). Moscow: Ekonomika.

Barlett C. A and Ghosal S. 1987. "Managing Across Borders: New Strategic Requirements." *Sloan Management Review* Summer: 7–16.

Bauer R. et al. 1965. *Zarys Teorii Gospodarki Socjalistycznej*. (Outline of a Theory of the Socialist Economy). Warsaw: Panstwowe Wydawnictwo Naukowe.

Bauer T. 1978. "Investment Cycles in Planned Economies." *Acta Oeconomica* 1: 17–54.

Beksiak et al. 1978. *Zarazadzanie Przedsiebiorstwami Uczestnikami Rynku Dobr Konsumpcyjnych*. (Management of Enterprises in Consumption Goods Sector.) Warsaw: Panstwowe Wydawnictwo Naukowe.

Berliner J. S. 1957. *Factory and Manager in the USSR*. Cambridge Mass.: Harvard University Press.

Bernthal W. F. 1962. "Value Perspectives in Management Decisions." *Academy of Management Journal* 5: 150–196.

Binder D. 1991. "More Economic Pain Seen for the Soviets." *New York Times* May 17: A2.

Bohlen C. 1991a. "Hungarians Debate How Far Back to Go to Right Old Wrongs." *New York Times* April 15: A1–A4.

————. 1991. "New York Restaurateur Plots a Revival in Budapest." *New York Times* May 15: B8.

Bokros L. 1990. "Fresh Priorities for Pioneer Market." *Euromoney* July: 49–50.

Bolshaya Sovetskaya Encyklopedia. 1952. Moscow: Nauka.

Boukharin N. 1928. *Zametki Ekonomista k Nachalu Novogo Khoziaistvennogo Goda* (Remarks of an Economist at the Begining of the New Economic Year.) Moscow–Leningrad: Gosizdat.

Breitkopf M. and Gorski M. and Jaszczynski D. 1991. *Prywatyzacja w Polsce.* ("Privatization in Poland.") Warsaw: Fundacja im. Friedricha Eberta w Polsce.

Brus W. 1961. *Ogolne Problemy Funkcjonowania Gospodarki Socjalistycznej.* (General Problems of Fuctionning of the Socialist Economy.) Warsaw: Panstwowe Wydawnictwo Ekonomiczne.

————. 1986. *Histoire Economique de l'Europe de L'Est.* Paris: Editions La Decouverte.

Brzezinski Z. 1991. *The Grand Failure: the Birth and Death of Communism in the Twentieth Century.* New York: Charles Scribner's Sons.

Buravoy M. and Lukacs J. 1985. "Mythologies of Work: a Comparison of Firms in State Socialism and Advanced Capitalism." *American Sociological Review* 12(50): 723–737.

"Capital Market–Act of Faith." 1990 *Banker* July: 34–39.

Cassel D. and Cichy E. V. 1987. "The Growing Shadow Economy in Socialist Planning Systems: Causes and Consequences." *Nauki o Zarzadzaniu* 1: 49–63.

Chelinski R. 1964. "Przedsiebiorstwo Jako Element Socjalistycznych Stosunkow Produkcji." ("Enterprise as Element of Socialist Production Relations.") *Zeszyty Naukowe SGPiS* 5 (53): 30–58.

Cushman D. and King S. 1990. "The Impact of High Technology on International Management." in: Shuter R. and Chatarjea S. (eds.) *International Management and Comparative Management Systems.* Wawatosa Wis.: Cultural Press: 247–286.

Czarny B. 1991. "Ciezki zywot twardej waluty." ("Difficult Life of Hard Currency.") *Polityka* 29. (July 25): 23.

Degtyarenko I. 1991. "Foreign Trade Boom Forecast. Foreign Investment Meanwhile Expected to Fail." *Commersant* March 11: 6.

Deutsche Bank 1991a. *Unification Issues: Economic Assistance to New Lander 1991.* Washington D.C.: Transatlantic Futures Inc.

————. *Focus Eastern Europe: Hungarian Success.* Washington D.C.: Translantic Futures Inc.

————. *Unification Issues: The State of Privatization.* Washington D.C.: Transatlantic Futures Inc.

Doktor K. 1975. *Socjologiczna Teoria Organizacji.* Warsaw: Instytut Organizacji i Kierowania.

Domanski G. E. 1991. "Nowe Prawo o Inwestycjach Zagranicznych." ("New Foreign Investment Law.") *Rzeczpospolita* 158 July 9: 3.

Domanski R. 1991. "Rentownosc Polskiego Przemyslu." ("Profitability of Polish Industry.") *Przeglad Organizacji* 11: 3–5.

Doz Y. 1986. *Strategic Management in Multinational Companies.* Oxford: Pergamon Press.

Dumas A. (ed.) 1981. *L'Autogestion–un Systeme Economique.* Paris: Dunod.

Dziadul J. 1991. "Na Pochylej Barykadzie" ("On the Slippery Barricade.") *Polityka* 25. June 20: 7.

Ehrlich A. 1960. *The Soviet Industrialization Debate 1924–1928.* Cambridge Mass. Harvard University Press.

Engelberg S. 1991. "Factories with Amenities Hinder Poland's Stark Turn to Capitalism." *New York Times*, June 3: A1–A3.

Fijalkowski M. 1991. "Gabor Szeles–Czolowy Przedsiebiorca Wegierski" (Gabor Szeles–Top Hungarian Entrepreneur.") *Rzeczpospolita* 186 (2921), August 10–11: III.

Fogel T. and Friedman J. 1990. "No Money Machine Can Run this Fast Forever." *Business Week*, April: 96–98.

Forss K. and Hawk D. and Hedlund G. 1984. *Cultural Differences–Swedeshness in Legislation, Multinational Corporations and Aid Administration*, Stockholm: Institute of International Business Stockholms Handelshogskola.

Fronczak K. 1991. "Z Przezyc Lezacego." ("Impressions of the Lying Down.") *Zycie Gospodarcze* 24. (June 16): 3.

Gabrisch H. et al. 1992. *Depression and Inflation: Threats to Political and Social Stability, The Current Economic Situation of Former CMEA Countries and Yugoslavia*, Vienna: The Vienna Institute for Comparative Economic Studies.

Gacs J. 1989. "Decentralization and Liberalization in the Hungarian Economy." *Revista del Instituto de Estudios Economicos* 4: 12–35.

Gardner H. S. 1989. "US–Soviet Trade–Old Problems–New Opportunities." *Baylor Business Review* Summer: 2–8.

Geremek B. 1990. *Rok 1989*. Warsaw: Plejada.

Golachowski E. 1991. *Procesy Prywatyzacyjne w Krajach Post-Socjalistycznych.* (Privatization Processes in Post-Socialist Countries.) Warsaw: Instytut Finansow (mimeographed).

Golan G. 1981. *The Czechoslovak Reform Movement: Communism in Crisis 1962–1968*. New York: Cambridge University Press.

Golcman A. 1924. "Soyouzy i Proizvodstvo." ("Trade Unions and Production.") *Priedpriatye* 8: 7–19.

Goldberg C. 1991. "Adventures in Red Tape: Preparing to Open Moscow Hotel." *Los Angeles Times*, May 26: D 16.

Gornov S. 1991a. "Danish Firm's Soviet Deal Sports Intriguing New Strategy." *Commersant*. February 25: 4.

———. 1991b. "Sozdana Pervaya Tchastnaya Firma Gramzapisi." ("First Private Audio Recording Firm Established.") *Delovoi Mir*, January 14: 7.

Gorski M. and Jaszczynski D. 1991. *Polityka Stabilizacyjna w Europejskich Krajach Socjalistycznych.* ("Stabilization Policies in the European Socialist Countries.") Warsaw: Instytut Finansow (mimeographed).

Greenhouse S. 1990. "General Electric Running on Fast Forward in Budapest." *The New York Times*, December 16: 7–8.

Gregory P. R. and Stuart R. C. 1990. *Soviet Economic Structure and Performance*. New York: Harper and Row Publishers.

Griffith D. 1934. *What is Socialism*. London: Allen and Unwin.

Grossfeld I. Hare P. 1991. *Privatization in Poland, Hungary and Czechoslovakia*. Discussion Paper Nr. 544. London: Center for Economic Policy Research (mimeographed).

Grossman M. 1923. "Trest, Fabrika, Zavod i Rabota Direktora." ("Trust, Enterprise, Plant and the Managers' Work.") *Predpryatye* 2: 5–12.

———. 1924. "Fayerverski blask." ("Firework's Light.") *Predpryatye* 8: 13–18.

Hamel G. and Doz Y. and Prahalad C. K. 1989. "Collaborate with your Competitors and Win." *Harvard Business Review* January–February: 133–139.

Harris P. R. and Moran R. T. 1987. *Managing Cultural Differences: High Performance Strategies for Todays Global Manager*. Houston: Gulf Publishing Co.

Hertzfeld J. M. 1991. "Joint Ventures: Saving the Soviets from Perestroika." *Harvard Business Review* January–February: 80–91.

Hirszowicz M. and Morawski W. 1967. "Z Badan and Spolecznym Uczestnictwem w Organizacji." ("From Research on Social Participation in Organizations.") Warsaw: Ksiazka i Wiedza.

Hopkins T. H. et al. 1982. *World System Analysis: Theory and Methodology*. Beverly Hills: Sage Publications.

Horvath B. 1982. *The Political Economy of Socialism*. Armonk N.Y.: ME Sharpe.

Horvath B. and Markovic M. and Soupek R. *Self-Governing Socialism*. New York: International Arts and Sciences Press.

Jarosz J. 1990. "Pracownicy o Prywatyzacji." ("Employeees on Privatization.") *Polityka* 36: 3.

Jasinski P. 1990. "Two Models of Privatization in Poland." *Communist Economies* 3: 373–402.

Jermakowicz W. and Bochniarz Z. 1991. *Direct Foreign Investment in Poland: 1986–1990*. (mimeographed).

Jezierski A. and Petz B. 1982. *Historia Gospodarcza Polski Ludowej*. (Economic Hisotry of Poeple's Poland). Warsaw: Panstwowe Wydawnictwo Ekonomiczne.

Jordan L. D. 1990. "How to Build Successful Strategic Alliances." *The Journal of European Business* November–December: 18–24.

Kadiroff R. 1991. "Otkrovenye Bankira: Kak Zarabotat Miliony." ("Banker's Confession: How to Make Millions.") *Delovoi Mir* 23–24: 13.

Karoly J. W. 1990. "Assignment: 90 Days on the Polish Front." *The New York Times Magazine*, September 23: 28–31.

Karpinski A. 1986. *40 Lat Planowania w Polsce*. (40 Years of Planning in Poland.) Warsaw: Panstwowe Wydawnictwo Ekonomiczne.

Katsenliboigen A. 1977. "Coloured Markets in the Soviet Union." *Soviet Studies* 1.

King T. 1990. *Foreign Direct Investment in the East European Transition*. Washington D.C.: Economic Development Institute of the World Bank (mimeographed).

Kohout J. 1970. "What Kind of Managers Do We Have." *Management Sciences in Czechoslovakia* 1: 17–70.

Koerner E. 1989. "GE's High Tech Strategy." *Long Range Planning* 4 (22): 11–19.

Konrad G. and Szelenyi I. 1979. *The Intellectuals on the Road to Class Power.* New York: Harcourt and Brace and Jovanovich.

Koptyaeff A. 1991. "Pervye Piat Leningradskikch Magazinov Stali Chastnymi." ("First Five Stores in Leningrad Became Private.") *Commersant* 1. January 5: 5.

Korani J. 1980. *Economics of Shortage.* Amsterdam, New York, Oxford: North Holland.

———. 1984. "Shortage–Fundamental Problems of Centrally Planned Economies and Hungarian Reform."—interview with A. Jutta-Pletsch. *Revue d'Etudes Comparatives East–Ouest* 3: 13–18.

———. 1990. *The Road to a Free Economy–Shifting from a Socialist System. The Example of Hungary.* New York and London: W. W. Norton and Co.

Kornai J. and Richet X. (eds.) 1986. *La Voie Hongroise: Analyse et Experimentations Economiques.* Paris: Coleman Levy.

Kostera M. 1990. *Szwedzki Styl Zarzadzania* (Swedish Management Style)—unpublished doctoral disssertation Warsaw University.

Kovari G. and Sziracki G. 1985. "Old and New Forms of Wage Bargaining on the Shop Floor." in: Galasi P. and Sziracki P. (eds.) *Labor Market and Second Economy in Hungary.* Franfurt: Campus Verlag: 264–292.

Kozminski A. K. 1974. "Les Entreprises Pilotes dans le Nouveau Systeme de Gestion de l'Economie Polonaise." *Revue de l'Est* 4: 31–42.

———. 1976. "The Role of the Manager in the Socialist Economy." in: Boddewyn J. (ed.) *European Industrial Managers: West and East.* New York: International Arts and Sciences Publishers Inc.: 393–415.

———. 1982. *Po Wielkim Szoku.* (After a Big Shock.) Warsaw: Panstwowe Wydawnictwo Ekonomiczne.

———. 1988. "Reformer l'Economie Socialiste: les Perspectives Polonaises." *Revue d'Etudes Comparatives Est–Ouest* 4 (19): 47–70.

———. 1990a. "Market and State in Centrally Planned Economies." in: Martinelli A. and Smelser N. J. (eds.) *Economy and Society.* London: Sage: 133–157.

———. 1990b. "Czy Mozliwe Jest Przyspieszenie w Gospodarce." (Is acceleration in the economy possible) *Gazeta Wyborcza* 197(364) August 25–26: 1–7.

———. 1992. "Global Management a New Road to Social Progress." in: Kozminski A. K. and Cushman D, (eds.) *Globalization: A Communication and Management Prespective.* Albany N.Y.: SUNY Press.

Kozminski A. K. and Obloj K. (eds.) 1983. *Gry o Innowacje* (Innovation Games). Warsaw: Panstwowe Wydawnictwo Ekonomiczne.

———. 1984. "Collaboration de la Recherche Scientifique et de l'Industrie pour l'Innovation." *Revue d'Etudes Comparatives Est–Ouest* 2 (15): 48–59.

———. 1989. "Macrochanges in Macroorganizations: the Case of Socialist Economies." *Communist Economies* 4: 409–419.

————. 1990. "From Innovative to Systemic Change: The Transformation of Communist Economies." *Communist Economies* 3: 335–345.

————. 1991. "Post-Communist Reforms from the Organizational Change Perspective." *Cybernetics and Systems an International Journal* 22: 459–479.

Kozminski A. K. and Tropea L. A. 1982. "Negotiation and Command: Managing in the Public Domain." *Human Systems Management* 3: 21–31.

Kozminski A. K. and Zawislak A. M. 1982. *Pewnosc i Gra* (Game and Certainty). Warsaw: Panstwowe Wydawnictwo Ekonomiczne.

Kreft J. 1991. "Pod Lupa." ("Under Magnifying Glass.") *Gazeta Bankowa* 46: 24.

Kuffner K. 1988. "English the Common Language of Europeans." *International Management* 4 (42): 24–29.

Kukushkine M. 1991. "Aktsii Menatepa: Teper my ikch kupim obratno i snova prodadim." (Menatep Shares: Now We Will Buy Them Back and Resell.") *Commersant* 4: 9.

Kurowski S. 1956. "Demokracjz i Prawo Wartosci." ("Democracy and the Value Law.") *Kierunki* 17–19 August: 1–3.

Leites N. 1985. *Soviet Style in Management.* New York: Crane, Russak and Co.

Levine J. B. 1990. "GE Carves out a Road East." *Business Week,* July 30: 32–33.

Levitas A. and Strzalkowski P. 1990. "What Does Uwlaszczenie Nomenklatury (Propertization of the Nomenklatura) Really Mean." *Communist Economies* 3: 413–416.

Lewin M. 1968. *Russian Peasants and Soviet Power.* London: Allen and Unwin.

————. 1987. *La Formation du Systeme Sovietique.* Paris: Gallimard.

Liberman E. 1968. "The Role of Profits in the Industrial Incentive System of the USSR." *Industrial Labor Review* 1: 17–29.

————. 1971. *Economic Methods and the Effectiveness of Production.* White Plains, N.Y.: International Arts and Sciences Press.

Lipton D. and Sachs J. 1990. "Creating a Market Economy in Eastern Europe: the Case of Poland." *Brookings Papers on Economic Activity* 1: 75–139.

List of 100 Richest Poles. 1991. *Wprost* 4 (447): 27–46.

Loktiev A. 1991. "Menatep Banking Group has Successful Stock Offering." *Commersant,* January 7: 3.

Magala S. (ed.) 1991. *Business as Unusual: a Report on Polish and Hungarian Transition to Market Economies.* Delft: Eburon.

Maney K. 1990. "GE Brings Good Things to Tunsgram." *USA Today,* June 23: 5.

Markiewicz W. 1991. "Afera." ("Scandal.") *Polityka* 33: 1–4.

Marx K. 1951. *Kapital.* Warsaw: Ksiazka i Wiedza.

Mayer C. 1991. "Agent of the State." *International Management* 2. February: 28–33.

Mazan L. 1991. "Mafia i Nomenklatury." ("Mafia and Nomenklatura.") *Polityka* 31. August 31: 12.

Mergers and Acquisitions Special Report 1991. "A Cold Eyed Agenda for Betting on the East." *Mergers and Acquisitions* March–April: 67–70.

Merill Lynch 1990. *Investing in Former East Bloc Countries: Obstacles and Opportunities.* New York. September 4.

Mering K. 1991. "Na Pochylni." ("On the Building Slip.") *Zycie Gospodarcze* 29 (July 21): 6.

Miliukov O. 1991. "Boisia Danaitsev Dari Prinosiaschtchikh." ("Be Aware of Danaians Gifts Bringing.") *Delovoi Mir* 45 (61) February 28: 6.

Millar J. 1970. "Soviet Rapid Development and the Agriculture Surplus Hypothesis." *Soviet Studies* 1: 109–117.

———. 1974. "Mass Collectivization and the Contribution of Soviet Agriculture to the First Five-Year Plan." *Slavic Review* December: 750–766.

Mintzberg H. 1988. "Opening Up The Definition of Strategy." In: Quinn J. B. and Mintzberg H. and James R. H. (eds.) *The Strategy Process*. Englewood Cliffs N.J.: Prentice Hall: 13–20.

Misiak M. 1991a. "Twarde Ladowanie." ("Hard Landing.") *Zycie Gospodarcze* 34 (August 25): 15.

———. 1991b. "W wymiarze pienieznym." ("In Monetary Terms.") *Zycie Gospodarcze* 35 (September 1.): 15.

Nagorski Jr. Z. 1974. *The Psychology of East-West Trade: Illusions and Opportunities*. New York: Mason and Lipscomb Publishers.

Naj K. A. 1991. "GE's Latest Invention: a Way to Move Ideas From Lab to Market." *Wall Street Journal*. June 17: A1–A9.

Newman B. 1991. "Poland has Plenty of One Thing: Crooks." *Wall Street Journal* April 9: A14.

Nove A. 1969. *An Economic History of the USSR*. London: Penguin.

Obloj K. and Davis A. S. "Innovation Without Change: Contradiction Between Theories Espoused and Theories In Use." *Journal of Management Studies* 4 (28), July: 323–337.

OECD 1989. *Investment Incentives and Disincentives: Effects on International Direct Investment*. Paris.

Ohmae K. 1985. *Triad Power: The Coming Shape of Global Competition*. New York: The Free Press.

———. 1987. "The Triad World View." *The Journal of Business Strategy* Spring: 8–19.

Papuzinska M. 1991. "Art B Story." *Gazeta Wyborcza*, August 10–11: 2.

Perlmutter H. V. and Heenan D. A. 1986. "Cooperate to Compete Globally." March–April: 132–152.

Podshivalov J. 1990. "From Young Communist to Money Lender." *Commersant* 23. (June 11–18): 15.

Porter M. E. 1986. "Changing Patterns of International Competition." *California Management Review* 2 (28): 9–40.

———. 1990. *The Competitive Advantage of Nations*. New York: The Free Press.

Powers C. T. "Poles Want Property Back." *Los Angeles Times* May 24: A5.

Prahalad C. K. and Doz Y. 1987. *The Multinational Mission: Balancing Local Demands and Global Vision*. New York: Free Press.

Preobrazhenski E. 1964. *La Nouvelle Economique*. Paris: Presses Universitaires de France.

Program Powszechnej Prywatyzacji (Program of Mass Privatization) 1991. Warsaw: Ministerstwo Przeksztalcen Wlasnosciowych.

"Prywatyzacja dla Bankrutow." ("Privatization for Bankrupts.") 1991. *Gazeta Wyborcza* December 1: 4.

Qickel S. W. 1990. "Welch on Welch." *Financial World,* April 3: 62–70.

Roberts P. C. 1971. *Alienation and the Soviet Economy.* Albuquerque: University of New Mexico Press.

Rosenthal J. 1991. "The First Capitalist in Prague." *New York Times* May 10 (48596): A18.

Rumelt R. 1988. "The Evaluation of Business Strategy." In: Quinn J. B. and Mintzberg H. and James R. M. *The Strategy Process.* Engleewood Cliffs, N.J.: Prentice Hall: 50–56.

Sachs, J. and Lipton D. 1990. "Poland's Economic Reform." *Foreign Affaires,* Summer: 47–66.

Sadowska-Cieslak E. and Olszewski J. "Niech Mowia Liczby." 1991. ("Let Figures Speak.") *Zycie Gospodarcze* 30 (2674): 6.

Sarabyanov S. 1924. "Voprosy Siezda Skvoz Prizmu Pryedpryatya" ("Congress Issues from the Enterprise Perspective" *Pryedpryatye* 5: 2–14.

Schein E. H. 1990. *Organizational Culture and Leadership.* San Francisco, Oxford: Jossey Bass.

Schonberger R. 1987. *World Class Manufacturing.* New York: The Free Press.

Seethi S. P. and Namiki N. and Swanson C. L. 1984. "The Decline of the Japanese System of Management." *California Management Review* 4 (24): 35–45.

Seurot F. 1983. *Inflation et Emploi dans les Pays Socialistes.* Paris: Presses Universitaires de France.

———. 1989. *Le Systeme Economique de L'URSS.* Paris: Presses Universitaires de France.

Shares G. E. 1991. "Czechoslovakia: Reluctant Reform." *Business Week.* 3209. April 5: 55–57.

Sherman H. J. 1969. *The Soviet Economy.* Boston: Little and Brown and Co.

Shihkine A. 1991. "Zapadnye Investitsii: Problem Bolshe Tchem Reshenii." ("Western Investment: More Problems than Solutions." *Delovoi Mir* 49 (65) March 6: 5.

Smith H. 1990. *The New Russians.* New York: Random House.

Smolar A. 1974. "L'Utopie et la Science: L'Economie Politique dans la Vision Marxienne du Communisme et Pendant l'Industrialization Sovietique." *Revue de l'Est* 4: 97–132.

The State of Small Business: A Report of the President, 1986, Washington, D.C.

Statistishe Jahrbuch fur Bundesrepublik Deutschland. 1989. Berlin.

Stewart T. E. 1990. "A Heartland Industry Takes on The World." *Fortune.* March 12: 10–11.

Szelenyi I. 1988. *Socialist Entrepeneurs: Embourgeoisement in Rural Hungary.* Madison Wis.: The University of Wisconsin Press.

Tardos M. 1988. "Stosunki Wlasnosci na Wegrzech." ("Property Relations in Hungary.") *Wektory* 8: 14–16.

Tarnowski P. 1991. "Dokerski Poker." ("Dokers' Poker.") *Polityka* 14. May 4: 4.

Taylor W. 1991. "The Logic of Global Business" an interview with ABB's Percy Barnevik. *Harvard Business Review,* March–April: 91–105.

Ternovszky F. 1991. *Foreign Investment in Hungary.* Budapest: Institute of Labor. (mimeographed)

Tichy N. M. 1989. "GE's Crotonville: Staging Ground for Corporate Revolution." *The Academy of Management Executive.* 2 (3): 99–106.

Tichy N. and Choran R. 1989. "Speed, Simplicity, Self-Confidence" an interview with Jack Welch. *Harvard Business Review* September–October: 112–120.

Tully S. 1990. "GE in Hungary: Let There be Light." *Fortune,* October 22: 137–142.

UNIDO (United Nations Industrial Development Organization) 1991. *Poland: Managing the Transition to a Market Economy.* Oxford UK. Cambridge USA.: Blackwell Publishers.

Utitsin O. 1991. "Artem Tarasoff: Teper Oni Mogut Menya Perestrelit." ("Artem Tarasoff: Now They Can Shoot at Me.") *Commersant* 6: 13.

Vasilieff A. 1991. "Jewish Business: How it Works at Joseph's." *Commersant* 9: 30.

Wandycz K. 1991. "Solidarity's Partner." *Forbes,* May 27: 168–170.

Wieczorkowska A. 1991. "Ucieczka Przed Upadkiem." (Escape from Collapse) *Zycie Gospodarcze* 27 (July 7): 7.

Wierzbicka E. 1991. *Polityka Stabilizacyjna w Europejskich Krajach Post-Socjalistycznych.* (Stabilization Policies in European Post-Socialist Countries) Warszawa: Instytut Finansow.

Wolf M. 1991. "The Giant Leap to a Capitalist System." *Financial Times.* May 3: VI.

Woycicki K. 1991. "Papierowy Tygrys." ("Paper Tiger.") *Zycie Warszawy.* October 25: 3.

Wrobel E. 1991. "Strajk w Sprawie Przyszlosci." ("Strike for the Future.") *Zycie Gospodarcze* 34 (August 25): 5.

Vernon R. (ed.) 1988. *The Promise of Privatization: a Challange for American Foreign Policy.* New York: Council on Foreign Relations.

Vlachoutsikos C. and Lawrance P. 1990. "What We Don't Know About Soviet Management" *Harvard Business Review* November–December: 50–63.

Vogal T. and Kelly K. 1991. "Will GE's New Jet Engine Ever Get Off the Ground." *Business Week* February 4: 98.

Zabkowicz A. 1991. "Wegierska Lekcja." ("Hungarian Lesson.") *Zycie Gospodarcze* 6: 3.

Zaitseva A. 1991. "Privatizatsya w Torgovle i Bitovom Obsluzivanii." (Privatization in Commerce and Services) *Delovoi Mir* 51. March 7: 2.

Zaleski E. 1980. *Stalinist Planning for Economic Growth: 1933–1952.* Chapel Hill: University of North Carolina Press.

Zielinski J. G. 1961. *Rachunek Ekonomiczny w Socjalizmie* (Economic Calculation under Socialism). Warsaw: Panstwowe Wydawnictwo Naukowe.

———. 1973. *Economic Reforms in Polish Industry.* Oxford: Oxford University Press.

Zvorykin A. A. and Geliuta M. M. 1977. "Engineering and Technical Personnel in the Social Structure of Soviet Economy." in Boddewyn J. (ed. *European Industrial Managers; East–West.* White Plains N.Y.: International Arts and Sciences Press Inc.: 491–540.

Index